Adult Learners

Understanding and Instructing

Robert E Ripley, PhD
and
Marie J Ripley, MA

International Award Winning Authors

Library of Congress Cataloging in Publication Data

Ripley, Robert E
Adult Learners: Understanding and Instructing

Includes Index and Bibliography
1. Adult Training 2. Training 3. Adult Education 4. Life Long Learning
5. Teaching 6. Adult Development 7. Adult Motivation

I. Ripley, Marie J   Title

First Edition, (1993) ISBN 0962113379
Second Edition, (1997) ISBN 1892794020
Third Edition, (2006) ISBN 1892794128

Fourth Edition, December, 2009

Library of Congress Catalog Carol

ISBN 1449962084

EAN-13 9781449962081

PREFACE - DEDICATION

On many occasions over a considerable period of years, various educational, business, industry, government and military professionals have asked us to share what we know about the process of adult education and training. They asked for learning that can be put to use in designing effective education and training classes and programs. This book is designed to answer their concerns in a comprehensive fashion.

We have educated and trained adults from over 24 different countries, representing undergraduate and graduate levels of education, worker position levels from the new hire to top International Fortune 500 executives. These students and employees have come from every aspect of education and the world-of-work. In the education level this has included from pre-school HEADSTART through Ph.D. programs in higher education.

Our experience with adult education and training also includes writing books and international publications on such diverse areas as child and adult development, parenting, career choice, career development, personal empowerment, woman power, innovation and empowerment in organizations, self-managing teams, strategies for implementing change, communication skills, knowledge management, patterns for success, financial planning and pre-retirement.

An additional area of expertise and experience is in organizational and individual assessment. Some of the assessment tools we have researched, developed and utilized which relate to adult educating and training include:
a   BestFit™ Performer Assessment
b   BestFit™ Leadership Assessment
c   Organizational Culture Inventory
d   Organizational Health Inventory
e   Adapted Baldrige Assessment for Education and Business
f   World of Work Inventory

The challenge and focus in writing this book is to present a coherent sequential body of knowledge for adult educating and training. This book has also been developed for use as a college or university textbook in adult learner and education classes. We hope you find the informative suggestions and processes useful in your interactions with other adults.

We dedicate this books to the memory of those who have passed on and to those who are still living on earth with whom we were and are granted the privilege of having them as mentors, professional colleagues, associates and many as close friends.

Many of the words and ideas originated with them and have just been passed through us to you.

Drs. Malcolm Knowles, Leonard Nadler, Roger Axford, Sidney Jourard, Robert Frank, William E. Edson, E. Paul Torrance, Rollo May, Kenneth B. Hoyt, Willard Abraham, John Krumboltz, Anne Roe, W. Lee Hoover, Harold W. Stevenson, Donald E. Super, Albert Ellis, S.I. Hayakawa, Wendell Johnson, Donald G. Paterson, Carl Rogers, Ralph Birdie, Theta Hagenah, Judith Osgood Shiner, William W. Willard III, J. Jeffries McWhirter, W. William Blaesser, Richard Rodriguez, Katherine Martyn, Ken Patch, Betty Kelley, Vivian Hewer, Len and Tina Reich, Carolyn DesJardins, Celia Halas, William Scofield, KaoruYamamoto, Maynard Reynolds, Fritz Perls, Abraham H. Maslow, Edward Williamson, C. Gilbert Wrenn, and Weldon Shoftstall.

Revisions and Additions

This edition contains major revisions and previously unpublished materials that the authors have researched, developed and used over the past 30 plus years.

The following are major sections not previously published but used extensively in college and university classes, workshops, seminars and consulting situations both public and private, nationally and internationally.

A Ripley Task - Data-Analysis - People Orientation

This adult understanding model has over a twenty-five year history of research and development. The model represents adults as having **TASK, DATA-ANALYSIS** and **PEOPLE** orientations. The orientation identifies the thinking and behaving style of an individual. Identifying the adult learners current style is a big part of knowing how to interact effectively with the them and also how he or she will interact with others. Significant differences in goals have been found for individuals if they are dominant in one area.

B Ripley Recurring Cycle: Cognitive and Behavioral

The key thing the adult learner wants is to be understood. The authors developed this personality - psychological theory and approach to enhance that understanding. The authors state there are two characteristic ways we look at an adult. One is physical appearance and the other is behavior, that which they call psychological identity. Just as the nose is part of the body there are various elements or characteristics of the psychological identity. Psychological identity is not observable as a whole as is the physical appearance. It is analogous to the difference between physical and chemical properties.   The physical we can touch, taste, and smell and it will always be relatively the same but the psychological identity differs under different conditions. You have to observe behavior under many different circumstances or conditions and combinations. This recurring cycle approach eases that process and provides multiple opportunities for further research and development

C Ripley Levels of Learning

Levels of learning
> (1) is a framework for talking about and solving everyday learning situations,
> (2) gives a theoretical framework on which to design the education and training,
> (3) assists the instructor and trainer to get from the beginning to the end of
>   learning or training without missing important steps and ensures starting the
>   learning on the right level, and
> (4) helps to explain why what the instructor or trainer is doing works.

The levels of learning explains the naturally occurring phenomenon of acquiring knowledge, skills, understandings and problem solving ability from the simplest to the most complex in a systematic manner.

This has been a pleasant challenge again revising and creating a manuscript that can meet the test of time for the next coming years.

May our knowledge and experience align with yours to explode into global learning.

Robert E Ripley, PhD and Marie J Ripley, MA

This Copy Belongs to:

Table of Contents

INTRODUCTION

Total Utilization of Individual's Talents

Adult Education/Training and Empowerment are critically important in enabling U.S. businesses, organizations and educational institutions to survive in this ever-expanding national and international marketplace. A company will not beat the competition with better products, facilities, or equipment alone. In mature markets with free global access of information, a competitive edge in these areas tends to be a short-lived illusion. Competitive strength is now derived from the ability to deliver quality, variety, customization, and convenience in a timely manner using increased specialization and service levels.

Today and throughout the 21st Century, organizations' and nations' competitiveness will be based on improved production processes and total utilization of workforce talents. One of the major blockages to increased utilization is management's underlying fear of trusting adult subordinates. Such trust includes empowering decision-making at the lowest level practical, belief in adults' brain power, and belief that others are motivated by more than money. Implementing adult training and empowerment in a company helps reduce or eliminate these non-productive and obstructive executive fears.

Through adult learning and empowerment, the strength of the whole workforce is harnessed and used most effectively to meet customer requirements with improved quality products and services. At its root, adult learning and empowerment says we trust our people; that we are, in reality, a team--not a loose collection of adults. Adult learning and empowerment can be utilized as the process for managing cultural change and for integrating the non-traditional worker into the workforce and college/university settings. Adult learning and empowerment allows managers to treat adult employees as a strategic fixed asset worthy of consistent maintenance and investment.

To improve your instructing you don't need to read, digest and utilize every page of this book. To each user specific parts are going to seem to be most useful at different times. People have told us they are still using specifics twenty and twenty-five years after they first learned them in our classes, seminars and workshops. We would like this to be your goal and privilege as you share your knowledge and experience in assisting your adult learners to identify and develop their talents to the fullest.

PART I
(☐) *UNDERSTANDING THE U.S.A. ADULT LEARNERS* (☐)

In the United States, mature adults today have acquired significant sets of beliefs and values. They are motivated by these perceived values of true adulthood, and by their behavior seek their personal fulfillment and gratification. To effectively instruct and train you must first understand these factors that give today's adult a sense of fulfillment and personal empowerment.

The organized beginning in the United States of understanding, educating and training the adult, vs the child or youth, is often given to the founding of the American Association for Adult Education in 1926. Such people as Thorndike (1928) and Sorenson(1938) presented scientific evidence that adults could learn and that they possessed interest and abilities that were different from those of children. However, Lindeman (1926) is usually given credit for laying the foundation for understanding the adult from a learning point of view. Some of the key points presented by Lindeman and later supported by research were that adults are motivated to learn as they experience needs and interest that learning will satisfy; adults' orientation to learning is life-centered; experience is the richest resource for adults' learning; adults have a deep need to be self-directing; and individual differences among people increase with age.

Jung (1921) introduced the approach that the adult possesses four ways of extracting information from experience and thereby achieving an internalized understanding. These four ways were sensation, thought, emotion, and intuition -the goal of the adult was to use all four to arrive at a balanced personality.

There has been a continuous surge of looking at the adult from the Freudians (Freud, 1904, Horney, 1939), to the Behaviorists (Bandura and Walters, 1963, Dollard & Miller, 1950, Skinner, 1953, Wolpe, 1969), to the Humanists (Maslow, 1970, Rogers, 1961, Jourard, 1958) and the Gestaltist (Perls, 1969). Then another group explained the total life span and the changes or developmental tasks of adulthood (Havinghurst, 1970, Bischof, 1969, Knox, 1977, Ripley and Ripley, 1974, 1988, 1992, 1994, 1997, 2009, Hoyer and Roodin, 2003, Santrock, 2004, Dacey and Travers, 2004).

There have also been some excellent learning theories and approaches that relate and are a foundation for this book. As this is not the major purpose of this book, a quick synopsis has been placed in some of the chapters and then a selected and more extensive bibliography provided for those individuals wanting to pursue these areas more in-depth.

Chapter 01
•□•□•□• *The Mature American Adult Learners and Their Motivation* •□•□•□•

Reasons For Seeking Learning -- Motivation

Although adults have been found to engage in learning for a variety of reasons (such as job advancement, pleasure, etc.), for most adults one of these reasons is **not** that learning is its own reward. The adult learner's primary motivation is the particular results that can come from the learning.

Most adults seek learning experiences dealing with *life-change events - *new job, new boss, divorce, retirement, new responsibilities, seeking new personal empowerment (physical, cognitive, emotional, social), etc. This is when they are most willing to learn - a window of opportunity. The more life-changing events or boredom an adult encounters, the more likely he or she is to seek out learning opportunities. The learning experiences adults seek are directly related, at least in their own perception, to the life-changing events that triggered the seeking. Adults are generally willing to engage in learning experiences for the duration of the particular life-changing events, they then too often arrive at a new comfort zone.

Another interesting fact is the more education people acquire, the more learning they want. They keep on attending other seminars and classes. They seem to keep demanding more knowledge about the known and unknown. During the ten years we consulted to Motorola senior management, some of the individuals in the company attended at least five different seminars ranging from a workshop for effective management to management of time, management of stress, team building, and managing your career. This was also true of individuals employed in other organizations such as those in the hospitality industry, home building industry, medical industry, government agencies (at all levels) and military units.

> **Note:** It works best to promote the person first and then send them to training, i.e. at Motorola when a person was promoted to a manager, they became eligible to attend our week long off-site Workshop For Effective Management.
>
> At Bobby McGee's combination full-service restaurants and discos, the new manager, regardless of their years of experiences, had to go through an extensive carefully planned and instructed 14 week education and training program starting at the back of the house and ending at the front of the house reception area before they could manage for one day. They became enculturated and instructed in the specific policies and procedures, selective retention of employees, and best methods of successfully motivating and serving the customer. This process became a major model for the industry.

We have noticed, as adults age they tend to take more time in some psychomotor learning tasks. They will often compensate by being more accurate and making fewer trial-and-error ventures. Adult learners want to do trial-and-success ventures. Adults tend to take errors personally

and are likely to let these affect their self-esteem. Because of this, they
may tend to apply tried-and-true solutions, take fewer risks, and some
may become more rigid and limited in their approaches. For these
reasons with the adult to widen their solution thinking, you need to
reward incremental risk taking and participative behaviors.

Adults learn faster when they know why a particular thing is performed.
Adults seek learning experiences primarily because they have a *use* for
the knowledge or skill. For adults, learning is a means to an end, not an
end in itself. The learning must be oriented towards the results, usable,
accessible and tied to the goal of the learner.

**MOTIVATION
FOR
LEARNING**

There is great benefit in knowing that a variety
of motives exist and how they originate and
develop within the individual. By being able to
determine learners' current wants and needs, you
can predict how these influence their current and
future behavior. Usually a motivation is the
fulfillment of a need.   Such intertwining of
needs and motives make the learners want to
seek knowledge, utilize their talents, desire self-
empowerment, relate to other people in a
satisfying manner, and become and remain
effective members of society.

If an instructor is to get the best performance
from each adult learner, he or she needs to be
concerned with two types of needs: *primary* and
psychological. The primary needs involve those
elements of the job that are fundamental to

performance, i.e., the tools and basic requirements that allow them to do their job. For example seeking basic sustenance and job security are primary needs. The task of the instructor is to see that these primary needs are met, for without fulfillment, major blocks to excellent performance will be encountered.

The learners' psychological needs must also be recognized and dealt with. Often the difference between superior and mediocre performance is whether or not these needs are filled. Here examples are self-esteem, self-worth, self-concept and self- confidence. An adult learner's primary needs can be completely filled, yet they can still be a marginal performer if they have unmet psychological needs.

> **Note:** As an outcome of unfulfilled psychological needs, many managers and leaders exhibit personalized power behaviors. This appears to be a substitute for their unmet psychological needs such as belongingness, self-worth, etc. It is thus understandable to see how psychologically inept adults end up "at the controls" through the use of intimidation and bullying.

Most of the clues to an individual's motivation will come from observing what they do and say over a period of time. You must be careful not to latch onto one or two words or actions that the learner uses as a way of assessing their behavior. Rather, you need to look for achievement, affiliation, and status/power, as well as, task, analysis or people orientation needs that tend to recur over time.

Next, when trying to decide whether another person has mostly primary or psychological needs, you must be careful not to confuse your own motivations with those of the individuals you are instructing. There is a natural tendency on the part of most people to see others as they see themselves. You must be careful to sort out your own feelings from what you actually observe, not what you think you are observing. A good technique to assist you in observing is to take a sheet of paper and put on the top half the facts of the observation of the individual in a particular situation at a particular time. On the bottom of the paper write your interpretations of what you feel or think the top half of the paper means.

This then helps you distinguish between the facts, the observed (top half) and your personal interpretation via your own needs (bottom half). You train yourself to separate out the objective data from your interpretation.

There is a tendency to attribute motivation to an individual when none is present. Just because he or she says "goals", talks about "people", or uses "strong language", it does not mean that he or she has a certain need. There must be some activity, action, behavior or concern before any of these motives should be acknowledged.

MOTIVATION TO ATTEND EDUCATION AND TRAINING

With respect to the practical problem of providing instruction to adult learners. It is evident that they want to place themselves in the to place themselves in the environment where such instruction occurs in order to be able to be effected by it.

Many adults have had negative motivation experiences regarding school. It is key to note that most adults do not have negative motivation regarding learning per se, or the value of an education, but only toward school attendance and the methods of instructing and testing.

For purposes of the present writing, desire or willingness to attend a learning situation is assumed.

MOTIVATION TO ACHIEVE

Usually individuals conceptualize their goals in terms of *action*. Wanting to comprehend, understand or appreciate a subject is *not* the type of learning   to which most adults aspire.

If the adult's motivation to learn means that he or she resolves to be *able to do something*, (a something that can be achieved as a result of learning,) then this is a substantial positive motivation.

Achievement motivation is the incentive to impel or move to action, to accomplish something successfully, especially by means of exertion, skill, practice, or perseverance. Achievement motivation is the inspiration, stimulation and resolution to stir to a behavior or feeling to acquire, attain and finish.

Motivation to achieve means wanting to be able to do something well.

Wanting to comprehend a subject, or to really understand it, or to appreciate it are not the kinds of learning results to which learners normally relate their own individual desires. Typically only a very sophisticated, mature individual understands what is meant by a desire to understand.

Note: That is why a system such as (TQM) Total Quality Management or the Deming (1982) method helps people stretch their understanding levels in order to perform better via objective feedback loops, etc.

Specific achievement motivation is using action and outcome ideas as a basis for training in the work place. Wise instructors know the power of telling a learner what he or she will be able to do when a particular learning session or topic in completed. Young learners of science may be told, for example, that the learning of certain principles will enable them to predict the size of a plant, or to express its rate of growth in graphic form. Young learner of mathematics may be told that, having learned certain principles, they will be able to find the lengths of the sides of triangles.

However, it is relatively easy to overlook this kind of motivation, and this is a common mistake of beginning instructors. An instructor may begin by saying, "Now we are going to learn about valence," but such a statement is extremely weak, from the standpoint of human motives. How much better if the instructor can initially inform the learner that the principles of valence will enable them to predict the molecular composition of compounds resulting from chemical reactions, or some other desirable action the learner can readily grasp. The key to achievement motivation is knowing and accepting the learner's conception of action.

The learner must want to be able to do something first before achieving it.

ACHIEVEMENT OF SUB-TASKS

It is perhaps not surprising to find additional usefulness for specific achievement motivation in maintaining interest in a learning task. In this case, though, the learner must undertake to achieve the goals of sub-tasks along the route.

If achievements of sub-tasks are to become sources of motivation, it is evident that they must be systematically communicated to the adult learner. This means simply that the learner must be told, "Next you will need to learn how to recognize the --------," or something equivalent to this, before the learner actually undertakes the learning. One cannot expect the learner somehow to infer the goal of the next sub-task before the learner has even begun it. In order to use achievement as a source of motivation, it must be communicated to the learner prior to the occurrence of learning. Obviously to do this for every subtask to be learned requires very careful planning of the whole instructional sequence for any topic.

Carefully constructed specific achievement motivation can be used to justify the learning to the organization or institution. Your job is easier if you can show how the vision and mission are being furthered through education and training.

ENJOYMENT OF LEARNING

If the learner can regularly seek and find rewards for his or her achievement motivation, it is not unreasonable to suppose this entire set of experiences will generalize into a positive enjoyment of learning itself.

The learners' personal internal "state of affairs" greatly influences their enjoyment of learning. What we have reference to as primary and psychological are kinds of needs that arise from within the individual. The next to be considered are the external events that influence the learning process. This is the instruction part. In terms of managing instruction, it is evident that certain steps must be taken to arrange establishment of suitable sequences of instruction and any possible consequences regarding outcomes. By suitable planning one can ensure that prerequisite learning has been accomplished or completed.

‹ ‹ ‹ ‹ ‹ ‹ ‹ **What the Adult Learner Wants** › › › › › › ›

There are five basic things a learner wants that can help you structure your instruction.

1. *They want to know the truth.* They want to really know the truth. Everyone believes that they are not getting the truth. They feel there is more margin than you say and that there are more fringes you could use. They want to be trusted just like you want to be trusted. They want to be recognized by their boss and others as a person of good, sound judgment.

2. *The adult always wants to feel good about themselves.* So do you. They want to feel that what they are doing definitely matters. They want to be listened to. They want to be liked. They really do. They may put on the facade of being mean and grumpy but they really want to be liked.

3. *They want to avoid the insecurity that comes from surprises and changes.* They want to avoid future troubles and risks. They want to avoid feeling boxed into a corner. They want to work easier, not harder. They want to keep their job and get promoted. They want to count on the instructor, now and in the future. While they certainly want to be the best now, they want to be able to count on the instructor in the future.

4. *They want to meet their personal goals and needs without violating their integrity.* They want to be treated nicely. Most want excitement. Most want adventure, travel, sex, good food, calmness and the good life.

5. *They want knowledge.* Yet, they want to get the education and training over with and get on to other things. Very few people want to

sustain an education or training for a long time. They are as eager and anxious to get on with other things just as the instructor is. Understanding this will help the instructor assume a more masterful position and posture in their instructing stance.

[•[•[•[•[•[•[Values and Beliefs   ]•]•]•]•]•]•]
Leading to Motivation and Gratification

As a small child, what gets gratified gives a person incentive to repeat or not repeat the action. These gratifications received the during the Basic Imprinting Stage, ages 0 to 6 (Ripley & Ripley, 1997) are then translated and adopted during the Values Acquiring stage, ages 7 to 12. (Ripley & Ripley, 1998) Later they are reexamined and accepted or rejected during the Era Impacting Stage, ages 13 to 18, (Ripley & Ripley, 2004) with the individual in possession of fairly solidified values and beliefs by their late 20's. (Your Child's Ages & Stages, Ripley and Ripley, 1995) Values and beliefs in turn lead to later motivations and gratification. The following specific items combine to show how today's American adult's values are reflected in their desires. The following are examples of what we have found that the American people value and how they want the world to operate.

ENJOY
DOING
GOOD

Today's mature adults enjoy doing good. They like to reward and praise talent, potential accomplishments and virtue. By loving to see virtues rewarded, they seek happy endings and good completions.

AVOID PUBLICITY

Today 's mature adults generally are publicity shy They tend to avoid publicity, or at least do not seek celebrity status. It seems to be not awfully important to them one way or another. They vicariously enjoy the status of others but acknowledge that publicity has a downside: *loss of freedom.* They have no sympathy for publicity seekers who whine about the lack of privacy after seeking publicity to attain fame and fortune.

HAVE NO NEED TO BE LOVED BY EVERYONE

Adolescents in our culture have a need to be liked and loved by everyone. Their subsequent inevitable experiences show that this places the person in a position of being approval dependent, letting others control their life. Along the maturing process, the young adult gets selective in their love - their requirement for the fulfillment of love becomes satisfied by a more select, fewer number of people. So the mature person does not need to be loved by everyone but acknowledges that they need to give and receive quality love.

EXPRESS GRATITUDE

Today's mature adults have an awareness that they alone are not responsible for their successes. They give credit where credit is due, to: mentors, parents, colleagues, educators, educational institutions, home towns, etc. Expressions of gratitude, or at least awareness of their good fortune, are common. This is demonstrated by the fact that whenever asked they quickly and easily give credit to a wide variety of people and institutions.

DELIGHT IN JUSTICE

Today's mature American adults find great satisfaction in bringing about justice. They delight in stopping cruelty and exploitation. They fight lies and untruths, and are good punishers of evil. Since they hate for sin and evil to be rewarded, they deplore people "getting away" with such behaviors. Law and order is something they enjoy bringing about in a chaotic situation, or in a dirty and unclean situation.

They try to set things right, to clean up bad situations. They may appear to be meddlers but they do not mean to do bad things and will respond with anger when other people do mean things. Their fighting is not indicative of open hostility, paranoia, grandiosity, authority, rebellion, etc., but it is for setting things right. Their behavior is problem-centered and improvement-oriented.

PICK OWN CAUSES

Today's mature adults generally pick out their own causes, which are apt to be few in number rather than responding to advertising or to campaigns or to other people's exhortations. The media has only a momentary impact, not the true lasting impact it thinks it has. When enough adults concur or focus on one cause, the resulting change becomes incorporated into the current culture and passed on to the next generation. Diversity as a concept is an example of such an incorporated change.

**ATTITUDE
ON
WAR AND PEACE**

Today's mature adults tend to enjoy peace, calm, quiet, pleasantness, etc., and they do not like turmoil fighting, war, etc. They are not generalized fighters on every front, but they can enjoy themselves in the middle of a particular "war". They also seem practical, shrewd and realistic about war and peace, more often than impractical or unrealistic. They like to be effective and dislike being ineffectual.

**ENJOY
SOLVING
MYSTERY**

Today's mature American adults tend to be attracted by mystery, by the unknown, and by unsolved problems. The challenging situation does not frighten them, but entices them. From uncovering a previous secret of nature to watching a TV mystery unfold, the unknown beckons them. They try to free themselves from illusions, to look at the facts courageously, to take away the blindfold and behold the truth.

**IMPROVE
WORLD
BEYOND THEIR**

Today's mature adults have concern for the world beyond their borders. They somehow manage to love the world as it is and yet try to

BORDERS

improve it. They feel in all cases there is some hope that people, nature and society can be improved. They realistically recognize both good and evil wherever these occur.

**GO BEYOND
WORK ETHIC**

Today's mature adults have evolved a work ethic that includes the whole work life environment. They respond with vigor to the challenges in a job. Uniformly, they all consider their work to be worthwhile, important, even essential. They enjoy creating greater efficiency by making an operation: more neat, more compact, simpler, faster, less expensive, turn out a better product, function with less parts, require a smaller number of operations, less clumsy, less effortful, more fool proof, safe, more "elegant", and less laborious. Being given a chance to improve the situation or the operation is considered a reward in itself. They enjoy improving. They like doing things well, "doing a good job", "to do well what needs doing". Many such phrases in use add up to "bringing about good performance". They enjoy taking on responsibility that they can handle well, and certainly don't fear or evade such accountabilities.

Americans receive their primary identity from their career. If you ask an American who they are, they tend to respond with the name of their career. The most mature workers move beyond the occupational label to give them meaning. Yet they receive vast enjoyment from the work environment, a satisfaction often equal to the home environment. Therefore what happens in their work world is important to them - they enjoy self-managing teams and love to be in-charge of their own work environment.

From the rewards of their work, they enjoy giving some of their money away to causes they consider important, good, and worthwhile. They take pleasure in philanthropy. One advantage they see of taking responsibility is eventuality of becoming the boss with the right to give away the corporation's money, to choose which good causes to help.

HELP THOSE COMING BEHIND

Today's mature adults enjoy helping-up those behind them. This is observable in how they take great pleasure in their children and in helping them to grow into good fulfilled adults. The mature adult has a sense of "noblesse oblige": it is the duty of the superior, of the one who sees and knows, to be patient and tolerant, as with children. By feeling it is a pity for talent to be wasted, the mature adult tends to acknowledge that every person should have an opportunity to develop to his or her highest potential, to have a fair chance, to have an equal opportunity.

They enjoy watching and helping younger workers develop self-actualization. They offer guidance and support to co-workers. The mature adult gets great pleasure from knowing admirable people. They respect courageous, honest, effective, "straight dealing", "big", creative, and playing by the rules people. "My work brings me in contact with many fine people." The mature adult enjoys watching happiness and helping to bring it about.

REPLICATE SOCIETY

The above characteristics all help to stabilize and replicate society yet also encourages creativity and innovation. The instructor needs to know who are the learners today. By taking into account and utilizing the motivations and satisfiers along with the personal empowerment needs of the individual adult attendee, more effective and lasting learning can result.

People may say "yes, this is us, but are others in other areas of the world really different?" It doesn't take much imagination (i.e. a quick look at current world events) to realize how some people cling to old ideas, shun the unknown, or may only be concerned for themselves.

Note: We need to repeat that these are characteristics of mature adult Americans. Our current subculture for teenagers seems to be so far away from these adult attributes that the federal government has instituted several legislated programs, such as the School-to-Work program(School-to-Work Opportunities Act, 1994) and the Workforce Investment Act (1998) for fostering values more consistent with the mature adult American, but at a younger age.

Chapter 02
∫◊∫◊∫◊∫ Adult Personal Empowerment ∫◊∫◊∫◊∫
In business, industry, government and educational institutions

Adult personal empowerment is a concept, a philosophy, a set of organizational behavioral practices, and an organizational program. (Ripley and Ripley, 1993) As a concept, empowerment is the vesting of decision-making or approval authority to adult employees where, traditionally, such authority was managerial prerogative. Empowerment as a philosophy and set of behavioral practices means allowing the self-managing teams and individual adults to be in charge of their own career destinies while meeting and exceeding company and personal goals through the shared company vision. Empowerment as an organizational educating and training program involves providing the framework and giving permission to the total adult workforce in order to unleash, develop, and utilize their skills and knowledge to their fullest potential for the good of the organization as well as for the adult themselves.

Empowerment as Decision Making Concept

Empowerment is placing the responsibility for decisions further and further within the organization. Empowerment is making all adults in the business, industry, government or educational institution a manager of their own workstation. Empowerment as shared decision making does not necessitate giving up control but rather changing the way control is exercised.

Empowerment as Meeting Goals Through a Shared Vision or Philosophy

Empowerment is the effective application of an organization's vision and mission to the selection, development and utilization of their total adult human resource asset. This organization could be government, a private enterprise or an educational institution. Empowerment is channeling the organizational culture in such a way that the aims and goals of the organization and those of adult employees are not in conflict. Empowerment is a process to better implement customer focus, quality and continuous improvement. Empowerment is the means and the quality finished product is the end. This result is carefully measured by customer satisfaction. Such empowerment requires the individual manager to believe himself or herself to be a force for change and improvement and to behave accordingly.

Empowerment as a Learning Culture or Organizational Practices

Empowerment can be described as a learning culture. Learning encompasses short-term skill requirements and longer term adult development needs. Learning culminates in problem solving and problem avoidance.

Empowerment is an employment relationship, a set of organizational practices for the optimum utilization of all adult human resources. Empowerment is any management practice that increases the team's or individual adult's sense of self-determination.

Empowerment refers to a process whereby an individual adult's or team's belief in their competency or effectiveness is enhanced. To empower then means either to strengthen this enhancement belief or to weaken the individual's or team's belief in powerlessness (helplessness). Empowering means enabling and raising adult employees' and students' convictions to successfully execute desired behavior rather than just raising their hopes for favorable performance outcomes. Learning, training and retraining are the keys to raising these convictions as well as competence.   Empowerment is the realization and actualization of potential and opportunity that are only just waiting to be unleashed.

Adult Instructing and Empowerment Involves Both Behavioral and Organizational Changes

As managerial and instructor behavior, empowerment involves talking with adults, training adults, building adults into teams, trusting adults, holding adults accountable, and giving recognition to adults.

In empowerment we are talking about the empowerment of the environment -- the organization and culture, of the self- managing team, and of the individual on the two dimensions of behavior and beliefs. All of these factors can be measured with assessment instruments first for baselining and later for recording the improvements and/or blockages. Adult instructing and empowerment allows for the creating and sustaining of an organization's or institution's vitality. (Lewin, 1951, Arguris, 1964, Likert, 1967, Lippitt, 1969, Knowles, 1975, 1998, Zander, 1977, Ripley and Ripley, 1988, 1992, 1993, 1994).

Due to their values and beliefs, the mature American adult seeks personal empowerment.   Personal empowerment to each individual adult is learning the tools to take control of their life and discovering and developing their talents, so they can find, build, and keep their personal success. Personal empowerment comes from within the individual. It is believing in themselves as a force for change and improvement in their life and environment. It is ensuring that their aims and actions do not conflict. It is being in charge of their own career destiny while meeting personal goals.

The 60's through the 90's swirled together and made a dynamic 21st Century populace with a broad balanced value system. Today's mature adult is carrying forward the basics of American heritage while continually adding small subtleties that also improve their personal empowerment. Younger Americans have already assimilated what the previous generations had to resolve through conflict resolution. We should not be surprised as the "X" and "Y" generations do well, for they have been raised by these previous system-changing generations. Revolutionary, society-changing actions are seen as no longer necessary since a large portion of the "60's" desired changes have occurred.

The happier and more motivated adult will have satisfied most of these personal empowerment needs, according to their individual criteria. The following are twenty of the most important personal empowerment needs and motives of the adult learner.

PERSONAL EMPOWERMENT NEEDS

•**Security** - self-preservation, survival: important to satisfy first to have energy left for other motives

•**Health-Wellness** - more people seek it, includes the development and maintenance of eight spokes of lifestyle. (Ripley, 2009).

•**Gratification of Appetite** - for physical, mental and emotional fulfillment

•**Entertainment** - amusement, games, movies, books, recreations, all forms of diversion.

•**Admiration** - the desire to be recognized for accomplishments.

•**Self-improvement** - life long learning - insatiable human need to know and grow, the seeking and understanding of information.

•**Beauty** - one's individual need to seek and incorporate it into his or her life.

•**To Be Understood** - the successful conveying of ideas.

•**Career Satisfaction** - when personal talents and skills can and are developed and used.

•**To Be Loved and To Love** - the basic need without which the other needs have no meaning.

•**Belongingness** - resulting from support and caring.

•**Creative Expression** - activities and accomplishments that use the individual's talents, giving great satisfaction.

•**Recognition** - helps earn self-respect and enhance self-esteem.

•**New experiences** - benefits come from planning for the next experience as well as from the experience itself.

•**Self-Confidence** - good habits performed daily create self-trust.

•**Financial Freedom** - the outcome of saving part of all that is acquired and the maturity of delaying gratification.

•**Responsibility** - seeking and satisfying commitments with their work, their home, their life and their community.

•**To Trust And Be Trusted** - the ability to risk and be vulnerable.

•**Time** - personal use and control of time resources without creating undo pressure or stress, prioritizing what is worth spending your time on.

Chapter 03
≈ • ≈ • ≈ • ≈   Time Frame Eras   ≈ • ≈ • ≈ • ≈
Why the Adult Learners Behave the Way They Do

BEHAVIOR AND ATTITUDE SCRIPTING STAGES

AGE GROUPING STAGES	SCRIPTING PROGRAMMING
0-1-2-3-4-5-6	Basic Imprinting
7-8-9-10-11-12	Values Acquiring
13-14-15-16-17-18	Era Impacting
19 and older	Changes Primarily by Re-Parenting or a significant event

Basic Imprinting Stage (0 - 6 Year Old)

There is little agreement on the exact phasing of our human scripting and programming. However, there is general agreement on what happens during the programming stages of these age groupings. During the **Basic Imprinting Stage,** simple behavior patterns are quickly adopted. Scripts are the mental messages you were given as a child that stay with you directing controlling and advising your attitudes and behaviors. Such as most of you learned the "normal" American way to eat. You take the fork in the left hand and put the prongs in your food. You have your knife in the right hand and cut the food, while being held by the fork in the left hand. Then you put down the knife, transfer the fork from the left hand to the right, and place the food in your mouth. But many European-Americans don't eat that way. They keep the fork in the left hand and the knife in right hand, don't place the knife down, don't transfer the fork from one hand to the other and place the food directly in their mouths while still holding both the knife and fork. Many Asian-Americans don't even use knives and forks. They use two chop sticks to squeeze the portion of food and then place the food in their mouths. You probably don't get up-tight about the manner in which other people eat, but you probably think: "That is not the right way to eat! My way is the right way to eat." When you feel your way is the right way, basic scripting judgment already comes into play.

Basic imprinting is the time of learning the family's weekly, seasonal and annual activities - answering the what, how, when and why of these activities until a person reaches a fairly deep understanding of what goes on in a household. Your root attitudes and behaviors are based on programming that was presented to you during your basic imprinting stage.

In addition to physical behavior development, a tremendous amount of mental, emotional and social development takes place in the basic imprinting stage. For example, for most Americans are scripted that it is wrong to steal and if you do, you should make restitution and feel guilty for having done the act. However, for another group of Americans it is not wrong for them to steal, but it is wrong to get caught and they feel remorseful only for getting caught. There are several sage sayings that illustrate the importance of the basic imprinting stage. "Give me a child until they are six and they are already molded for life." "As the twig is bent, so the tree shall grow." Children observe and conclude, "That's what a mother is; that's what a father is; that's what adults do! If I become an adult that's what I'm going to do!" This is when you get your initial scripts and mental computer tapes for storage and future replay.

During the basic imprinting stage children have varying exposures and influences from the time-frame era occurring during the child's 0-6 years. The family protects and filters the messages from the outside world, isolating this age child from cruel realities, etc. The time-frame era most impacting to the 0-6 year old is the parent's and care-giver's one that occurred during their own era impacting stage. Also impacting the young child are older siblings or neighbors in the values acquiring stage. (see *Your Child's Ages & Stages: Ages 0 to 6*, Carefree Press)

Values Acquiring Stage (7 - 12 Year Old)
In the **Values Acquiring Stage** the formal learning process of the school, religious institutions and the media come into play to influence you. There is also the continuing influence of the family.

The schools provide the lockstep, sequential and cultural input that helps provide a common basis for our society. The skills and knowledge are provided that the society at that time deems to be important, such as science and mathematics vs one-hundred years ago when agriculture and literature predominated.

Religious institutions teach specific belief doctrines, resulting in varying values and sub-culture orientations.

The media, meaning the mass communication systems inputs of the times, (i.e. TV, video, Internet, etc.) presents a wider culture range of input to the "captive" audience of one to twelve year olds. Marketing of even extreme and atypical heroine and heroes can become the models for the target group.

This is the time of skills and talents identification and initial development.   Musicians, athletes, artists, mathematicians, budding scientists and electronic whizzes benefit from this process at this age.

New attitudes and behaviors are combined with your basic imprinting stage ones. Your heroes and heroines become models in your life that you secretly look up to, try to imitate in the way you talk, walk, dress and are influenced by as to the way you want to be when you grow up. This is the time of value accumulation. You may accumulate conflicting values from your family and from forces in your environment. Since these values become so deeply imprinted at this time, this is the prevention stage for drugs, violence and teen pregnancies of the next stage. It is up to parents and societal institutions to use this precious time to "inoculate" children against future pressures.

Your resulting values are demonstrated by your behaviors and attitudes and are programmed in you like software in a computer. Your mental computer is put to use in filtering, categorizing and shaping the new information. This information comes through the time-frame era happening then. The information is formed into concepts, which are combined into principles and laws of living. The combination of new knowledge and experiences, as well as identification and modeling after family members, friends, and external "heroes and heroines" in the world around you, helps create your values and standards. Your group memberships start to influence you.

During the values acquiring stage, the time-frame eras have more influence than before. The national and world conditions via the media, school, etc. influence the forming values of the child. Siblings, school mates and neighbors in the era impacting stage expose and initiate the 7-

12 age group to the sub-cultural norms around them. These norms are influenced by the time-frame era occurring then. (see *Your Child's Ages & Stages: Ages 7 to 12,* Carefree Press)

Era Impacting Stage (13 - 18 Year Old)

In the **Era Impacting Stage** the group pressure and "everyone is doing it" takes over. "Birds of a feather, flock together," but now the individual does the choosing of which flock. If you fail to choose, it is chosen for you. Now you start associating more and more with people of like interests, behaviors, attitudes and developing value systems. You associate intensively with one another and reinforce each other in these areas. You and your group are all more susceptible than before to time-frame era influences. This vulnerability can be positive if good things are occurring, negative if bad. This particular time-frame era will continue to influence this group for decades to come. The era becomes your fantasy, nostalgia, and the "yard stick" by which you measure future time-fame eras. These fads are going to be interacting in your mental pathways and emotionally in your responses and decisions for many years to come. You are now in the process of defining and integrating values, beliefs, and standards of your particular culture and sub-culture into your own personality. It is the task of a person in this stage to re-examine and question all previously acquired values and imprinted scripting. And this is often flamboyantly done, to the dismay of those close by, ie parents, siblings and grandparents. It is during this period when you achieve physical maturity and a "dominant core value system." It is during this time that you engage in experimentation, verification and validation of your basic life plan and script. This is inclusive of the time frame eras from when you were born to around age eighteen. Your generation group will go through life with a little different set of values and experiences than any other generation group that you come in contact with throughout your life. Your individual set of values were greatly influenced and partly determined by this set of values experiencing of your generational group. (see *Your Child's Ages & Stages: Ages 13 to 18,* Carefree Press)

Adult Script Changes Can Happen At Any Time
After this Era Impacting Stage about 80% of your behaviors and attitudes are pretty well set. However, dramatic change in your core value system may occur at any time during your life. It takes **learning** or a significant event to change your attitudes and behaviors after this time. Conflicts of values that accumulate during the previous three stages may also come to light at any time and cause internal or external distress. Assisting the individuals in resolving these conflicts is another job of **instructing**.

Changes in attitudes and behaviors can occur in a slow buildup by such things as continuous exposure to media messages, job changes, geographical moves, etc., or through dramatic events such as involvement in a divorce, being fired, a war, an accident causing a disability, or a new job or accomplishment. The common denominator of significant events is a challenge and a disruption to the adults' present behavior patterns and beliefs. The trainer must be careful to distinguish between events that actually change adults' value system, and events which simply modify their behavior. The trainer can control the changes in the adult and their outlook if the instructor is aware of learning techniques. The adult can change their attitudes and behaviors by new learning and new skill development when they receive appropriate reinforcement with new or old peer approval. The adults' public behavior and attitude may be outwardly changed because of new laws and new "correctness." However, the adults' core values are still basically the same. If there is little actual contact or interaction with the avoided or ignored, or never having a new experience or new knowledge on the subject, there will probably be no significant event to create either a slow buildup or dramatic permanent change to the core.

When change challenges the adults' value system, the likely reactions are rejection, frustration, or hostility. This is because it is threatening to the adults' core values. For most adults, it is much easier to maintain the status quo. To accept the possibility that a completely different way is equally as correct and as right is very unsettling.

Throughout history each new generation has probably challenged, to some extent, the older generations' ways of doing things. Recently the rate of change of technology, legal dimensions, social behavior, education and global economic systems have created vastly diverse scripting and programming experiences between generations. The differences in these experiences have created a spectrum of widely varying value systems within our society. The basic and cultural value systems are, in fact, dramatically different between the generations that presently exist simultaneously in our society. The focus should not be so much on how to change the learner to conform to the trainer's standards and values. Instead, the instructor must learn how to accept and understand the learner in their own right, acknowledging the existence and validity of their values and their behaviors. As many Native American Indians believe, "to know another person you must walk a mile in their moccasins." This is the classic challenge for understanding others. If the instructor can understand and respect other people and their values, then they can interact with them in a more effective manner. Most of the instructor's problems in communication, motivation, and interaction will diminish through such simple respect and understanding. Today's instructor must become a life-long student of the on-going process of cultural differences, time-frame era changes and their influence factors on the learner.

Time-Frame Eras

As instructors it is important to learn what was occurring when the various age groups in the United States ranging in age from 0 to 90 years old were *basic imprinted, value acquired*, and *era impacted*.   This provides you with an understanding of their normal core behavior and attitudes that are the result of what was going on when they were in the three stages.   By observing another person's period of history i.e. time-frame eras, and understanding the major influencing factors that programmed their age group contrasted to your age group - you can begin to understand the **why** and **how** that motivates them to do what they do in today's world.

The following is a quick snapshot of:
(((§))) Why American Learners Behave the Way They Do (((§)))
Due to Time Frame Eras

Time Frame Eras	**Behavior and Attitude Influence Factors During Basic Imprinting, Values Acquiring & Era Impacting stages.**
1920s	Post World War I
	Close and extended family
	Honored participations of elders in a close extended family
	Flappers - Charleston
	Model T
	Neighborhoods
	The "Old Country" - European influence
	"Jazz" age begins
	Black Sox baseball scandal
	Women receive vote
	First municipal airport opens in Tucson, Arizona
	Prohibition enacted
	First Miss America crowned
	Cigarettes first legalized in Iowa
	Inflation in Europe reaches levels requiring wheelbarrows of money to buy bread
	First birth control clinic opens in New York City
	Pancho Villa is gunned down in Mexico
	Mickey Mouse first appears
	First "Oscar" awards
	Babe Ruth hits 60 home runs
	First motel opens in San Luis Obispo, California
	First "Talking" Movie
	U.S. citizenship conferred on all Native American Indians
	Stock Market Crash
	Frank Lloyd Wright perfects organic architecture
	Modern kitchen - electric stove, refrigerator available
Time Frame Eras	**Behavior and Attitude Influence Factors During Basic Imprinting, Values Acquiring & Era Impacting stages.**
1930s	The Great Depression
	Security becomes important

Radio program become mainstream
Dionne quintuplets are born
Automobile becomes widely owned
Planet Jupiter discovered
First packages of frozen food - Birdseye
Empire State Building completed
Right of Negroes to serve on juries
"Star Spangled Banner" becomes the national anthem
Adolph Hitler appointed chancellor of Germany
"New Deal" proposed by Franklin D. Roosevelt
Prohibition ends
Tennessee Valley Authority formed as the first
 publicly owned utility in America
Social Security Act is passed
John L. Lewis emerges as the voice of organized labor
Rural Free Delivery - rural mail delivery
Rural electrification
Modern kitchen - electric stove, refrigerators available
Joe Louis becomes heavyweight champion
Parker Brothers introduces the game Monopoly
Jesse Owens wins four gold medal at the Berlin Olympics
Hindenburg zeppelin explodes in New Jersey
Golden Gate Bridge dedicated in San Francisco
Orson Welles delivers "War of the Worlds" broadcast
Jitterbug born in New York with Count Basie and Benny Goodman
Snow White and Seven Dwarfs movie
The Grapes of Wrath by John Steinbeck, published
Gone With the Wind Movie
Hollywood society in full swing
The Wizard of Oz movie with Judy Garland

Time Frame Eras	Behavior and Attitude Influence Factors During Basic Imprinting, Values Acquiring & Era Impacting stages.
1940s	World War II Win is the dominant value Mobility of families becomes mainstream Family Decay begins Women in the work force becomes new phenomenon Right and Wrong are emphasized values Hardy Boys books Nancy Drew books Hattie McDaniel becomes first Negro to win Oscar Nylon stockings go on sale Grandma Moses has her first art show "White Christmas" written by Irving Berlin

The Withholding Tax Act is signed
GI Bill of Rights signed
Grand Rapids, Michigan adds fluoride to water supply
Atomic bombs dropped on Hiroshima and Nagasaki
German annihilation of six million Jews is discovered
United Nations is chartered
Negroes vote for the first time in Mississippi
First "auto-bank" service - Chicago
Berlin airlift
"Long-playing" 331/3 rpm record introduced
Kinsey Report released
Truman upsets Dewey
"Rudolph the Red-Nosed Reindeer" sung by Gene Autry
Television stations and public television begins

Time Frame Eras	**Behavior and Attitude Influence Factors During Basic Imprinting, Values Acquiring & Era Impacting stages.**
1950s	McCarthyism is new "witch hunting" on TV
	Korean Conflict (Pretty much ignored)
	Affluence (The "good life" arrives)
	Indulged kids - Dr. Spock
	Berlin Wall built
	Television arrives to the masses
	Permissiveness
	Male length of hair becomes public concern
	Sex change operation - Copenhagen -
	Douglas MacArthur relieved of his duties
	Mt. Everest conquered
	Playboy begins publication
	Salk's polio vaccine distributed in the U.S.
	Brown v. The Board of Education decided by Supreme Court
	Frank Lloyd Wright designs Guggenheim in NY
	"Rock Around the Clock" by Bill Haley and the Comets begins the rock and roll era
	Elvis Presley becomes the "King of Rock and Roll"
	Dr. Martin Luther King becomes recognized
	Blacks becomes the popular new name for Negroes
	Grace Kelly marries Prince Rainier
	Peyton Place become best seller
	Edsel is major failure
	Explorer I, circles the globe
	Hula hoops the rage
	Fidel Castro takes control of Cuba
	Alaska and Hawaii become States
	Malls Open - Southdale in Minneapolis

Barbie dolls emerge
Track housing developments spread across U.S.
Jackson Pollock - Lead Artist: Abstract Expressionism
Sputnik launched

Time Frame Eras	Behavior and Attitude Influence Factors During Basic Imprinting, Values Acquiring & Era Impacting stages.
1960s	Sun City opens in Arizona Payola scandal involving over 200 disc jockeys The "pill" Peace Corps founded U.S.S.R. sends a cosmonaut into space Alan Shepard into space one month later Bay of Pigs invasion fails in Cuba HUD started Vietnam John Glenn, first American to orbit the earth Roger Maris hits 61 home runs First major "skyjacking" in the U.S. Supreme Court bans prayer in public schools Thalidomide babies born in Europe and U.S. Second Vatican Council James Meredith, first black student to attend the University of Mississippi Marilyn Monroe dies Andy Warhol - Artist & Filmmaker makes impact The first "singles only" weekend in the Catskills Cuban Missile Crisis Beatles tour the U.S. Dr. Martin Luther King - "I have a dream . . . ." John F. Kennedy assassinated Malcolm X assassinated Civil Rights Act signed Dr. Strangelove movie popular Dr. Zhivago movie popular Campus protests begin at Berkeley Timothy Leary lead LSD cultist to "turn on" and "drop out" Ralph Nader begins consumerism movement "Hippies" are born - "Flower Children" Six Days War - Israel First human heart transplant U.S.S. Pueblo captured by North Koreans Musical "Hair" opens in New York Dr. Martin Luther King assassinated

Robert Kennedy assassinated
Woodstock
Chappaquidick
First trip to the moon - Neil Armstrong
The Chicago Seven and Charles Manson make big news
Businesses and Institutions use Computers
Home computers made from kits.
Food Stamps
Medicare - Medicaid
Toffler's Future Shock book published
Rolling Stones introduce conspicuous menace and
sexuality in music
Sexual revolution - Helen Gurley Brown
NOW founded - Betty Friedan first president

Time Frame Eras	Behavior and Attitude Influence Factors During Basic Imprinting, Values Acquiring & Era Impacting stages.
1970s	"Hot pants" hit the streets
	18 year olds get right to vote
	Watergate
	Jaded expectations
	Skylab missions
	Patty Hearst kidnapped
	Muhammad Ali regain heavyweight title
	U.S. celebrates its 200th birthday
	Affirmative Action takes over in hiring
	Elvis Presley dies
	Baby conceived in test tube
	Star Wars movie starts the space craze
	Ayatullah Khomeini overthrows Shah of Iran
	Reusable space shuttle
	Generation gap becomes popular topic
	Disco dancing becomes trendy
	Masters and Johnson's research
	"Free Sex" hits the campuses and the Discos
	Generation Gap widens
	Women's Rights Groups
	Cross-cultural marriages
	Book: Silent Spring - Enviornmentalists begin
	1st Heavy Metal Bands
	Vietnam war ends
	Wounded Knee, S.D. - Native American Indian movement gains national recognition
	Roe vs Wade - U.S. Supreme Court decision

Time Frame Eras	Behavior and Attitude Influence Factors During Basic Imprinting, Values Acquiring & Era Impacting stages.
1980s	AIDS acknowledged, projected to be worldwide problem
	Video Tape- Beta and VHS
	Cable TV
	Atari become popular game
	Japanese automobiles
	Drugs
	Legos
	Commodore - Apple Computer
	Food Stamps become largest funded U.S. welfare program
	Home Schooling spreads
	Welfare expands to include more
	Immigration opens up
	Soccer leagues for children
	Heavy Metal and Acid Rock at peak
	Asian influence
	Gays and Lesbian Rights
	Gender Communication Differences
	Interactive Video
	End of the Berlin Wall
	Cellular Phones
	Nintendo
	Movie - Pretty Woman
	CD-ROM
	Challenger Explosion
	Health Clubs - Jogging
	Stock Market Crash
	S&L Scams and Collapses
	Capital Gains Tax
	TV - Dallas, Moonlighting, Charlie's Angels
	Rambo starts the adventure/violence macho movies
	Movies - Terminator and Die Hard
	Vietnam War movies
	Transformation from records to tapes
	Madonna
	Michael Jackson
	Music - CDs
	Video rental stores
	Global Warming Projected
	Afro-Americans becomes popular name for Blacks
	Mexican-Americans go through popular name change become Chicanos, then Chicanos become Hispanics
	Line Dancing

Multi-Plex movie complexes
Stone washed jeans
Springsteen brings the hard working man into
 mainstream
Memorabilia nostalgia stage of the 50s and 60s
Me - materialistic generation
Home camcorders
Cabbage Patch Dolls
Greenpeace
Minority and women's rights activists make major
social-economic changes
Global economy impacts to all size communities
Country music again brought back into mainstream
Reganomics takes over in a growth economy
First Space Shuttle flight

Time Frame Eras	**Behavior and Attitude Influence Factors During Basic Imprinting, Values Acquiring & Era Impacting stages.**
1990s	American Disabilities Act
	GATT and NAFTA
	Outcome based public education
	Computer software explosion
	Dismemberment of the Soviet Union
	Virtual Reality
	Gangs
	Violence
	Internet - World Wide Web
	1st Computer Graphic Arts Movie - Toy
	Movie - Pocahontas and The Lion King
	Global Interdependence
	Professional Sports Marketing
	Rappers
	Amusement parks change to Theme Parks
	Single Parents
	Majority of adult women in workforce
	Day-Care and Pre-School child care explosion
	Teenage pregnancy explosion
	African-Americans becomes new popular name for Afro-Americans
	Charter Schools spread
	Concern rises over athlete violence
	Christmas Barbie Doll Sells Out
	Renewal of romantic classic movies
	Movie Harry met Sally sets the stage
	3 Jane Austen books made into movies
	Latch-key children

New Age books and music
Legal and illegal immigration reaches new high
First Republican congress in 40 years
Generation "X" emerges
TV program Friends emerges as a voice
"Politically Correct" controls open communications
TV program Friends emerges as a voice
Gangster rock music and clothing
Superstores emerge - Books, sports, electronics
Super Highway of Information expands at lighting speed
Space - joint national ventures and sharing
Softer rock - Hootie and the Blowfish
Astronomers change ideas with Jupiter exploration
Pay of professional athletes now multi-million dollar deals
UN worldwide - war "peace keeping" missions
TV becomes main political impactor
Lawyers and courts become major society values interpreters
Movie Jurassic Park
Hubbell telescope expands look at the universe
Malls become center of social activity
American troops sent to variety of countries to ensure the "peace"
Environmentalists become heavy activists

Now look and see what the influence factors were and are for those who are in their childhood and teens today. What will be the basic imprinting, cultural values scripting, and era impacting factors as this adult learner group moves through the **21st Century**?

Chapter 04
< • // • # • >   Styles of Learning   < • // • # • >

While adult learners do not approach every learning task exactly the same way they do develop a set of behaviors with which they are most comfortable. The purpose of examining learning styles is to get to know those behavior patterns so that you can better see when they are helpful and when not in your instructing the adult learners in the various learning event settings. These learning situations can vary from colleges and university courses, business and industry education and training sessions, government agency seminars, military training settings, public workshops, and specialized retreats.

Learning styles refer to the ways adult learners prefer to approach new information. Each learns and processes information in their own special ways, though they all share some learning patterns, preferences, and approaches. As the instructor, knowing your own style also can help you realize that other people may approach the same situation in a different way from your own.

The research and literature on learning styles has given instructors new directions for making changes in their instructing. The broadest change has been to open adult learning to more than one approach in the cognitive realm. Different social groupings, alternative activities, more complex projects have all been introduced as efforts to create opportunities for adult learners to use their various strengths in dealing with course material.

Despite the wide range of models, the concept of learning styles has gained growing acceptance because it provides a stable-enough characterization to plan instructional strategies. These varied strategies appear more responsive to adult learner needs. They seem to provide better learning opportunities.

For the purpose here, we will present a synoptic review of the numerous and varied theories or approaches to styles of learning. Then follow with a short self-assessment of your learning style.

To start, Knowles (1975, 1998) theory of <u>andragogy</u> (adult learning) was an attempt to differentiate the way adults learn from the way children learn. Assumptions made based on this theory was outlined by Cantor (1992)

- adults are autonomous and self-directed
- adults are goal oriented
- adults are relevancy oriented (problem centered)--they need to know why they are learning something
- adults are practical and problem-solvers
- adults have accumulated life experiences

This means that instruction for adults needs to focus more on the process and less on the content being taught. Here, instructors adopt a role of facilitator or resource rather than lecturer and utilizes such approaches as case studies, role playing, simulations, and self-evaluations.

Differences Between Men's and Women's Learning Styles
Not only do adult learners have different learning styles than children, but a great deal of literature and research is being conducted on how men and women do not approach the cognitive world in quite the same way.

William Perry (1968) did a study of undergraduate New England college students (male). From this study he determined that young men pass

through a developmental sequence in their thinking modes. Perry isolated nine stages in the sequence, but in outline the stages form this pattern:
Perry's "Developmental Process"

- male students see the world as black/white, right/wrong--they are convinced there is one right answer.
- male learners see there is diversity of opinion, but feel that authorities that describe diversity are poorly qualified, or just "exercising learners" so learners will be forced to find the "right answer" themselves.
- male learners begin to feel that diversity is temporary. They feel that maybe the "right" answer just hasn't been found yet.
- male learners understand that diversity is a legitimate state, but they would still prefer to know what is "right".
- male learners see that everyone has a right to his or her own opinion
- finally the male learners develop a personal commitment to the relativistic world.

Then Belenky et al., (1986) building of the theory and writings of Gilligan (1982) showed how women did not fit into this "male" scale. They reported that women have different "ways of knowing." Belenky et al. chose not to describe the way women think in a staged sequence, although women do move from one style of thinking to others as they mature and gain life experience. Belenky et al. concluded that women have the following possible "ways of knowing."
Belenky et al. "Women's Ways of Knowing"

- silence: women learners feel mindless and voiceless, subject to whims of external authority.
- received knowledge: women learners feel they can receive knowledge, but not create it.
- subjective knowledge: truth and knowledge are private and subjectively known or intuited.

- procedural knowledge: women learners are invested in learning and applying objective procedures for obtaining and communicating knowledge.
- Constructed knowledge: women learners view knowledge as contextual and can create knowledge found objectively or subjectively.

With those two "thinking structures" in the background, let's turn to some specific theories on learning styles that have come out of writings in education and psychology.

Then a number of theorists catalogued the ranges of learning styles in more detail. One of the best known and dominant in references is Kolb (1984)
.

Kolb proposed and illustrated how learning styles could be seen on a continuum running from:
- concrete experience: being involved in a new experience .
- reflective observation: watching others or developing observations about own experience.
- abstract conceptualization: creating theories to explain observations.
- active experimentation: using theories to solve problems, make decisions.

Kolb's Learning Style Model
This model classifies learners as having a preference for 1) *concrete experience* or *abstract conceptualization* (how they take information in), and 2) *active experimentation* or *reflective observation* (how they internalize information). The four types of learners in this classification scheme are:

Type 1 (concrete, reflective). A characteristic question of this learning type is *"Why?"* Type 1 learners respond well to explanations of how course material relates to their experience, their interests, and their future careers. To be effective with Type 1 students, the instructor should function as a *motivator*.

Type 2 **(abstract, reflective).** A characteristic question of this learning type is *"What?"* Type 2 learners respond to information presented in an organized, logical fashion and benefit if they have time for reflection. To be effective, the instructor should function as an *expert*.

Type 3 **(abstract, active).** A characteristic question of this learning type is *"How?"* Type 3 learners respond to having opportunities to work actively on well-defined tasks and to learn by trial-and-error in an environment that allows them to fail safely. To be effective, the instructor should function as a *coach*, providing guided practice and feedback.

Type 4 **(concrete, active).** A characteristic question of this learning type is *"What if?"* Type 4 learners like applying course material in new situations to solve real problems.

To be most effective, the instructor should stay out of the way, maximizing opportunities for the learners to discover things for themselves.

Some adult learners best perceive information using concrete experiences (like feeling, touching, seeing, and hearing) while others best perceive information abstractly (using mental or visual conceptualization.)

Once information is perceived it must be processed. some people process information best by active experimentation (doing something with the information) while others perceive best by reflective observation (thinking about it).

This results in four learning dimensions in this model:

Concrete experience
learning from specific experiences, relating to people, and sensitivity to feelings and people.

Reflective observation
careful observation before making a judgment, viewing things from different perspectives, and looking for the meaning of things.

Abstract conceptualization
Logical analysis of ideas, systematic planning, acting on intellectual understanding of a situation.

Active experimentation
ability to get things done, risk taking, influence people and events through action.

By combining these two opposite dimensions we get four quadrants of learning behavior.

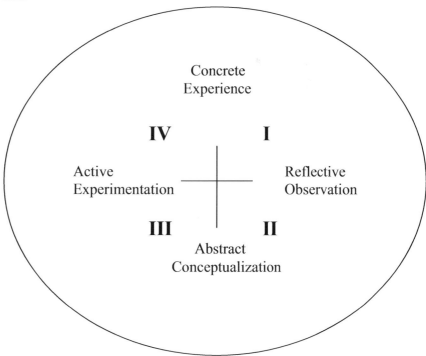

Type I learner:
They are primarily a "hands-on" learner. They tend to rely on intuition rather than logic. They like to rely on other people's analysis rather than your own. They enjoy applying their learning in real life situations.

Type II learner:
They like to look at things from many points of view. They would rather watch rather than take action. They like to gather information and create many categories for things. They like using your imagination in problem solving. They are very sensitive to feelings when learning.

Type III learner:
They like solving problems and finding practical solutions and uses for their learning. They shy away from social and interpersonal issues and prefer technical tasks.

Type IV Learner:
They are concise and logical. Abstract ideas and concepts are more important to them than people issues. Practicality is less important to them than a good logical explanation.

Kolb's model is only one of many. Anthony Gregorc (1982, 1990) modified Kolb's dimensions by focusing on random and sequential processing of information. This is similar to top-down and bottom-up processing. Top-down learners look at the whole task (random) while bottom-up learners proceed one-step-at-time. (sequentially)

Others proposed cycling through all four of Kolb's dimensions. That is first experience the problem, then reflect on it, then analyze it, then act on it. In this approach the learner will recognize that some modes in the cycle are easier than others and will be able to identify the types of learning that should be worked on.

Although Kolb indicated these learning styles as a continuum that one moves through over time, usually people come to prefer, and rely on, one style above the others. And it is these main styles that instructors need to be aware of when creating instructional materials.

Hartman (1995) later took Kolb's learning styles and gave examples of how one might teach to each them:
- for the concrete experiencer--offer laboratories, field work, observations or trigger films..
- for the reflective observer--use logs, journals or brainstorming.
- for the abstract conceptualizer--lectures, papers and analogies work well.
- for the active experimenter--offer simulations, case studies and homework..

Those who prefer the cognitive mode of learning probably learn best by developing overviews, abstracting information, making precise notes, going to lectures, and working in a solitary environment.

Those who prefer the relational/emotional mode of learning probably learn best by working in groups, verbalizing information, and working in relaxed environment.

Those who prefer the physical mode probably learn best by hands- on applications, daily repetitions, taking good notes, allowing time for demonstration and imitation, and allowing free-flowing movement from one task to another.

Gardner (1993) chose to approach learning styles from his theory of multiple intelligence. provided the following summary of Gardener's Multiple Intelligences:
- plays with words (Verbal/Linguistic)
- plays with questions (Logical/Mathematical)
- plays with pictures (Visual/Spatial)
- plays with music (Music/Rhythmic)
- plays with moving (Body/Kinesthetic)
- plays with socializing (Interpersonal)
- plays alone (Intrapersonal)

Probably each adult learner uses some, if not all of these styles when learning, but tend to prefer a small number of methods over the rest.

Schroeder (1996) pointed out that the "typical" student learning style profile is changing on campuses today and there is a much greater variation in the range of learning style preferences to be considered. Therefore it would be wise to understand what learning style preferences are, and how to address them when preparing instructional materials for adults.

Litzinger & Osif (1992). proposed that each of us develops a preferred and consistent set of behaviors or approaches to learning and break it down into the following processes:
- cognition--how one acquires knowledge.
- conceptualization--how one processes information. There are those who are always looking for connections among unrelated events. Meanwhile for others, each event triggers a multitude of new ideas.
- affective--people's motivation, decision making styles, values and emotional preferences will also help to define their learning styles.

Felder and Silverman (1988) proposed that a person's learning style may be defined in part by the answers to five questions:

What type of information does the student preferentially perceive: *sensory*---sights, sounds, physical sensations, or *intuitive*---memories, ideas, insights?

Through which modality is sensory information most effectively perceived: *visual*---pictures, diagrams, graphs, demonstrations, or *verbal*---sounds, written and spoken words and formulas?

With which organization of information is the student most comfortable: *inductive*---facts and observations are given, underlying principles are inferred, or *deductive*---principles are given, consequences and applications are deduced?

How does the student prefer to process information: *actively*---through engagement in physical activity or discussion, or *reflectively*---through introspection?

How does the student progress toward understanding: *sequentially*---in a logical progression of small incremental steps, or *globally*---in large jumps, holistically?

Felder-Silverman Learning Style Model

This model classifies learners as:

- *sensing learners* (concrete, practical, oriented toward facts and procedures) or *intuitive learners* (conceptual, innovative, oriented toward theories and meanings).
- *visual learners* (prefer visual representations of presented material--pictures, diagrams, flow charts) *or verbal learners* (prefer written and spoken explanations).
- *inductive learners* (prefer presentations that proceed from the specific to the general) or *deductive learners* (prefer presentations that go from the general to the specific).
- *active learners* (learn by trying things out, working with others) or *reflective learners* (learn by thinking things through, working alone).

- *sequential learners* (linear, orderly, learn in small incremental steps) or *global learners* (holistic, systems thinkers, learn in large leaps).

Felder & Silverman (1988) in their learning style model proposed the following approaches to reach different adult learners.

Sensing Learners

sensing learners (sensors) favor information that comes in through their senses and *intuitive learners* favor information that arises internally through memory, reflection, and imagination. (These categories derive from Carl Jung's theory of psychological types. Sensors tend to be practical; intuitive learners tend to be imaginative. Sensors like facts and observations; intuitive learners prefer concepts and interpretations. A student who complains about courses having nothing to do with the real world is almost certainly a sensor. Sensors like to solve problems using well-established procedures, don't mind detail work, and don't like unexpected twists or complications; intuitive learners like variety in their work, don't mind complexity, and get bored with too much detail and repetition. Sensors are careful but may be slow; intuitive learners are quick but may be careless.

Sensing learners learn best when given facts and procedures, but most science courses (particularly physics and chemistry) focus on abstract concepts, theories, and formulas, putting sensors at a distinct disadvantage. Moreover, sensors are less comfortable than intuitive learners with symbols; since words and algebraic variables---the stuff of examinations---are symbolic, sensors must translate them into concrete mental images in order to understand them. This process can be a lengthy one, and many sensors who know the material typically run out of time on tests. The net result is that sensors tend to get lower grades than intuitive learners in lecture courses; in effect, they are selectively weeded out, even though they are as likely as intuitive learners to succeed in scientific careers.

Visual Learners

Visual learners get more information from visual images (pictures, diagrams, graphs, schematics, demonstrations) than from verbal material (written and spoken words and mathematical formulas), and vice versa for *verbal learners*. If something is simply said and not shown to visual learners (e.g. in a lecture) there is a good chance they will not retain it.

Most people (at least in western cultures) and presumably most students in science classes are visual learners while the information presented in almost every lecture course is overwhelmingly verbal---written words and formulas in texts and on the chalkboard, spoken words in lectures, with only an occasional diagram, chart, or demonstration breaking the pattern. Professors should not be surprised when many of their students cannot reproduce information that was presented to them not long before; it may have been expressed but it was never heard.

Visual learners remember best what they see—pictures, diagrams, flow charts, time lines, films, and demonstrations.

Verbal learners get more out of words—written and spoken explanations. Everyone learns more when information is presented both visually and verbally.

Inductive Learners

Inductive learners prefer to learn a body of material by seeing specific cases first (observations, experimental results, numerical examples) and working up to governing principles and theories by inference; *deductive learners* prefer to begin with general principles and to deduce consequences and applications. Since deduction tends to be more concise and orderly than induction, students who prefer a highly structured presentation are likely to prefer a deductive approach while those who prefer less structure are more likely to favor induction.

Research shows that of these two approaches to education, induction promotes deeper learning and longer retention of information and gives students greater confidence in their problem-solving abilities.

Sensing and intuitive learners

Sensing learners tend to like learning facts; intuitive learners often prefer discovering possibilities and relationships. Sensors often like solving problems by well-established methods and dislike complications and surprises; intuitions like innovation and dislike repetition. Sensors are more likely than intuitive learners to resent being tested on material that has not been explicitly covered in class.

Sensors tend to be patient with details and good at memorizing facts and doing hands-on (laboratory) work; intuitions may be better at grasping new concepts and are often more comfortable than sensors with abstractions and mathematical formulations

.

Sensors tend to be more practical and careful than intuitive learners; intuitive learners tend to work faster and to be more innovative than sensors.

Sensors don't like courses that have no apparent connection to the real world; intuitions don't like "plug-and-chug" courses that involve a lot of memorization and routine calculations.

Active Learners

Active learners tend to learn while doing something active---trying things out, bouncing ideas off others; *reflective learners* do much more of their processing introspectively, thinking things through before trying them out. Active learners work well in groups; reflective learners prefer to work alone or in pairs. Unfortunately, most lecture classes do very little for either group: the active learners never get to do anything and the reflective learners never have time to reflect. Instead, both groups are kept busy trying to keep up with a constant barrage of verbiage, or else they are lulled into inattention by their enforced passivity.

The research is quite clear on the question of active and reflective versus passive learning. In comparing instructor-centered classes (lecture/demonstration) with student-centered classes (problem-solving/discussion), lectures appear to be marginally more effective when students are tested on short-term recall of facts but active classroom environments are superior when the criteria involves comprehension, long-term recall, general problem-solving ability, scientific attitude, and subsequent interest in the subject. Substantial benefits are also gained from instructing methods that provide opportunities for reflection, such as giving learners time in class to write brief summaries and formulate written questions about the material just covered.

Active learners tend to retain and understand information best by doing something active with it—discussing or applying it or explaining it to others. Reflective learners prefer to think about it quietly first.

Active learners tend to like group work more than reflective learners, who prefer working alone. Sitting through lectures without getting to do anything physical but take notes is hard for both learning types, but particularly hard for active learners

Sequential Learners

Sequential learners absorb information and acquire understanding of material in small connected chunks; *global learners* take in information in seemingly unconnected fragments and achieve understanding in large holistic leaps. Sequential learners can solve problems with incomplete understanding of the material and their solutions are generally orderly and easy to follow, but they may lack a grasp of the big picture---the broad context of a body of knowledge and its interrelationships with other subjects and disciplines. Global learners work in a more all-or-nothing fashion and may appear slow and do poorly on homework and tests until they grasp the total picture, but once they have it they can often see connections to other subjects that escape sequential learners.

Before global learners can master the details of a subject they need to understand how the material being presented relates to their prior knowledge and experience, but only exceptional teachers routinely provide such broad perspectives on their subjects. In consequence, many global learners who have the potential to become outstanding creative researchers fall by the wayside because their mental processes do not allow them to keep up with the sequential pace of their science courses.

Sequential learners tend to gain understanding in linear steps, with each step following logically from the previous one. Global learners tend to learn in large jumps, absorbing material almost randomly without seeing connections, and then suddenly "getting it."

Sequential learners tend to follow logical stepwise paths in finding solutions; global learners may be able to solve complex problems quickly or put things together in novel ways once they have grasped the big picture, but they may have difficulty explaining how they did it.

Myers-Briggs Type Indicator (MBTI)

Scores obtained from the MBTI indicate a person's preference on each of four dichotomous dimensions. Myers and McCaulley (1986)
The first two dimensions are particularly helpful in understanding learning styles:

> extroversion (E) versus introversion (I) indicates whether a person prefers to direct attention toward the external world of people and things or toward the inner world of concepts and ideas;
> sensing (S) versus intuition (N) indicates whether a person prefers perceiving the world through directly observing the surrounding tangible reality or through impressions and imagining possibilities.

This model classifies adult learners according to their preferences on scales derived from psychologist Carl Jung's theory of psychological types. Adult learners may be:

- *extraverts* (try things out, focus on the outer world of people) or *introverts* (think things through, focus on the inner world of ideas);
- *sensors* (practical, detail-oriented, focus on facts and procedures) or *intuitives* (imaginative, concept-oriented, focus on meanings and possibilities);
- *thinkers* (skeptical, tend to make decisions based on logic and rules) or *feelers* (appreciative, tend to make decisions based on personal and humanistic considerations);
- *judgers* (set and follow agendas, seek closure even with incomplete data) or *perceivers* (adapt to changing circumstances, resist closure to obtain more data).

The MBTI type preferences can be combined to form 16 different learning style types. For example, one student may be an ESTJ (extravert, sensor, thinker, perceiver) and another may be an INFJ (introvert, intuitive, feeler, judger).

Letting the adult learner assess the accuracy of the descriptions is essential. Like all other assessment instruments, the MBTI provides clues, not infallible labels. The adult learner is the ultimate judge of his or her behavior patterns.

ISTJ (introvert, sensor, thinker, judger) learners tend to rely heavily on memorization and drill (traits of ISTJs) as approaches to problem solving.

ENTJ (extravert, intuitive, thinker, judger) learners tend to go directly into derivation on every homework and test problem (behavior consistent with extroverted intuition) rather than using routine procedures for routine problems. The resulting demands on the learner's time may cause problems with assignment completion and test performance. They need to learn to apply their analytical talents when needed rather than using them indiscriminately and inefficiently.

During the past 20 years, a great deal of research utilizing the MBTI has focused on the relationship between psychological type and various aspects of the educational process. Our understanding of learning pattern differences is further enhanced when the preferences for extroversion/introversion and sensing/intuition are combined to produce the following patterns:

ES pattern: concrete active
IS pattern: concrete reflective
EN pattern: abstract active
IN pattern: abstract reflective

Concrete active learners are action-oriented realists, the most practical of the four patterns, and learn best when useful applications are obvious. The concrete reflective (introverted sensing) learners are thoughtful realists preferring to deal with what is real and factual in a careful, unhurried way.

The abstract active learners (extroverted intuitives) are action-oriented innovators having wide- ranging interests and liking new possibilities as challenges to make something happen.

Finally, the abstract reflective learners (introverted intuitive) are thoughtful innovators, introspective and scholarly, interested in knowledge for its own sake; they value ideas, theory, and depth of understanding. The concrete active pattern is the most pragmatic and least academic of the four, whereas the abstract reflective is the most academic and least pragmatic.

The internet has hundreds of links to information and ideas about the Myers-Briggs and there are numerous books and Myers-Briggs specialty organizations with extensive literature and "certification" training. So this would serve little purpose to expand more other than include this very popular approach.

Gregorc's (1982) based his Delineator Approach on studies into the functions of the left and right brain hemispheres. His system of learning takes into account the different ways of perceiving and ordering information. We either perceive things in methods that are concrete-oriented (from our physical senses) or abstract-oriented (from logical, deductive reasoning). Ordering is making sense out of what we perceive. Ordering can either be sequential (organized, systematic) or random (unorganized).

These different means of perceiving and ordering information form Gregorc's four categories of learning styles:

Concrete-Sequential	Learning is linear and sequential.
Concrete-Random	Learning is concrete and intuitive, and the person thrives on problem solving.
Abstract-Sequential	Learning is abstract and analytical, and the person thrives on a mentally challenging but ordered learning environment.
Abstract-Random	The person is emotional and imaginative, and prefers an active, interesting, and informal learning environment.

Herrmann Brain Dominance Instrument (1990)
His method classified learners in terms of their relative preferences for thinking in four different modes based on the task-specialized functioning

of the physical brain. The four modes or quadrants in this classification scheme are

Quadrant A (left brain, cerebral). Logical, analytical, quantitative, factual, critical;

Quadrant B (left brain, limbic). Sequential, organized, planned, detailed, structured;

Quadrant C (right brain, limbic). Emotional, interpersonal, sensory, kinesthetic, symbolic;

Quadrant D (right brain, cerebral). Visual, holistic, innovative.

Today and in the future, more and more information will be discovered and shared about the multiple dimensions of the human brain. For the purpose here this separate section is provided to explain what is known as it affects current understanding of the adult learners.

§©§©§©§©§©§ Left Brain and Right Brain §©§©§©§©§©§
Dominance and Style of Learning

In general the left and right hemispheres of your brain process information in different ways. We tend to process information using our dominant side. However, the learning process is enhanced when all of our senses are used. This includes using your less dominate hemisphere. Listed below are information processing styles that are characteristically used by your right or left brain. (original research and literature sources for the following unknown)

Linear vs. Holistic Processing

The left side of the brain processes information in a linear manner. It processes from part to whole. It takes pieces, lines them up, and arranges them in a logical order; then it draws conclusions. The right brain, however, processes from whole to part, holistically. It starts with the answer. It sees the big picture first, not the details. If you are right-brained, you may have difficulty following a lecture unless you are given the big picture first. Do you now see why it is absolutely necessary for a right-brained person to read an assigned chapter or background information before a lecture or to survey a chapter before reading? If an instructor doesn't consistently give an overview before he or she begins a lecture, you may need to ask at the end of class what the next lecture will be and how you can prepare for it. If you are predominantly right-brained, you may also have trouble outlining (you've probably written many papers first and outlined them latter because an outline was required). You're the student who needs to know why you are doing something. Left-brained students would do well to exercise their right-brain in such a manner.

Sequential vs. Random Processing

In addition to thinking in a linear manner, the left brain processes in sequence -- in order. The left-brained person is a list maker. If you are left-brained, you would enjoy making a master schedule and doing daily planning. You complete tasks in order and take pleasure in checking them off when they are accomplished. Likewise, learning things in sequence is relatively easy for you. For example, spelling involves sequencing; if you are left-brained, you are probably a good speller. The left brain is also at work in the linear and sequential processing of math and in following directions.

By contrast, the approach of the right-brained student is random. If you are right-brained, you may flit from one task to another. You will get just as much done but perhaps without having addressed priorities. An assignment may be late or incomplete, not because you weren't working, but because you were working on something else. You were ready to rebel when asked to make study schedules for the week. But because of the random nature of your dominant side, you must make lists, and you must make schedules. This may be your only hope for survival in college. You should also make a special effort to read directions. Oh yes, the mention of spelling makes you cringe. Use the dictionary, carry a speller, or use the spell checker on your computer. Never turn in an assignment without proofing for spelling. Because the right side of the brain is color sensitive, you might try using colors to learn sequence, making the first step green, the second blue, the last red. Or you may want to "walk" a sequence, either by physically going from place to place or by imagining it. For the first step of the sequence, you might walk to the front door; for the second, to the kitchen; for the third, to the den, etc. Or make Step One a certain place or thing in your dorm room or study place and Step Two another. If you consistently use the same sequence, you will find that this strategy is transferable to many tasks involving sequence.

Symbolic vs. Concrete Processing

The left brain has no trouble processing symbols. Many academic pursuits deal with symbols such as letters, words, and mathematical notations. The left-brained person tends to be comfortable with linguistic and mathematical endeavors. Left-brained students will probably just memorize vocabulary words or math formulas. The right brain, on the other hand, wants things to be concrete. The right-brained person wants to see, feel, or touch the real object. Right-brained students may have had trouble learning to read using phonics. They prefer to see words in context and to see how the formula works. To use your right brain, create opportunities for hands-on activities. Use something real whenever possible. You may also want to draw out a math problem or illustrate your notes.

Logical vs. Intuitive Processing

The left brain processes in a linear, sequential, logical manner. When you process on the left side, you use information piece by piece to solve a math problem or work out a science experiment. When you read and listen, you look for the pieces so that you can draw logical conclusions. Your decisions are made on logic--proof. If you process primarily on the right side of the brain, you use intuition. You may know the right answer to a math problem but not be sure how you got it. You may have to start with the answer and work backwards. On a quiz, you have a gut feeling as to which answers are correct, and you are usually right. In writing, it is the left brain that pays attention to mechanics such as spelling, agreement, and punctuation. But the right side pays attention to coherence and meaning; that is, your right brain tells you it "feels" right. Your decisions will be based on feelings.

Verbal vs. Non-verbal Processing

Left-brained adult learners have little trouble expressing themselves in words. Right-brained students may know what they mean but often have trouble finding the right words. The best illustration of this is to listen to people give directions. The left-brained person will say something like "From here, go west three blocks and turn north on Vine Street. Go three or four miles and then turn east onto Broad Street." The right-brained person will sound something like this: "Turn right (pointing right) by the church over there (pointing again). Then you will pass a McDonalds and a Walmart. At the next light, turn right toward the BP station." So how this is relevant to planning study strategies? Right-brained students need to back up everything visually. If it's not written down, they probably won't remember it. And it would be even better for right-brained students to illustrate it. They need to get into the habit of making a mental video of things as they hear or read them. Right-brained students need to know that it may take them longer to write a paper, and the paper may need more revision before it says what they want it to say. This means allowing extra time when a writing assignment is due.

Reality-Based vs. Fantasy-Oriented Processing

The left side of the brain deals with things the way they are--with reality. When the environment affects the left-brained adult learners they usually adjust to it. Not so with right-brained adult learners; they try to change the environment! Left-brained people want to know the rules and follow them. In fact, if there are no rules for situations, they will probably make up rules to follow! Left-brained adult learners know the consequences of not turning in papers on time or of failing a test, but right-brained students are sometimes not aware that there is anything wrong. So, if you are right-brained, make sure you constantly ask for feedback and reality checks. It's too late the day before finals to ask if you can do extra credit. Keep a careful record of your assignments and tests. Visit with your professor routinely. While this fantasy orientation may seem a disadvantage, in some cases it is an advantage. The right-brained student is creative. In order to learn about the digestive system, you may decide to become a piece of food! And since emotion is processed on the right side of the brain, you will probably remember well anything you become emotionally involved in as you are trying to learn.

These are just some of the differences that exist between the left and right hemispheres, but you can see a pattern. Because left-brained strategies are the ones used most often in the classroom, right-brained adult learners sometimes feel inadequate. However, you now know that you can be flexible and adapt material to the right side of your brain. Likewise, those of you who are predominantly left-brained know that it would be wise to use both sides of the brain and employ some right-brained strategies.

The implications for adult learners instructing is that they are probably as many ways to instruct as there are to learn. The most important thing is to be aware that adult learners and adult learning instructors may not all see the world in the same way. Other instructors, as well as the adult learners may have very different preferences than you for how, when, where and how often to learn. You need to find your own way that is adaptable and flexible to the specific learning event and to the specific group of learners.

While none of the above models or the many not mentioned here are perfect, they give you an opportunity to explore yours and others your preferred learning style. It is up to you to pull together those parts of the different theories and approaches to integrate into your personal theory and approaches of learning styles. However, to provide a start a short learning styles assessment to provide a distinct and synoptic picture of your current learning style.

My Typical or Usual Way of Doing*

This assessment will assist you in identifying your preferred learning style
   *Ripley Adapted Learning Style Assessment - Adapted from work developed by Neil D. Fleming, New Zealand

Choose the answer which best explains your preference and circle the letter next to it. You may circle more than one answer if that is your normal/typical action or behavior for that situation.

1.   You are not sure whether a word should be spelled occurrence or occurrence. I would:
   a.   look it up in the dictionary.
   b.   see the word in my mind and choose by the way it looks
   c.   sound it out in my mind.
   d.   write both versions down on paper and choose one.

2.   You are about to purchase a new stereo. What would influence your decision?
   a.   the salesperson telling me what I wanted to know.
   b.   reading the details about it.
   c.   playing with the controls and listening to it.
   d.   the smart and fashionable look.

3.   You are with a couple from out of town that is visiting for the first time. You are at their hotel, they are going to come to your house later, and have a rental car.
   I would:
   a.   draw a map on paper
   b.   tell them the directions
   c.   write down the directions (without a map)
   d.   collect them from the hotel in my car

4.   You have just received a copy of your Mediterranean cruise trip. This is of interest to some friends. I would:
   a.   phone them immediately and tell them about it.
   b.   send them a copy of the printed itinerary.
   c.   show them on a map of the Mediterranean..
   d.   share what I plan to do at each place I visit.

5. You are going to cook something special for some friends.
    a. cook something familiar without the need for instructions.
    b. thumb through the cookbook looking for ideas from the pictures.
    c. refer to a specific cookbook where there is a good recipe.
    d. Try out the recipe myself first, and possibly making some changes in the recipe.

6. Recall a time in your life when you learned how to play a new board game. I learned best by:
    a. visual clues -- pictures, diagrams, charts
    b. written instructions.
    c. listening to somebody explaining it.
    d. doing it or trying it.

7. A group of tourists has been assigned to you to find out about botanical gardens.
    I would:
    a. drive them to a botanical garden.
    b. show them slides and photographs
    c. give them pamphlets or a book on botanical gardens.
    d. give them a talk on botanical gardens.

8. Do you prefer an instructor or teacher who likes to use:?
    a. a textbook, handouts, readings
    b. flow diagrams, charts, graphs.
    c. field trips, labs, practical sessions.
    d. discussion, guest speakers.

9. You have a problem of wax collecting in your ear. I would prefer the doctor to:
    a. tell me what is wrong.
    b. show me a diagram of what is wrong.
    c. use a model to show me what is wrong.
    d. have me practice while reading instructions and then correcting.

10. You are going to learn to use a new program on a computer. I would:
    a. sit down at the keyboard and begin to experiment with the program's features.
    b. read the manual which comes with the program.
    c. telephone a friend and ask questions about it.
    d. draw a diagram on paper or the computer screen.

Ripley Adapted Learning Style Assessment Scoring Chart

Circled Letters	ITEMS									
	1	2	3	4	5	6	7	8	9	10
a	T	A	V	A	K	V	K	T	A	K
b	V	T	A	T	V	T	V	V	V	T
c	A	K	T	V	T	A	T	K	K	A
d	K	V	K	K	A	K	A	A	T	V

Total number of Vs circled _____ =   **VISUAL**

Total number of As circled _____ =   **AUDITORY**

Total number of Ks circled _____ =   **KINESTHETIC**

Total number of Ts circled _____ =   **TRADITIONAL**

A Synoptic look at your results

VISUAL LEARNING STYLE
You like textbooks with diagrams and pictures.
You like pictures, videos, posters, and slides.
You like flowcharts and graphs.
You probably underline or use a highlighter and even of different colors.
You like instructors or trainers who use gestures and picturesque language.
You may doodle in your notes and your checkbook..
You want the whole picture so you are probably holistic rather than a reductionist in your approach.
You are often swayed by the look of an object.

You are interested in color and layout and design and you know where you are.

You are probably going to draw something.

AUDITORY LEARNING STYLE

Your class notes may be poor because you prefer to listen.

You my often need to expand your notes by talking with others and collecting notes from the textbook.

You may need to put your summarized notes onto tapes and listen to them.

You probably ask others to 'hear' your understanding of a topic.

You may often read your summarized notes aloud to understand them.

You may need to explain your notes to another auditory person.

You may spend time in quiet places recalling the ideas of class or the textbook.

You may need to practice writing answers to old test questions.

You probably prefer to have this entire page explained to you. The written words are not as valuable as those you hear.

You will probably go and tell somebody all about this.

KINESTHETIC LEARNING STYLE

You like to use all your senses – sight, touch, taste, smell and learning.

You probably like laboratories, field trips, applications, hands-on approaches (computing), trial and error.

You like instructors or trainers who give real-life examples and recipes for solutions to problems.

You may like exhibits, samples and photographs.

You may have had or have collections of rock types, plants, shells, etc.

You class notes may be poor because the topics were not concrete or relevant.

You will remember the real things that happened.

You like case studies and applications to help with the principles and abstract concepts. You like pictures or photographs that illustrate and idea.

You will go back to the laboratory or your lab manual to understand the topic.

You like the lab or similar experience or an exam so that you can understand it. The ideas are only valuable if they seem practical, real, and relevant to you.

You need to do things to understand.

TRADITIONAL LEARNING STYLE

This is the learning process that was probably the dominant methodology of your pre-adult years of schooling and learning. This was learning to read and to write, add and subtract, and multiply and divide. You learned to look it up, read the details and write down the directions or information. This was the common denominator of pre-post secondary education and training.

MULTI- PREFERENCE

If you have multi-preference you are in the majority. As you can see this can be quite varied with a combination of any of the four styles.

A multi-style preference gives you choices of two or three or four modes to use for your interaction with others.

If you have two dominant or equal preferences, read the information that apply to your two choices. If you have three preferences read the three lists that apply and similarly for those with four. You will need to read two or three or four lists of information.

Chapter 5
≈◊≈◊≈◊≈◊≈◊≈ *Ripley* ≈◊≈◊≈◊≈◊≈◊≈
TASK - DATA-ANALYSIS - PEOPLE ORIENTATION

The Adult Learners TASK - DATA-ANALYSIS and PEOPLE ORIENTATION

This adult understanding model has over a twenty-five year history of research and development.   The model represents adults as having **TASK, DATA-ANALYSIS** and **PEOPLE** orientations. The orientation identifies the thinking and behaving style of an individual.   Identifying the adult learners current style is a big part of knowing how to interact effectively with the them and also how he or she will interact with others.

The difference between people is a matter of degree in each area. For instance, Engineers and Accountants very often have a high degree of data-analysis orientation with far less in task and less in people orientation. A production manager may be very high in task and medium on data-analysis and have a lower preference in people orientation.   A human resource specialist may be very high in people orientation and less in data-analysis and far less in task orientation.

What is the best orientation? **IT DEPENDS.** The most effective orientation or combination style will depend on many things: the particular desired decision outcome, the short-term or long-term effect, and the style others perceive the adult as using most consistently.

Differences in goals have been found for individuals if they were dominant in one area.

For example:
DOMINANT TASK ORIENTED ADULTS Goal: To have competency and progress measured by results.

DOMINANT DATA-ANALYSIS ORIENTED ADULTS Goal: To collect facts and data before making decisions and to be measured as an individual contributor.

DOMINANT PEOPLE ORIENTED ADULTS Goal: To be measured by personal contributions through influential means.

Combinations:
TASK – DATA-ANALYSIS = Competing /Judicious

TASK - PEOPLE = Assertive/Nurturing

DATA-ANALYSIS - PEOPLE = Cautious/Supportive
These differences and combinations refer to the individuals being in charge of their own behaviors. The individual selects which behaviors will most often get the desired result in a particular personal or business situation. This takes conscious effort on the part of the individual, but may become intuitively habitual after years of experience.

TASK ORIENTATION ADULT LEARNER
Full of conviction, self-reliant. Likes directing and getting things done through other people, urge others to move to a belief, position or course of action, has a strong capacity to persuade or convince. Will respond without delay or hesitation, fast to act, makes quick, effective responses. Willing to take a chance based on probability of winning. Has a habit of deciding definitely and firmly. Likes to have the power of deciding. Firmness, conclusiveness and determination. Is productive and effective without waste. Characterized by confidence, is trustful and self-reliant. Has a sense of urgency, will call for immediate action and have an

insistence to continue toward an activity or goal. Wants to have competency and progress measured by results.

DATA-ANALYSIS ORIENTATION ADULT

Will collect facts and data before making decisions. Likes to be measured as an individual contributor. Is skilled at using analysis in thinking or reasoning. May be somewhat subdued in manner, not joking or trifling. Is disposed to action and usefulness rather than speculation or theoretical. Will continue in spite of interference and be persistently active and regularly occupied. Pays attention to the small elements that collectively constitute a whole. Will spend a great deal of attention to particular items or parts. May be restrained in words and silent in meetings. Will work long hours to get something done. Focuses on operating with little waste, careful and efficient with use of resources. May like to deal with figures, statistics and accounts. Busy, constantly, regularly or habitually occupied. Very firm in determination and a course of action.

PEOPLE ORIENTATION ADULT

Indicates a high willingness to modify and adjust, make adjustments to differences, people or situations, capable of responding to changes or new situations, can be relied on, trusted, and is prompt to act or respond.

This person shows a high interest in work that involves dealing with people. Likely to prefer employment that involves a high degree of contact with others and would not be happy working on his or her own. Will enjoy work that requires difficult and demanding interpersonal skills. Likes to support and assist to keep something going. Will show excitement and strong feelings when attached to a pursuit. Willing to reconcile differences. Will motivate others, influence, be animated and enliven a situation to get something done. Also is tactful and can handle delicate situations. Will maintain good relations and avoid offense with others.

POINTS FOR COMPARISON
BETWEEN THE ADULT LEARNERS DOMINANT
ORIENTATIONS

TASK	*DATA-ANALYSIS*	*PEOPLE*
SENSE OF WORTH BASED UPON		
Being successful, winning leader of others	Being self-sufficient, self-reliant, independent	Being genuinely helpful to others
DERIVES PERSONAL FULFILLMENT THROUGH		
Success in directing fulfilling accomplishments	Success in managing resources	Success in others
BASIC APPROACH TO OTHERS		
Getting things done done Through others	Getting things done independent of others	Getting things for others
UNDERSTANDS THE PRODUCTIVITY BEHIND		
The exercise of power and control over others welfare	The exercise of judicious foresight	The exercise of concern for of others
EXERTS INFLUENCE AND LEADERSHIP THROUGH		
Challenging, arguing, differences, persuading, directing will and competing	Establishing order, planning ahead, analyzing/reserving judgment	Reconciling promoting good and harmony
FEELS REWARDS SHOULD GO TO THOSE WHO ARE		
The strongest	The most judicious	The most helpful
JUDGES OTHERS IN TERMS OF		
Who is strong vs. vs. who is weak Who is a winner vs. who is a loser	Who is bright vs. who is stupid Who is right vs. who is wrong	Who are helpful who is selfish Who is friendly vs. who is aggressive
VIEWS SELF AS NEEDING TO BE		
More considerate and and more playful	More sensitive and more self-assertive	More aggressive more hard headed
EXPERIENCES GREATEST SATISFACTIONS FROM		
Being challenged Being followed Being a winner	Being respected for logic, perseverance and fairness	Being thanked Being needed Being liked

EXPERIENCES DISCOMFORT AND THREAT FROM

Withdrawal of loyalty and indifference	Over helpfulness and invasion of rights	Anger and indifference

WANTS TO PROTECT SELF FROM ACTING IN

A soft and gullible manner	A dependent and emotional manner	An angry or selfish manner

TYPICAL STRENGTHS

Ambitious	Analytic	Supportive
Competitive	Cautious	Loyal
Self-confident	Thorough	Trusting
Persuasive	Methodical	Adaptable
Organizer	Principled	Modest
Forceful	Fair	Optimistic

OVERUSE CREATES RISK OF BEING SEEN AS

Ruthless	Nit-picking	Submissive
Combative	Suspicious	Slavish
Arrogant	Obsessive	Gullible
Pushing	Rigid	Spineless
Controlling	Purist	Self-effacing
Dictatorial	Unfeeling	Impractical

Chapter 6
≈◊≈◊≈◊≈◊≈ *Ripley Recurring Cycle:* ≈◊≈◊≈◊≈◊≈◊≈
Decidep, Solidep, Recidep

Explanations and Descriptions

There are two characteristic ways we look at an adult. One is physical appearance and the other is behavior, that which we call psychological identity. Just as the nose is part of the body there are various elements or characteristics of the psychological identity. Psychological identity is not observable as a whole as is the physical appearance. It is analogous to the difference between physical and chemical properties. The physical we can touch, taste, and smell and it will always be relatively the same but the psychological identity differs under different conditions. You have to observe behavior under many different circumstances or conditions and combinations.

In order to better describe and explain the observed adult behavior we had to invent three new words: DECIDEP, SOLIDEP and RECIDEP. There is a dual nature to the terms decidep, solidep and recidep. Used in one sense they describe the observed behavior of an individual in the specific environmental setting. The other meaning of the words is similar to what the scientists in the field of biology call, "Ontogeny Recapitulates Phylogeny". In other words the psychological life history or development of an individual repeats or goes through the history of cultural development.   In the same sense as the phylum charts stages in the evolutionary growth of a plant or animal family, these are the stages of psychological development in one's growth to adult psychological maturity.   Just as no phylum in biology can be said to have reached fulfillment, but still developing, so is each adult still developing, and we can use the three positions terms to describe, show and designate the general positions on the ontological psychological development scale. The adults psychological identity is seen as a recurring cyclical process of *DECIDEP, SOLIDEP AND RECIDEP* behaviors in the three recurring *Decidep, Solidep, and Recidep* situational stages throughout life.

An individual goes through these three situational stages throughout their lifetime with recurring behavior in each of them.   First, a *Decidep* where things are provided for the adult and he or she is told what is proper behavior.   Decisions are made for the adult and he or she is unsure of everything.   This is the infant of any phase where the food for substance or thought is provided.   It is the world outside the individual acting on him or her to effect their behavior.

The second situational stage and behavior is the *Solidep* where the adult is acting upon the environment. It is the adolescent stage of development, whether it is a job, period of life between childhood and adulthood, or educational development.   The child thinks he or she knows better than the parent and the employee knows better than the "Boss". He or she is simply rebellious and does not want to be dependent on anyone.   This is also the period of ambivalence because he or she wants to be "free".   He or she enjoyed the *Decidep* stage or behavior and the security of others making their decisions.

The *Recidep* is the most mature situational stage and behavior. This is the period of realizing the worth of the other individual and yourself. It is the period of discovering that you can accomplish more together than alone. The *Recidep* tries to help others in the *Decidep* stages to be able to make their own decisions and further their development. It is now realized that they themselves are responsible for their actions and are willing to accept this responsibility and accountability. It is now a period of using their knowledge and skills. It is a time of realizing that others have a fear of the unknown and that others are also somewhat creatures of habit. The individual now realizes their part in the community and the responsibility for its action. The *Recidep* realizes he or she cannot maintain themselves alone so is reciprocally dependent upon others and for others. This is the point of mature psychological adulthood.

Definitions

DECISION DEPENDENCY
Dedicep or
DECIDEP

One who lacks self-reliance. His or her behavior is determined by someone else. He or she habitually seeks the help of others in making or carrying out actions. A person who by necessity or choice relies on another individual, individuals or on a stage of life, or a behavior of subordination and subjection. The consistent unwillingness, or lack of desire, or lack of knowledge to choose between alternatives or to take risks. A helplessness with minimal acceptance for ownership and accountability.

The small letters-**Decidep** refer to the situational Stages of Life. The capital letters-**DECIDEP** refer to the observed behavior.   This relates the same to the following Solidep and Recidep definitions.

A Situational Stage of Life (Decidep): This is the infancy or the beginning stage in any of life's choices; be it in a job, at home, at school or in the community. All humans start with this stage in life and then advance to the Solidep stage. The human cycles through the Decidep, Solidep and Recidep Stages over and over again as they go along their life line. These are stages of life all humans pass through. These do not indicate the observable behavior at any moment in time, although there are expected norms of behavior at each stage.

Observed Behavior-(DECIDEP): This is the classification of an individual's behavior in a particular environmental setting in any one of the stages of life as one of dependence. The normal progress is for the individual to advance to the SOLIDEP level of behavior at the different stages of life.   There is expected DECIDEP behavior limits at each stage of life and in the different environmental settings. The human cycles through the DECIDEP, SOLIDEP and RECIDEP levels of behavior just as they do through the situational stages of life. However, the individual may revert to a previous level of behavior that was appropriate at a different situational stage of life. Also, an individual may demonstrate DECIDEP behavior in one environmental setting, such as at home, and SOLIDEP or RECIDEP behavior at work. (See Table 1) The individual may also remain with DECIDEP behavior and make no attempt to move to a more advanced level of behavior no matter what the environmental setting.

SOLITARY DEPENDENCY
Solidep or
SOLIDEP

A person who attempts to be self-reliant, confident and governing without regard for other individuals or the environment. The purposeful attempt not to be dependent on another person or persons and to avoid being responsible for others. One who is disrespectful and exclusive toward others. He or she does not rely on other people for decisions and guidance but habitually, when making decisions, reverts to "outside" authority and does not accept personal responsibility for decisions they make. A stage or state of independence and purposeful non-subordination and non-subjection. Resistance to control by others by deliberately not seeking the help of others or considering the welfare of others in making decisions or in carrying out actions.

A Situational Stage of Life (Solidep): This is the situational stage of ambivalence. The individual wants to take control of their existence but still wants the security of others setting the limits and taking the responsibility for final decisions.

Observed Behavior (SOLIDEP):
Classification of an individual's behavior in a particular environmental setting in any one of the stages of life as one of purposeful independence. This is the observed behavior that occurs between the DECIDEP and RECIDEP classification. There is expected ambiguity behavior that is appropriate at the different situational stages of life. However, a person may never go beyond this SOLIDEP behavior and not move into RECIDEP behavior. Many adults have arrested development of SOLIDEP behavior. This is commonly known as adolescent behavior. A mature RECIDEP individual may revert to this behavior when under undue stress or placed in difficult decision making situations. No matter what the situational stage of life this observed behavior is one of an ambivalence struggle between dependency and independence.

RECIPROCAL DEPENDENCY

An adult who is self-reliant, confident and self-empowering while taking into account

Recidep or
RECIDEP

other individuals and the environment. One who has the conscious willingness to seek the help of others in making decisions or carrying out actions. Also accepts the responsibility for his or her decisions and actions and those of the team or group with whom he or she participates. An adult who neither attempts to be disrespectful or exclusive toward others nor remains in a state of unempowerment or subjection. An adult who has their existence or nature determined by himself or herself while realizing the influence of other individuals on him or her and on the environment. An adult who is willing to take risks and make decisions, but does this while realizing his or her dependency on others and others dependency on them. A situational stage or behavior of mutual dependency and empowerment and the realization and acceptance of responsibility with accountability.

A situational stage of life (Recidep): This is the mature adult in the various situational stages of life. This follows the Solidep stage in any situation. Few adults are at the Recidep stage of development in all situations. The adult may be at a Recidep stage in one part of their job and at a Decidep or Solidep stage in another part of their job. This is also true   of the parts of parenting or community involvement.

Observed Behavior (RECIDEP):
A classification of an individual's behavior in a particular environmental setting in one of the situational stages of life as one of interdependence and mutual empowerment. This is the most mature behavior within any stage of life . This is the most mature behavior within any environmental setting and any human relationship. This is the observed acceptance of ownership, responsibility and accountability for one's behavior, attitudes and decisions. The observed RECIDEP behavior may vary according to the environmental setting. (See Table 1) This is the optimum level the individual attempts to achieve for their *Psychological Identity*. There are very few individuals who will demonstrate RECIDEP behavior in all settings.

PSYCHOLOGICAL IDENTITY

The characteristic behavior of an individual in a particular *psychological environment*. The way other individuals perceive a person and the way that a person perceives themselves. The way an individual is observed by others. This is the DECIDEP, SOLIDEP or RECIDEP.

PSYCHOLOGICAL ENVIRONMENT

The particular setting, location and place in which the individual is in at that time. It is the summation of the physical location in a particular culture, in a particular geographical area at a particular time. It includes the past psychological environment of the individual, the present observation and future perception of the physical location and surroundings at that time.

PSYCHOLOGICAL EXPRESSION   That which is emitted by the individual in the psychological environment. That which is necessary for the life of the psychological identity.

PSYCHOLOGICAL NOURISHMENT   That which is received by the individual in a psychological environment after having given a psychological expression. It is not necessary for a person to give a psychological expression prior to receiving a psychological nourishment in situations, such as: art, radio, TV, computers, books, compliments or symbols. This is the necessary force or factors for the continuance of the adult's psychological expression and thus for the maintenance of life of the individual's psychological identity.

PSYCHOLOGICAL INJURY   That which results from thwarting, lack of nourishment or too stressful conditions in the individual's psychological environment. The result of intolerable psychological nourishment of the individual's psychological expression. That which may be caused by psychological nourishment which is incompatible with the individual's psychological expression or identity.

PSYCHOLOGICAL
CREATION

That which the individual has when they are born and which is developed into a psychological identity. The original beginning of the *Decidep* stage and *DECIDEP* behavior of the individual.

The development of an individual's psychological identity through various and ever differing psychological environments.

Psychological needs are as urgent as physical needs. Psychological expression is as necessary as food. If individuals are to maintain their psychological identity they must obtain psychological nourishment from their psychological expression.

Psychological identity is an active, not a static property. Little worthwhile observation can be made of the psychological identity during sleep or after death. Persons can no more afford to give up their psychological development as they cannot afford to give up breathing. In order to maintain their psychological identity an individual must exhibit psychological expression and receive some type of psychological nourishment. The human can survive in physical isolation but cannot live in a psychological vacuum.

What we are interested in adults is sanity or some form of normality. Psychological environments in which a person is able to perform successfully--the tasks of managing a home, taking care of themselves and performing a function whereby he or she can maintain a living. Such a state is defined as one in which a person possesses a psychological identity and is satisfactorily performing. The maintenance of this condition or conditions is dependent on psychological creation and is developed so that the *DECIDEP* behavior may eventually flower into the *RECIDEP* behavior. Some psychological environments are dead or the individual's psychological identity is in *DECIDEP* or *SOLIDEP* behavior. However, it should be realized that some individuals do not have the mental or physical capacity, need or desire to rise above these behaviors.

This psychological creation is the developmental approach where the individual is born into a psychological environment that allows for psychological expression so that a person can have a psychological identity. If this does not occur or is refused a psychological injury results. To heal or repair a psychological injury one must develop a new psychological expression that allows for psychological nourishment in a new psychological environment. When a person loses his or her "sanity" it is liken to losing their physical life. We try to restore life and develop a new psychological identity which will allow for psychological expression and nourishment. Neurosis is psychological injury just as a broken arm is a physical injury. Without proper treatment this could lead to a permanent impairment (Compulsion, Obsession, Hysteria, etc.), or the complete destruction of the psychological identity (psychosis). In repairing the injured personality you do not want to re-create the old psychological identity because that is what caused the psychological injury. This must be done in a new psychological environment because the old psychological environment is where the injury occurred. This does not mean the individual cannot return to his or her home, family or job but that the psychological expression--DECIDEP, SOLIDEP or RECIDEP--must be developed and in a new manner to ensure that the psychological nourishment will not again cause the same injury.

Even with **psychological injuries** an individual still continues **psychological expressions.** Everyone has psychological injuries which they overcome without professional help. Psychological injuries can be minor as the common cold with little note or notice on of the part of other persons, or they may be major enough to cause the death of the **psychological identity**.

Psychological expressions and **nourishments** are the ways in which a person is most likely to sustain the situation. A person drives rather than walk, unless he or she realizes that walking is good for their health or some other pertinent reason. He or she will only use what is necessary to survive any situation in relation to how it is perceived by that individual.

Bizarre behavior could be a situation in which psychological identity is overtaxed or not experienced enough in a wide enough variety of psychological environment activities. Foolish behavior could be in a situation where the individual is so used to or the behavior is so rote that he or she does not attend to what they are doing or what is going on in the psychological environment. He or she may act as if there was no psychological environment surroundings. This is like what is commonly called daydreaming.

Some people cannot receive **psychological nourishment** from certain **psychological environments** so go to different or bizarre situations as in the case of the male who has a home, wife and children yet goes to a prostitute in a drunken condition to receive this **psychological nourishment** in that **psychological environment**. For some reason the psychological environment of the home, family and children does not allow all people the psychological expression and required nourishment.

Psychological strength is like physical strength. Psychological strength (Identity) is developed through many psychological environments without too many or too serious injuries. Psychological strength is developed through wide and varied psychological environments. A person may have a strong psychological identity in a small town but have a weak one in a large city.

Then a robust individual is one who can establish an identity under a variety of psychological environmental conditions. That is, the psychological nourishment can be taken, by means of psychological expressions under many varying conditions of psychological environments. This is done with minimal amount of psychological injuries and the maximum amount of recovery of the desired psychological identity--*DECIDEP, SOLIDEP* or *RECIDEP*. This is a satisfactory psychological environment where the individual can give psychological expression and receive psychological nourishment while developing and maintaining the psychological identity.

Table 01 **Developmental Behavior Cycle in a Work Environment**

Environmental Setting	Psychological Behavior	Employee Cycle
Work	DECIDEP	Embarrassed, unsure of tasks, trial and error, orientation time
	SOLIDEP	"Knows better than supervisors" Can do everything alone, can do the job better and lets you know
	RECIDEP	Sees job in relation to whole, sees importance of working together coordinates, empowers self and others

Table 01 illustrates a specific behavioral developmental process when a person starts a new job. The individual goes through the three situational stages (decidep, solidep and recidep) with the three sequences of behavior or personality identity (DECIDEP, SOLIDEP and RECIDEP). At work he or she first demonstrates *DECIDEP* behavior. It is a trial and error time with embarrassment, orientation and unsureness in most tasks. His or her behaviors are those of a *DECIDEP* and they turn to others to made their decisions and are dependent on them. He or she then arrives at a time when they believe they could operate the organization better than their supervisors or upper management. He or she ask for no assistance but are very ready to give advice (*SOLIDEP*).

Then with a more complete maturity on the job (*RECIDEP*) he or she realizes the role of each individual in the organization and their value to the whole picture. He or she now coordinates and sees the importance of working together. Many persons will be demonstrating *DECIDEP* behavior and will never advance beyond this in their work environment and may not desire to develop beyond this point. An individual may be limited by the work environment or his or her own mental or physical capacity to develop through all three behavior levels. An organization policy or immediate boss may maintain a *decidep* situation stage in order to maintain their necessary feeling of superiority or power. Some work situational stages may be maintained at the *solidep* situational stage in order to sidestep accountability with responsibility. In a *recidep* situational stage the work requires shared power with individual and team empowerment for appropriate decision making and maintaining of their quality of work life.

Table 02 **Behavior Cycle in a Manager Environment**

Environmental Setting	Psychological Behavior	Employee Cycle
Manager's Office	DECIDEP	Wants to be told, expects manager to "tell" what to do
	SOLIDEP	Knows all the answers, "stupid" policies and procedures.
	RECIDEP	Realizes value of working together. Sees manager' role and their own role. Accepts ownership and responsibility for their actions

Table 02 shows how the individual's developmental behavior cycle relates to employee coaching. When a direct report or associate comes into the manager's office and they are demonstrating *DECIDEP* level behavior they first look to the manager for answers and to give the manager their problems to solve. He or she wants the rules and the manager to tell them what to do. The direct report or associate then arrives at a behavior cycle point, *SOLIDEP*, when they know all the answers and no policies or procedures can control their behavior because they are the exception to the rules. He or she can solve their own problems and do not need someone to assist them who might know something better. Then if the individual arrives at a full employment maturity they will realize the value of working together, being empowered, but that they are ultimately responsible for their own actions and decisions. He or she can then see that the manager and their employment role are not conflicting but supplementing. By observing behavior as going through these developmental processes one can see that an individual could have conflicting areas within his or her total behavioral framework. If the manager is at a *Recidep-SOLIDEP* level and the individual is in a *DECIDEP* behavior level they may have a difficult time being able to communicate. The manager must attempt to discover at what stage of psychological development and what type of psychological identity the individual has in the various psychological environments in which the individual perceives himself or herself as having problems. It should be realized that few persons will arrive at the Recidep stage with a *RECIDEP* behavior in all environments. The stage of development and psychological identity the individual presently has may determine the methods, procedures used, and the predictability as to the outcome or level of attainment the individual may reach.

In the coming decades the study of human behavior will become more and more important to business, industry, government agencies, and educational organizations within each country and throughout the global economy. There is a greater and greater need to understand how the individual develops psychologically and how to maximize the development of each individual. The key thing an individual wants is to be understood. The Decidep, Solidep, Recidep model assists in developing that better understanding.

PART II
⊓⊓⊓⊓§⊓⊓⊓⊓ *Instruction-Training* ⊓⊓⊓⊓§⊓⊓⊓⊓
How the Adult Learner Learns

Few things are as intriguing to wonder about as the development of human learning. The skills, knowledge, reasoning, problem solving, planning, and performance in all their great variety, as well as human values, hopes, and aspirations are all dependent for their development largely on the events called **learning.** Learning is one's interaction with the environment, externally and internally, which results in behavioral change.

Instructing causes some specific kind of purposeful learning. While good instructing is often described as being a "gift" or mystery, it is actually definable and obtainable by the instructor.

The instructor's first step is accepting learning as an occurrence that can be examined and understood.

Learning is not only an event that happens naturally; it is also an event that happens under certain observable conditions. These conditions can be altered and controlled.

It becomes possible to observe the conditions under which learning takes place and to describe them in objective language. By observing changes in behavior, you can investigate what conditions made change (learning) take place. It is therefore possible to construct training models to create and account for the changes observed, just as it is with other types of natural events. When you know what works, you can reproduce the process to create the same result.

> Definition: Learning is a change in human beliefs or behaviors, which can be retained, and which is not simply ascribable to the process of physical growth.

> The instructor can conclude that learning from training actually happened by comparing what behavior or attitude was present prior to the instructing or "learning situation" and what behavior or attitude is exhibited after such treatment.

This means the change may be, and often is, an increased capability for some type of performance. It may also be an altered disposition of attitude, interest or value. The change must be capable of being retained over some period of time and distinguishable from the kind of change that is attributable to adult aging.

For example, on one and the same day the adult may learn to find the company restroom and may also learn to call the boss by his or her name. Somehow the events in the adult's environment, whether deliberately arranged or not, conspire to bring about these changes in the individual's performance. The changes are also in his or her capabilities, as shown by the fact that he or she can now go to the bathroom or call the boss by the correct name any time the needs arises. The question here is what elements in either or both situations can be deduced as having to do with learning?

1. **First, there is a learner, who is the adult human being**. Events in the environment affect the learner's senses, and start changes of nervous impulses that are organized by his or her central nervous system, specifically, by the brain. This nervous activity occurs in certain sequences and patterns that alter the nature of the previous organizational pattern. This effect is exhibited as learning. Finally, the nervous activity is translated into action that may be observed as movement of muscles in executing responses of various sorts.

2. **The events that stimulate the learner's senses are spoken of collectively as the stimulus situation**. When a single event is being distinguished, it is often called a stimulus.

3. **The action that results from stimulation and subsequent nervous activity is called a response**. Responses are often described in terms of their effects rather than in terms of their appearances. When so classified, they are called performances. For example: A response might be "moving the finger rhythmically over a small area of the scalp." But it may often be more useful to refer to the performance as "scratching the head."

A *learning event*, then, takes place when the ***stimulus situation*** affects the learner in such a way that his or her ***performance*** changes from a time ***before*** being in that situation to a time ***after*** being in it . The ***change in performance*** is what leads to the conclusion that learning has occurred.

The framework for the events of learning consists of a constant set of elements. With the simplest kind of learning that can be observed or even imagined, there is the unvarying relation between the **stimulus** and the **response**

The learning change is from: Stimulus -> (nothing)

                                                          to

                                                          Stimulus -> Response

This basic kind of learned capability is called an association. If an adult who previously could not supply the English word "horse" for the French word "cheval" now does so, it is appropriate to call this newly learned capability a verbal association.

Thorndike's Law of Effect,(1928) stated that *the correct responses are progressively strengthened by being followed immediately by motive satisfaction.* The motivated adult learner engages in various tries to attain satisfaction (Trial and Error Learning). Then the person tends to repeat those that were completed and followed by a satisfaction. Skinner (1953) substituted Reinforcement for motive satisfaction. To him recurrence of an action is due to reinforcement.

It will be seen that the learning of single associations in adult instructing is a rare event. This merely constitutes a fundamental "building block" for the more complex performances of recalling, recognizing, thinking, choosing, playing former internal mental learning tapes, combining, associating, etc. Adults can call upon their "personal learning computer" for various retrieval combinations. Adults come into instruction with a lot of "stuff" from previous education, training, learning, experiences and multiple self-developed capabilities.

Previous learning, acquired though a number of encounters with similar problems, can establish a kind of internal capability that makes the experienced adult learner quite different from the "naive adult" of the same age. Just because the two adults are placed in the same structured situation, don't expect the two to function or learn the same. One may have more accumulated experiences based on many individual trials of previous learning.

> The acquisition of knowledge then is a process in which every new capability builds on a foundation established by previously learned capabilities.

The adult is ready to learn something new when he or she has mastered the prerequisites, that is, when he or she has acquired the necessary capabilities through preceding learning. Planning for learning means specifying and ordering the prerequisite capabilities and levels of learning within a topic, and later perhaps among the topics that make up a "subject."

Maslow (1970) saw the goal of learning to be self-actualization, "...the full use of talents, capacities, potentialities, etc." He conceived of growth toward this goal as being determined by the relationship of two sets of forces operating within each individual. The one set clings to safety and defensiveness out of fear, tending to regress backward, hanging on to the past. The other set of forces impels the individual forward toward wholeness to self and uniqueness of self, toward full functioning of all capacities. We grow forward when the delights of growth and safety are greater than the anxieties of safety.

Rogers (1969) stated that learning has a quality of personal involvement - the whole person in both feelings and cognitive aspects being in the learning event. It is self-initiated. Even when the impetus or stimulus comes from the outside, the sense of discovery, of reaching out, of grasping and comprehending, comes from within. It is pervasive. It makes a difference in the behavior, attitudes, perhaps even the personality of the learners. Learning is evaluated by the learner. Learners knows whether it is meeting their needs, whether it leads towards what they want to know, whether it illuminates the dark area of ignorance they are experiencing. The locus of evaluation, resides definitely in the learner. Its essence is meaning. When such learning takes place, the element of meaning to the learner is built into the whole experience. Learning is a "being there" kind of experience.

Jourard (1958) developed the concept of independent learning. He saw that independent learning was problematic as it was peculiar, because the human always and only learns by him or herself. He said that learning is not a task or problem; it is a way to be in the world. Humans learn as they pursue goals and projects that have meaning for them. They are always learning something. Perhaps the key to the problem of independent learning lies in the phrase "the learner has the need and the capacity to assume responsibility for their own continuing learning." Two people can be presented with the same learning situation and come away with different learning.

In cooperative learning (Johnson and Johnson, 1975) the adults' knowledge and experiences are shared with the other learners and the instructor to maximize their own and each other's learning. The adults participate in small groups and receive guidance and instruction from the instructor. The instructor is a facilitator of learning. The group then works through the assignment until all group members have successfully understood and completed the task or knowledge comprehension.

Oneself and one's colleagues mutually cause one's performance and this cooperative effort results in participants recognizing that in this learning situation.   There is a positive interdependence among the group. (Johnson, Johnson and Smith, 1991)

This newer model fills the need of the adult for belongingness, to be a part of something, The value and personal reward received from sharing knowledge and experience, as well as the multiple reinforcements received from the group members and not just from the instructor. This learning approach places the adult learning in an active learning mode and places a shared responsibility and accountability for the knowledge or skills gained on the individual. This learning model moves the individual more toward a level of self-actualization and the reward of sharing in the responsibility of training others in team.

Through this theoretical and practical model of learning, we have demonstrated with adults over and over again the increased ability developed in problem solving, decision making, transfer of learning and the value of having fun in learning. (Nienstedt, 1979, Ripley and Ripley, 1992, 1994) We have used this technique and refer to it as experiential learning. The experiential learning emphasizes task accomplishment as well as the group process. It combines discovery learning, learning by doing and shared group learning.

Here again the reader can become almost overwhelmed by the number of writers and variety of theories related to learning. However, most of the theories and research on learning was and has been done on animals and children. Our focus is on the adult. Our attempt has been to weave together a practical, usable understanding and techniques rather than focus on the hundreds and hundreds of writers on learning theory.

However no matter who the theorist and researcher is today, they still build from the same foundation   For those who desire more exposure as to who formulated what piece of learning theory, Knowles (1973, 1998) presents a good historical thread review of the different theories and their authors.

The model, the **Ripley Levels of Learning** makes clear the sometimes confusing sequential learning processes.   A different type of learning takes place when a new sound is learned versus when a new company policy is learned.   This learning model describes how knowledge is organized.   It accounts for how learning is acquired, from the concrete to the abstract, from the simplest to the most complex.   By understanding the **Ripley Levels of Learning**, appropriate instructing can be designed to enable the learner to reach the desired performance level. (See Ripley *Levels of Learning:*)

Chapter 07
•∫ •∫ •∫ •∫ •∫ • Practical Points   •∫ •∫ •∫ •∫ •∫ •
on Adult Instructing

•People learn at different speeds. Be patient with "slow learning" adults, offer them reassurance, encouragement, and a positive reinforcer when they perform closer to the standard of what is correct. Remember we sell learning, experience and peace of mind, and that our learners are also our customers.

•Adult learners do not progress smoothly. Expect "ups" and "downs" in the adult's learning progress. Learning is generally faster during the first few practice sessions, then slows down until the ultimate skill is acquired. Once the adult reaches the desired skills and behavior, they will not continue at the desired standard unless they are periodically rewarded when you observe the desired skill or behavior.

•Adult learners get discouraged. Frequently, learners reach a "learning plateau" at which point they don't improve noticeably. In fact, performance may become worse. Expect this and be prepared to reassure the learner with encouragement until the desired skill is again attained. Remember you are the model, *Pygmalion* and selective reinforcer and that they are shadows of the leader. Think and be enthusiastic, and they will become the same.

•**Nervousness is natural.** The adult learner needs to be reassured and encouraged frequently during the learning. Remember to only reward and reinforce the desired outcome you want. This reduces the learner's nervousness by removing ambiguities and inconsistencies.

•**Poor instruction often hinders the learner.** Instruction should be planned and administered with utmost care, or not administered at all. The sequence, selective reinforcers, and outcome rewards for successes need to be carefully thought through before you begin.

•**The whole learning process-experience should be shown first to adult learners.** The individual parts of a learning or training program should be explained only after the adult learner has an understanding of the overall learning or experience. This is called the "whole-part-whole" method.

•**Instruction should be properly timed**. Usually several short periods are more effective than one long period of instructing. On the other hand in particular situations, immersion techniques, i.e. Workshop for Effective Management - one week long off-site retreat, can have more impact. Rest periods between learning segments help to refresh the trainee. It is easier to reinforce learning, peace of mind and a specific desired skill or behavior for short periods of time.

•**It is important to explain "why"**. Adults learn faster when they know why a particular thing is performed in a certain way, how something came about or reasons for a point-of-view.

•**The adult learner should know how they are doing.** Adults left in the dark about their progress become frustrated and their learning progress suffers.   We all want feedback, a progress report on how close we are coming to the desired goal.   Remember the learner wants to do right and to please. Reinforce what they are doing right and do corrective coaching to help them become more effective.

•**"Form" rather than "speed" should be stressed.** Speed without accuracy of delivery in the human interaction and technical manipulations is not a desirable goal.   Once proper form is acquired, speed follows through practice and experience.

Knowledge and application of these principles will enable the instructor to prevent most problems.

PRACTICAL POINTS

<u>**Use Their Experience**</u>   They have a wealth of material for you, too. Learning is a two-way process.

<u>**Adults must want to learn.**</u>   They must be properly motivated and see the purpose of the learning.

<u>**Adults will learn only what they feel a need to learn.**</u>   Give them information they can put to use now. Practicality must be the key word.

<u>**Adults learn by doing.**</u>   There is less forgetting with more use of the senses: i.e., actually doing something. This is why on-the-job training with selective reinforcement of the desired learning is so very effective.

<u>**One-half of instructing focuses on the correct process and the other half on solutions to problems**</u>.   The problems to be solved must be

realistic. Adults will learn faster if you take actual business problems and then work out practical solutions from which principles may be deduced. Use of the case method and role playing are excellent.

Experience affects adult learning. Make use of the experience of your group. Take the learners from where they are at to where you want them to be.

Adults learn best in an informal environment. This may sound like trivial advice, but is a very important concept in business and industry training. In most cases the stiff, formal air of a "classroom" is not conducive to good learning. Informality should be the key.

Use the learners' time wisely.   They are in the learning event for a reason. The sooner they can accomplish their goal, the better for both of you.

Use a great deal of positive reinforcement. Use pressure sparingly.

Give them a break.   An hour of learning new skills can be tiring. Take a break. Have refreshments available if possible.

Set a good climate. Be honest and frank with adults. Remember, they aren't grown-up children, and they are not high school students, either.

Be sure the surroundings are comfortable -- lighting, heating, etc.

Encourage adult learners to participate. Their input will enrich your facilitating and coaching.

Always remember to have them be accountable and take ownership for their learning and training application outcomes.

To get what you expect, always remember you are their model, Pygmalion and primary reinforcer.

Remember: words are magic, so select words carefully to get the desired outcome..

A DOZEN MORE IMPORTANT POINTS FOR NOW OR SOMETIME IN THE FUTURE

Use those of the following that seem important to you now. Others of these may seem more relevant to you at a later date. In his classes, Dr. Bob always said, "Take the best and leave the rest."

- Adults need to be able to integrate new ideas with what they already know if they are going to keep and use the new information.

- Increasing or maintaining one's sense of self-esteem and sense of pleasure are strong secondary motivators for engaging in learning experiences. Acquiring a new skill or extending and enriching current knowledge can increase both, depending on the individual's personal perceptions.

- Information that has little conceptual-overlap with what is already known is acquired slowly.

- In any media, straight forward how-to is the preferred content orientation. The adult wants a plan of how and why they will use this information.

- Even for the learner who is a self-proclaimed "expert," structured but flexible learning seminars get positive ratings, especially when these events give the learner face-to-face, one-to-one access with true expertise.

- Adult learners tend not to be interested in survey courses, but instead prefer single-concept, single-theory courses that focus heavily on the application to relevant problems. This tendency increases with age.

- Too fast-paced, complex or unusual learning tasks often interfere with the learning of the basic concepts they are intended to teach or illustrate. Too many instructors take the adult learner directly to the unknown rather than building on the known. The learner needs time to incorporate new concepts.

- Programs need to be designed to accept viewpoints from people in different life stages and with different sets of values.

- The learning environment must be physically and psychologically comfortable. Long lectures, periods of interminable sitting and absence of practice opportunities are high on the adult irritation scale.

- Bad experiences in traditional education, feelings about authority, and the preoccupation with events outside the classroom effect in-class experience. Self-esteem and ego are on the line when learners are asked to risk trying a new behavior in front of peers and cohorts. Expectations from prior negative events can be neutralized by successful, results oriented instructing.

- Adults have expectations, and it is critical to take time *up front* to clarify and articulate all expectations before getting into content.

- Adults enter learning with broad experiences and like to share and/or apply these experiences in the learning setting.

Chapter 08
~Ω~Ω~Ω~ Adult Instructing   ~Ω~Ω~Ω~

What it takes to learn something is called the levels of learning. These influence how adult learning will take place. Adult instructing means arranging the conditions of learning that are external to the learner. These conditions need to be constructed in a stage-by-stage fashion, taking due account at each stage of the just previously acquired capabilities of the learner, the requirements for retention of these capabilities, and the specific stimulus situation needed for the next stage of learning.

DEFINITION OF INSTRUCTION

Control of the external events in the learning situation is what is typically meant by the word "instruction." These are the events that are manipulated by the trainer, the textbook writer, and the designer of films or television lessons.

Instruction needs someone to do the manipulating. In just reading a book you are not getting the feedback loop. In the experiential and cooperative learning you received feedback from other adult learners as well as the instructor/facilitator.

The description of the various conditions for the different levels of learning contained in the Ripley Levels of Learning, should make possible the derivation of principles of control over external instructional events. This works best when the specific content to be taught has been related to the levels of learning.

The material to be learned should progress from the least personally threatening to the most personally threatening, from the known to the unknown, from the objective to the subject, from the factual to opinion and either from the concrete to the abstract or the abstract to the concrete in a progressive, sequential manner.

Sometimes adult instruction is pre-designed, as in the case of a well-constructed textbook or workbook, or, more typically in the programmed instruction of an interactive simulated video or computer program. Sometimes it is extemporaneously designed by a instructor. In any case, instruction very often involves communicating verbally with the adult learner for the purposes of informing him or her of what he or she is going to achieve, reminding them of what they already know, directing their attention and actions, and guiding their thinking and behaviors along certain lines. All these events are instituted for the purpose of establishing the proper external conditions for learning. Assuming that the necessary internal capabilities have been previously learned, a suitable arrangement of instructional events will bring about efficient learning.

Instructing is an activity that is at the heart of the adult learning process. It is far more challenging to do with a group of adults. It is easier to accomplish under the rare conditions in which a single trainer or coach communicates with a single adult learner. Alternatively, it can be largely if not wholly pre-designed and used in video and computer programs of self-instruction. There is reason to suppose that an instructional mode which requires self-instruction may be very efficient, when properly designed, and may also help to establish valuable habits of independent study on the part of the adult learner. Obviously most mature adult learners have developed their own very efficient habits of self-instruction.

TRANSFER OF LEARNING

One aspect of instructing deserves special mention because it takes a special form. This pertains to the function of Transfer of Learning, which is to be contrasted to the initial learning of knowledge. Knowledge transfer is frequently emphasized as a purpose of learning. It is said learning should be concerned not simply with the acquisition of knowledge, but more importantly with the use and generalization of knowledge in novel situations. First of all, it is evident that little knowledge transfer cannot occur if the knowledge itself has not been initially mastered. But beyond this, there is an important question of what conditions of instruction are required to encourage transfer of knowledge. For a number of reasons, the instructional mode of organized group discussion is one that appears to be well designed to accomplish this function of transfer of learning. When properly led, such group discussion not only stimulates the production of new extensions of knowledge by the adult learner but also provides a convenient means of critical evaluation and discrimination of these ideas.

COMPONENTS OF INSTRUCTION

Three major part of the instructional complex that may be controlled:

1.   It is possible to *control the stimulus situation*, by which is meant the objects or events that are the focus of learning interest. The objects and events that make up the stimulus situation, naturally enough, vary according to what is being learned. The desired content of instruction will determine whether the stimulus situation is primarily composed of computer methods, collections of rocks, or of geometrical shapes. But the general forms taken by stimuli, whether objects, pictures, or printed texts, are importantly determined by the level of learning that must be undertaken. To deal with this question adequately will require you to consider the stimulus situation applicable to the level of learning.

2.   The *verbal communication* is employed to direct the learner's attention, to guide their learning, and to institute the proper sequence of actions, among other things. Strictly speaking, such communication is not a part of the content to be learned, but only that part of the instruction which exerts a control over the learner's behavior during learning. When simple forms of learning are being undertaken, this distinction between guidance and content is easy to make. Another important reason for verbal communications in instruction is to tell the learner what to do -- giving directions. Such communications have the form of instructions of the sort printed on packages to tell purchasers how to open them.

3.   The key to retention and maintaining of motivation is *feedback to the learner* from the events of learning. Consideration must be given to

the question of how the learner knows he or she has achieved the objective of a learning act, and how such information can be manipulated to bring about reinforcement.

CONNECT THE LEARNING IDEAS TO EXPERIENCES

Examples observed in the learning session or from outside experiences connect the learning ideas to real situations. Using this method helps that adult learner understand the presented concepts in terms of their own or others' experiences. It helps the adult translate an abstract idea into a job related skill.

Solicit a wide range of inputs from the trainees, asking particularly about job related experiences.

Strongly reward ("thank you for sharing.") the learner when their inputs make the connection between what is being presented or discussed and their experiences.

However, when using a learner's experience-based example to illustrate a point or of what is being presented, if possible, have the participants analyze it, determine the relevancy to the discussion, and highlight its relationships to the learning under discussion.

Before the learning event session, prepare interesting relevant examples that relate to key learning points. Remember the examples must be realistic and meaningful to the adult learner. Also have questions prepared to elicit examples from them.

Having the learners supply personal examples encourages them to fit the learning points into their experiences. Their examples help to indicate how well they understand the lesson concepts. Adult learners learn to appreciate the value of their background as well as how to learn from each other's experiences. This participation also works as a motivator to increase the learner's desire to learn.

However, only use your example when the trainees are unable to provide the inputs you are seeking. When creating your own examples make sure they relate directly to the learning points, and illustrate how the concepts or skills relate to the situation. Only present one or two examples, at most, because too many illustrations can be confusing or create confusion for the specific learning point. Examples should only be used where appropriate, not to often and must be in good taste, neither sexist, racist or offensive in any other way.

When opportunities arrive in one module of learning that relates to a previous lesson content this allows you to tie the information together and show the common elements between the two learning sessions. On the other hand, a learner will sometimes ask a question which will be dealt with in an upcoming module. Rather than covering the point right then, tell the learner to hold that point until you reach the module to which it applies. Then you must jot down a note as a reminder to yourself. Then when you get to the future module, remind the learners about the question and identify who originally asked the question and discuss the topic at that time. This gives you a lot of credence and believability in future learning sessions.

"BIG PICTURE" TECHNIQUE

In order to tie the modules and materials together you must thoroughly understand all the learning points of the training course. As you facilitate the learning sessions you must know where all the learning points are and be well prepared for questions and discussion. You must be ready to integrate and relate any ideas brought forth to previous modules or the upcoming learning sessions.

GROUND RULES FOR THE INSTRUCTING TECHNIQUES

Adult learners who are going to be in a group together like guidelines and ground rules as to how the training will be conducted.

Some of the common ground rules you should include each time are: Class start and stop times, being prompt about returning from breaks, no side conversations, decisions will be reached by consensus, one person talks at a time, no interruptions, and attack ideas not people. You may want to put these on a flip-chart, or other visual means, and then ask them for any more, such as smoking, room temperature, telephone calls, messages, etc. When all is taken down, get total trainee agreement on the ground-rules. They you have a contract for training room behavior. This not only provides a positive learning room environment but also allows the participants to control each other. With ground rules adults feel more comfortable to police each if some member is becoming disruptive. However, this does require that you model and maintain the ground-rules for yourself throughout the training.

Another ground rule we have used effectively is we don't start until everyone is here. "Is George coming?" "You saw him park his car?" "Okay, we will wait for him." Then just wait. When he shows up have everyone start clapping and then begin. This negative reinforcement will almost 100% of the time change behavior, he will not want to come late again. On occasion to an habitual later comer, a comment such as "Oh, so I see you didn't care about the time you stole from the other peoples learning?" can be very effective.

EXPERIENTIAL ACTIVITIES, PROJECTS AND TASK GROUP METHODS

A key in our instruction presentations is experiential-cooperative learning.

When having a team, which could be two or six to a group, give clear, concise instructions for the activity and take time before they break into teams to answer any questions for clarity. Provide the trainees with the objective of the activity, what is expected of them as a team and as individuals. Let them know how long they have to complete the activity and any directions about appoint a spokesperson and a recorder for presentation of results.

At the completion of the activity have a debriefing and sharing. This is the time to tie the activity to the objectives of the lesson and summarizes what has take place. You job as the facilitator of the learning activity is to listen to and acknowledge trainee's insights about the activity. Concentrate to keep the focus on the purpose of the activity. Remember, some experiential learning activities cannot present the clear objective or purpose until the activity is completed.

Example of an Experiential-Cooperative Learning Project

PLANNERS AND IMPLEMENTERS Experiential Activity
Facilitator:

Step 1 - Number off the total group by fours. So if you have 20 participants you will have 4 teams of 5 adults. (You want 5 or 6 in a group.)

Step 2 - Have participants go to the four corners of the room, "All number ones go to that corner.", etc.

Step 3 - Hand out **PROJECT INSTRUCTIONS** explanation sheet.

PROJECT INSTRUCTIONS

Step I   You are to select 2 or 3 members from your team who you feel will be the best **PLANNERS**.

Step II   Then select 2 or 3 members from your team who you feel will be the best **IMPLEMENTERS.**

Step III   Select a person from your team to represent your team as a **TOTAL QUALITY EVALUATOR** for determining criteria for judging the process and finished product, and then selecting the winning team.

When these decisions have been made, your Planners will stay where you are and wait for further instructions. Your Implementers will go outside and wait for further instructions. The Total Quality Evaluator will go to the kitchen and wait for further instructions.

Facilitator

Now hand out to the Planners their **Planners Instructions** sheet. Have them read the instructions   Go around to each team and answer their questions and then hand them their construction materials.

   Construction Supplies to be given to each team:
       100 drinking straws
       100 rubber bands
       100 paper clips

PLANNERS INSTRUCTIONS

You are to design a Bridge for your Implementers to build.

You will have only three materials for them to build the structure with - straws, paper clips and rubber bands. All teams have the same number of each of the materials. You may only handle one of each of the different materials when going through the process of designing the Bridge.

The winning team will be determined by the height and width of the bridge and other criteria determined by the Evaluators.

After you have finished designing your bridge you may call your Implementers in. When your Implementers come in you will have 5 minutes to explain your design to your implementers and answer any questions they may have. Neither you or the Implementers may handle the building materials during this design explanation time.

You may use drawings, written instructions, verbal instructions - that is up to you. After the 5 minute instruction period is up, you, the Planners cannot verbalize anymore or use any hand gestures or other types of activities for instruction to the Implementers. At this point, you the Planners, may only observe, non-verbally, during the building phase of the Bridge project.

While you are designing, your Implementers may communicate to you through written memos. However, whenever your Implementers send a memo and ask any questions, you must stop your Planning until you have answered the memo in writing and given it back to the messenger, who will deliver it to your Implementers.

There will be a 45 minute Planning Time maximum. And the project must be completed within 60 minutes of the start of the Planning Time. The Facilitator will give you the signal when that starting time is beginning. You do not need to take the full 60 minutes. In fact, you will be given points for completing your planning time before 45 minutes, as determined by the Total Quality Evaluators.

You do not need to use all materials to complete the structure. However, the finished structure must stand by itself for at least one full minute without any human assistance, such as touching or holding, and must be at least two inches off the floor at the lowest point of the Bridge.

Your Implementers will inform the Total Quality Evaluators when they want their completed Bridge project to be judged. The Evaluators will determine the starting time for the one minute and the two inches measurement.

After you have given each team their materials, then you go out to the **IMPLEMENTERS** and give them the following sheet of instructions.

IMPLEMENTERS INSTRUCTION SHEET

You are to remain out here until your Planners call you in.

You are allowed to write memos to your Planners. A professional messenger will deliver all memos.

(**Facilitator**, you are the "professional messenger" running memos between the Implementers and the Planners.)

Next go to the **Evaluators**. Treat them as a new team and give them the Evaluators Instruction sheet. Have them read the instructions and answer any questions they may have.

EVALUATORS INSTRUCTION SHEET

You Evaluators will first determine what criteria you will select for judging each teams' process and each teams' finished product.

Givens: The team project is to build a Bridge. A Bridge score must be given for height times the length of the finished product. The Bridge must stand by itself without any human assistance for one minute and must be at least two inches off the ground at the lowest point. You will determine when the one minute starting time begins and do the measuring of the lowest point. All Evaluators will judge the teams' finished product, one team at a time and all Evaluators together.

Planners may only handle one piece of each of the three materials during the planning phase. Planners will have five minutes to explain their design and give instructions their Implementers. Planners may use written and verbal forms of instruction. However, after the Implementers begin constructing the Planners must become non-verbal, and cannot give any more instructions, not even with gestures.

Planners have a maximum length of time to plan of 45 minutes. However, they have been instructed that you will give them extra points for completing their planning quicker and calling their Implementers in earlier. The teams have a total maximum of 60 minutes to complete the Bridge building project.

At the completion of all the Bridge product building and presentations, you will leave the room and go and share your Judgments with each other, negotiate your evaluations and determine a team winner.

QUALITY DELIVERY SYSTEM
SUGGESTED CRITERIA FORM

		TEAMS			
		A*	**B**	**C**	**D**
Results Criteria	**Weight x**				
Height x Weight	_____	___ = ___	___ = ___	___ = ___	___ = ___
Completion Time	_____	___ = ___	___ = ___	___ = ___	___ = ___
Product Design					
Use of Material	_____	___ = ___	___ = ___	___ = ___	___ = ___
Aesthetics	_____	___ = ___	___ = ___	___ = ___	___ = ___
Parsimony	_____	___ = ___	___ = ___	___ = ___	___ = ___
_____	_____	___ = ___	___ = ___	___ = ___	___ = ___
_____	_____	___ = ___	___ = ___	___ = ___	___ = ___
Construction					
Use of Material	_____	___ = ___	___ = ___	___ = ___	___ = ___
Replicability	_____	___ = ___	___ = ___	___ = ___	___ = ___
Direction Following	_____	___ = ___	___ = ___	___ = ___	___ = ___
_____	_____	___ = ___	___ = ___	___ = ___	___ = ___
_____	_____	___ = ___	___ = ___	___ = ___	___ = ___
Team Process					
Use of Talents	_____	___ = ___	___ = ___	___ = ___	___ = ___
Cooperation	_____	___ = ___	___ = ___	___ = ___	___ = ___
Planners	_____	___ = ___	___ = ___	___ = ___	___ = ___
Implementers	_____	___ = ___	___ = ___	___ = ___	___ = ___
_____	_____	___ = ___	___ = ___	___ = ___	___ = ___
TOTALS	100%	A	B	C	D

*Give each team a rating from 1 to 5, (5 being high) on each criteria.

Multiple the team's criteria score times the weighted percentage for that criteria category. When completed then add the team category scores together for a total score.

You may negotiate about the score on each category. You may just want a single total percentage for the three major areas. Just so your total weighted percentage adds up to 100%.

Facilitator - Some suggestions or ideas

Step 1   When the Evaluators return to the room, have the Planners and Implementers return to their original team corners.

Have the Evaluators go to the center of the room. Then instruct the Evaluators to give summary evaluations of each team's process and product, team by team. Then have them present the scores on a flipchart and announce the winning team. Then have the Evaluators return to their original teams.

Step 2   Have the teams discuss what they learned from this activity and put their key points on a flipchart and tape on the walls.

Step 3   Ask the Planners to comment first. "Planners how did you feel about the Implementers didn't understanding and couldn't following your simple instructions?"

Step 4   Implementers how did you feel about being outside and not knowing what was going on with the Implementers?" "What was your thinking and how did you feel about your memos and your Planners responses?"

Step 5   "Evaluators how did you feel about your task?" "What were you thinking and how did you feel when you returned to your team and it was the loser or the winner?"

Step 6   "Planners and Implementers what was your thinking and feelings about the TQ Evaluators?"

Step 7   "Let's review what you wrote on your flipcharts and see what we learned."

Step 8   Now let's relate this back on the job with the manager, the designers, the implementers and evaluators.

Hints to the Facilitator/Instructor:

1) The responsibility comes to be seen as lying with the Planners. The can't blame the Implementers, they designed the system and the process,

2) lack of effective communications up, down and across in an organization leads to many unintended consequences, and

3) when people don't know the criteria ahead of time or its relation to the mission or goals, the results by which they are rewarded or punished leads to frustration and no one feels good about the outcome. Such ambiguity on the job leads to a low level of continuous stress.

Let the discussion flow freely, but keep the focus on relating this experiential activity to actual job experiences and then have them give a summary of what they learned. You can relate this to the now historical but ingrained Total Quality Management methods.

Chapter 09
◊∑◊∑◊∑◊∑◊ Outline of the Five Phases   ◊∑◊∑◊∑◊∑◊
of Group and One-on-One Instruction

THE FIVE PHASES OF INSTRUCTING
   I.   Pre-instructing: planning and preparation
   II.   The beginning, establishing the learning environment
   III.   Presenting the modular sequence
   IV.   Summary, measurement and the future
   V.   Post-instructing, continuous process improvement

Often the course content is already determined. Yet you, the instructor, need to go through the five phases of instructing in order to ensure the conducting of the most effective instructing possible. This will guide you to become a master instructor, not just a syllabus reader. This process answers the question: "Is this learning appropriate for this group of learners?"

A recommendation for you is to take some blank sheets of paper and follow down this outline answering the questions to yourself so you can answer them to someone else. This will assist in assuring you haven't overlooked a significant area or point.

PHASE I   PRE-INSTRUCTING: PLANNING AND PREPARATION

A. Purpose - The reason for learning.
1. What caused this learning or course to come into being?
2. What purpose is it to serve?
3. What will be the subject of the learning?
4. Who are the people that will influence this learning?
   a. Presenters
   b. Learners
   c. Others affecting this learning
5. Where will the learning take place?
6. When will the learning take place?

B. Objectives - Identifying the outcomes.
1. Write a positive statement of the purpose, in objective terms.
2. Write statements of the objectives of the learners' outcomes from attending this learning.
3. What are the desired outcomes? Are they clearly stated, are they understandable and measurable?
4. Does the flexibility exist to accept adult learner variations?

C. Planning - Giving full consideration to the preceding questions.
1. Use the following criteria for planning learning presentations:
   a. Capability level and background of the learners.
   b. Capability and personality of the instructor.
   c. Subject matter content, scope and depth.
   d. The objectives and desired outcomes to be met in each module.

e. Available resources (human, facilities, equipment and materials).

f. Time available, both for preparation and presentation of learning.

2. Make sure to provide flexible alternatives so that a presentation won't collapse if conditions change.

3. Check to ensure there are a variety of practical learning experiences to appeal to as many learner senses as possible and to avoid monotony.

D. Organizing - giving substance to the plan.

1. Formalize the specifications of the learning presentation.

a. Identify the major levels of learning to be emphasized.

b. Detail the logical order or sequence of learning.

c. Draw up agenda giving content outline and time frame.

d. Define learner activities and responsibilities.

e. Decide on general methods and specific techniques to be used in learning presentations: lecture, demonstration, discussion experiential-cooperative.

2. Establish communications, where necessary, to coordinate outside individuals contributing to or affecting the learning presentation.

3. Develop resources and arrange for facilities, equipment and materials needed for the learning presentation.

E. Measurement Tools - Assessment of learning outcomes.

1. Determine how the desired outcomes will be measured.

a. Objectively by

•Work sample

•Productive activity using performance or academic tests,

quizzes, and assessments.
b. Subjectively by
•Class activity, problem solving, solution thinking, discussion, etc.

F. Preparation - completion of physical and psychological readiness.
1. Make sure all documentation required for both instructor and learners are completed (guides, handouts, references, administrative, etc.).
2. Make sure all instructional aids are produced and tested.
   a. Equipment (projectors, computers, films, PPTs, slides, mock-ups) are tested using actual visuals, ideally at the place where they will be used.
   b. Rehearse all demonstrations and check them out carefully during this time of preparation.
3. Confirm final communications and procedures to all coordinating activities (including back-up and alternate plans i.e., if remote computer is to be used).
4. Have instructor's personal preparation critiqued, including rehearsal with feedback on both technical content and delivery if necessary.
5. Make final "on site" preparations of room arrangement, appearance, lighting, heat, noise, other physical distractions, equipment, materials and any other pertinent details prior to the learning presentation.
6. Have technical assistance ready if needed.

PHASE II   THE BEGINNING, ESTABLISHING THE LEARNING ENVIRONMENT

A. First Meeting Model

As all learning starts with a first meeting the following seven points may be a guide.

1. **Greet them.** Introduce yourself, have your name written, either on a name tag, blackboard, or bulletin board where they can see it. Give them name tags also.

2. **Keep things on an informal basis, but on an adult level.** Try to put the learners at ease. Remember, this is probably an embarrassing situation for most of them.

3. **Review the program/learning objectives.** Discuss it with the group Ask questions so the group will respond. Try to get the feel of the group and their reactions so that you can plan accordingly.

   a. The desired outcomes (objectives) must be clearly stated and receive at least tacit approval if not sanction of the learners.

   b. Other conditions or "ground rules" must also be tactfully established (especially administrative or learner accountability)

   c. The relationships between this learning and any preceding or following learning needs to be established.

4. **Make yourself understood.** After all, you want adult learners to learn to be effective in communications, so be a good example. Speak slowly and distinctly, but with enthusiasm.
   Use large writing when using the whiteboard. Speak to your group and not to the whiteboard. Finish your sentences before you turn around again to the whiteboard.

5. **Fill out necessary forms, explaining clearly why they are necessary.** Assist each individual as needed. Be sure there is plenty of time so that the adults do not feel pushed or hurried by time.

6. **Ask for questions, suggestions, or comments.** You may not get any at the first meeting because the group probably will be shy, but if you're doing a good job they will comment in forth-coming sessions.

7. **Be relaxed.** They are adults, too, and know you're not perfect. So don't try to be. If you plan your sessions and your sessions are well organized, the participants will know it.

PHASE III   PRESENT THE MODULAR SEQUENCE

A. Application – of the planned and prepared methods and techniques.
   1. Based on agenda. Beginning with the first learning activity. conduct learning with appropriate learning methods:
      a. Lecture
      b. Demonstration (if applicable)
      c. Discussion
      d. Experiential-Cooperative
         It is not important that these methods be mutually exclusive, usually one is typically dominant when combinations are used.
   2. Techniques are the subsets of these methods and are used to treat the details of the training presentation and assist in reaching the desired outcomes.
      a. Some techniques used with lecture may be combined with the "speech" or telling:

•Visuals: slides, PPTs, overheads, films, videos, flipcharts, chalk board, felt and flannel boards, models, mock-ups, samples photos.

•Learner aids: handouts, reference guides, texts, exhibits, and exercises.

•Q & A: instructor questions, learner questions and brief discussions.

•Audio tape, telephone recording, telephone speaker.

•Video-Tapes, Film, Video Conference: Q & A.

b. Some techniques used with demonstrations - super planning is required for successful demonstrations. Preparedness for any eventuality is cardinal to avoid failure. Multiple alternatives must be available.

•Closed circuit TV, recorded interviews, telephone speaker, remote demonstration using computer terminals.

•Simulation, mock-up.

•Learner or audience participation.

These techniques are employed for two major reasons:

•To increase the communication potential: appeal to a variety of learning senses, to manifest thoughts, pictures, ideas, concepts, relationships, notions and to reinforce the basic verbal communication.

•To maintain learning activity and awareness of their responsibility and ownership for their own and other participants' learning.

c. Connect learning modules to concrete experiences.

B. Feedback -- Observing feedback from participants is key at this time.

1. You are fully responsible for receiving and analyzing not only the reactions and responses of the learners, but also maintaining an awareness of all other environmental conditions affecting the learning.

   a. The learners are constantly providing feedback tht must be analyzed against the responses that are anticipated as a result of planning. If you are not obtaining verbal or nonverbal feedback then ask the group or an individual for it.

   b. These learner responses range from negative aggression; through passiveness and tacit approval; to enthusiastic accord.
      •Use effective communications skills to deal with the disruptive or inattentive individuals.

   c. Environmental conditions that may cause personal discomfort will detract from the learning, these include heat, light, noise, furniture, and equipment.

2. Your making adjustments as the result of observed feedback analysis increases learning effectiveness.

   a. Minor adjustment is natural with a good instructor (e.g. appropriate and timely references for each situation, adapting to different facilities).

   b. Major adjustments may be required to:
      •Change technical detail level or rate in learning of subject matter.
      •Abandon an obviously unsuccessful technique.
      •To circumvent the loss of key material, equipment failure, abrupt time or duration change, or absence of a guest presenter.

PHASE IV   SUMMARY, MEASUREMENT AND THE FUTURE

A. **Ending** -- An effective ending must be planned and prepared, but feedback may dictate an adjustment. The instructor must be able to determine when and how to make an unscheduled stop.

B. **Summary** -- a summary is normally given in the ending.

    1. Have the learners present the summary on a flip chart or board. This provides them another means of interacting and reviews the learning. This also provides a means for seeing how far the learners' perceive it and alerts you to where the emphasis was in the learning and what specific points were missed.

    2. A summary serves to reinforce those key points and the relationships among them.

    3. Avoid re-presenting in the summary. The summary should be unique, although some aids (visuals, models, examples) may be reviewed.

C. **Sustain Learning** -- For a lasting learning, project the learner activity forward into actual situations.

    1. The learner must not be permitted to quit participating at the end, rather the learner needs to continue to feel ownership and responsibility for continuing the learning process in the future.

    2. The learners' responsibility for learning needs to be projected by some type of assignment - either actual or rhetorical, i.e., future goals list or have them write three things they will be able to do at work or at home as a result of this learning.

D. **Measurement** -- a measure needs to be provided regarding attainment of goals.

    1. If the body of the learning has been designed to provide some type of progress or performance evaluation, if their performance has

been evaluated module by module it may only need to be finalized in the ending.

2. A successful learning must communicate the progress toward or achievement of the stated objectives clearly to the learners. It is the instructor's duty to project a positive attitude and provide positive reinforcement of the group's and individual's accomplishments, i.e., whether it was of 10% or 90% of the learning goals. Even 10% is twice as much as 5% and a start toward the eventual goal.

3. Have all participants complete a feedback form that has the learners give objective and subjective responses to both the learning and the instructor. (This is not the thorough professional one in Part IV, but a short form that can be completed in ten minutes or less. This can be adapted from the longer professional form.)

E. **Presence To The End** -- The physical and psychological presence of the learner must be as positive and engaging as at the beginning.

1. It is the first impression that sets the standard for acceptance of the instructor and the learning by the learner, but it's the last impression, the close, that determines what the learner is going to do with what he or she has received.

PHASE V   POST-LEARNING ANALYSIS AND CONTINUOUS PROCESS IMPROVEMENT

A. **Outcomes** -- The degree to which desired outcomes were attained must be examined: objectives, goals, etc.

1. Isolate the factors that contributed to the success of the learning. If the factors were spontaneous and have enduring value, take steps to incorporate them into subsequent learning.
2. Isolate any factors which detracted from the success of the learning. If the factors were spontaneous and unlikely to occur again, they may be dismissed. If the factors resulted from poor planning, preparation or execution, take immediate steps to eliminate or neutralize them.
3. Summarize and reviews the written feedback results obtained from the learners. Look for recurring themes and responses related to the predetermined desired outcomes.

B. Refinement Of The Learning
1. Any weakness in your communication techniques needs to be analyzed and strengthened, modified or replaced.
2. Any faulty learning aids, equipment or documentation materials needs immediate attention to rectify them.
3. Check the subject matter content for any necessary updating. Determine if any parts need to be eliminated, replaced or added.

C. The Final Phase --The final aspect of the post-learning analysis blends into the pre-learning, planning and preparation phase of the next learning of this material. Make certain that all recommendations and summary evaluations are placed in the permanent course learning packet so that if you are not the next instructor of the material, the new instructor will have access and the advantage for improving the next learning.

Instructing The Individual Adult Worker
[1]   A One-On-One Model   [1]

Besides a course for a group of adults there is also the situation of instructing the individual adult. The following is a checklist model for conducting this individualized instructing.

I.   **Prepare the**
     adult worker
     for the learning

• Put the adult learner at ease.
• State the job and find out what he or she already knows about it.
• Get him or her interested in learning the job.
• Place him or her in position.

II. **Present the**
     modular
     sequence
     to be learned

• Tell, show, and illustrate one IMPORTANT STEP at a time.
• Explain the whole and then present the parts in correct sequence.
• Stress each KEY POINT.
• Instruct clearly, completely, and patiently.
• Take up one point at a time, but no more than he or she can master.

III. **Try out**
     performance
     of each module

• Have him or her do the job once – you correct the errors
.• Then have him or her explain each KEY POINT: a teachback as he or she does the job again.
• Use chaining, shaping and successive approximation learning methods. (See Appendix)
• Make certain he or she understands.
• Have them train the job or task back to you.
• Continue until YOU know the person has correctly sequenced the learning; they know when they have

reached a terminal point of the job at an acceptable standard; and when it is satisfying to them.

IV. Follow-up
Appraisal

•Put the worker on their own. Designate whom they go to for help.
•Check back frequently to reinforce the   correct process and to correct mistakes.
•Encourage questions.
•Taper off extra coaching and close follow-up.

Chapter 10
X◊X◊X◊ Planning and Building a Course ◊X◊X◊X
-Content Organization-

Very often the instructor will be facilitating someone else's learning materials or course. However, sometimes the instructor will need to know how to design a course from scratch. This knowledge will also help evaluate existing courses. The ideal situation is where the instructor can take the time to design the course so it meets the organization or institution's vision and mission and the personal goals of the learner.

This model assumes the course designer will be instructing or facilitating the course as well. How effectively the adult learns and retains what is learned is dependent on how effective the instructor is in using the tools of instructing. This is where most instructing falls down. There are too many experts in subject matter who are ineffective in transferring their knowledge to adult learners. Even enthusiastic experts can go only so far without effective instructing know-how.

First there are the questions and
second the designing of modules.

First: Framework Questions

A. What course or learning specific questions need answering?
   1. What are the desired outcomes and objectives in the areas of attitudes, skills, knowledge and problem solving?
   2. Who are the participants?
   3. What will be the size of the class?
   4. What will be the length of the course?
   5. Who will be the instructing staff?
   6. Where will the learning take place?
   7. What is the current situation before the learning?
   8. What levels of learning will be involved?
   9. What instructing methods and techniques will be used?
   10. What evaluation and measurement methods will be used?
   11. What are the resources to conduct the course?

B. What do you need to build a course?
   1. Knowledge of the subject matter of the course
   2. Tools and skills of the most effective techniques to enable the learners to acquire and retain this particular learning.

The instructing is the intervention to provide the means for the adult learners to move from where they are to the desired outcome. This can be new learning or refresher training. A course can contain all eight levels of learning. The following example has all eight levels of learning with a major emphasis on Level 6 - Concept Learning. (See Building a course with Bloom's Taxonomy and Levels of Learning)

EXAMPLE:

Course: Management Effectiveness Workshop

First: **Course Objective and Desired Outcome**
   a. As the result of this workshop all participants will be more
      effective managers and leaders back on the job.
   b. The participants will demonstrate an understanding of the
      objectives of the learning and the outline of the sequence of
      events.
   c. The participants will demonstrate an understanding of how
      management effectiveness has progressed over the past fifty
      years.
   d. The participants will demonstrate a gain in the appreciation of the
      natural developmental process and how the future is building
      normally on its own history.

Second: Participants
   Supervisors who are being promoted and currently employed
   managers who have been recommended for attendance.

Third: Size
   Limit to 24 - Selected by executive staff, need to be nominated
   and recommended to attend.

Fourth: Length
   5 Days - Arrive on Sunday and Leave on Friday

Fifth: Staff
   2 Full-time Instructors and 1 Workshop Administrator
   Senior Executive Presentations
   Topic Area Experts for Single Presentation

Sixth: Training Location
Off-Site resort hotel with sufficient break-out rooms, large general meeting room, flexible eating requirements and recreational facilities.

Seventh: Situation Before Learning Event
Authoritative, top-down management style with top management desirous of changing to a participative management style.

Eighth: Levels of Learning and Modular Sequence of Instructing
See model of modular sequence and levels of learning on following pages.
For evaluation of the total learning and the instructor see Part IV.

Ninth: Training Methods and Techniques

Example: Module I of *Management Effectiveness Workshop*

•**Structured Participation** - Introductions, ice breaker and overview of week long workshop rules, dress, timeliness, casual, refreshments always available, phone calls, etc.
Acknowledging the individual differences as to expertise and experience.
Emphasize the importance of being responsible for their own learning and the importance of assisting of other participants in their learning.

•**Lecturette with Overheads** (Transparencies, foils, etc., or may be done in slides or powerpoints)
Start with WWII and Ohio State model and sequentially add additions to management effectiveness knowledge up through the Baldrige and participative management of TQM. Learning Level 3 - Verbal Chaining - Establishing glossary of terms - then Learning Level 6 - Concepts are presented. (Too often adult instructing

starts at Learning Level 6 - Concepts and never brings the audience up to that level. The instructor is "over the heads" of the participants from the start. **Remember:** start where they are at, not where you want them to be.)

•**Discussion** - Q & A of Lecturette

•**Small Group Interaction** - Sharing of knowledge and group presentations.

Each group looks at: "where we are and projects where we will possibly be in the 21st Century."

•**Visual Media with the Lecturette -** Overhead transparencies or powerpoints with hard copies

•**Time Frame -** 3 Hours

•**Materials**

Syllabuses

Handouts of Visuals - Transparencies - Slides, powerpoints

Pencils, pens

Writing Pads

Name Tags

Coffee, Tea, Orange Juice, Water

Fruit, donuts, rolls

Folders

•**Equipment and other Supplies**

Overhead Projector or slide projector or laptop with LCD

Large Screen

5 Flip charts - 10 flip chart pads

Marking Pens - 3 colors, at least

Masking Tape & map tacks

Lectern

Long Table for Materials

Pointer - lazer

•Seating Arrangement

Large open U with enough room on the outside for small groups

Tenth: Evaluation and Measurement

For course questions see Module I example on following pages

For total evaluation of the learning and the instructor see Part IV

Assessing of Learners by the Instructor: At the completion of the Module I presentation, develop written notes of visual and auditory assessments of individual participants.

Who are the contributing participants?

Who are the isolatives or shy ones?

Who has and is willing to share real expertise?

Who are the over-controlling ones?

Who is supportive?

Who is resistant to learning?

Make strategies for overcoming individual behaviors and barriers to full participation.

Eleventh: Resources to Conduct the Course

Determine resources to include any prizes, t-shirts, memorabilia, guest presenters, transportation and a small contingency fund.

Determine appropriate menu with balance of food and liquids.

Second: Designing the Modules

A course and the modules within a course need to be broken down into the attitudes, skills, knowledge and problem solving areas to be covered. Then how much time and emphasis on each of the four areas needs to be determined for each module. The following is a continued example of the *Management Effectiveness Workshop.*

Management Effectiveness Workshop

Modular Sequence and Levels of Learning

	MODULE I	MODULE II	MODULE III	N---
	Objectives Manager-From There To Now and On to the Future	Getting To Know You Getting To Know Leadership	Your Style--Using vs Effectively Doing	
ATTITUDE 50% Ripley Levels of Learning--5 & 6	50%	20%	20%	10%
SKILLS 10% Ripley Levels of Learning-1 to 5	10%	20%	10%	50%
KNOWLEDGE 30% Ripley Levels of Learning- 5 to 8	30%	40%	30%	20%
PROBLEM SOLVING 10% Ripley Levels of Learning-8	10%	20%	40%	20%
Equals:	100%	100%	100%	100%

Learning Evaluation Questions

	MODULE I	MODULE II	MODULE III	MODULE N
Attitude	5	2	2	1
Skills	1	2	1	5
Knowledge	3	4	3	2
Problem Solving	1	2	4	2
Total:	10	10	10	10

Desired Outcomes and Levels of Learning for Module I

Some of these are behavioral learning objectives:

.

Attitude: Increased appreciation for management effectiveness development. Appreciation of their own knowledge and understanding. Appreciation of who the other participants are and what they have to contribute to the learning. Appreciation of the purposefulness of the workshop. Appreciation for the amount of preparation effort and attention to detail given to structuring the learning environment and learning process. (Accomplish with learning experiences emphasizing Levels of Learning 5 - Multiple Discrimination and 6 - Concept.)

Skill: All participants can distinguish one stage of development of the manager from another stage of development. (Create a sequential experiential team or individual exercise illustrating Ripley Levels of Learning 1 through 5 - Signal Learning, Reward the Response Learning, Chaining, Verbal Chaining and Multiple Discrimination.)

Knowledge: An understanding of what has been combined along the way from each management theory or approach; the forming of concepts, then new principles and now the development of new problem solving methods. (Using Ripley Levels of Learning 6 - Concept Learning, 7 - Principle Learning and 8 - Problem Solving.) Emphasize inductive reasoning.

Problem Solving: The combination of presented concepts and principles into the possible new management approach for the future. (Using Ripley Levels of Learning 8 - Problem Solving.) Emphasize strategies and creativity.

Other Desired Objectives of Module I
- The beginning of building team cohesiveness, openness and trust.
- The development of an open atmosphere of learning.
- The development of participants' ownership and accountability for their own learning.
- The modeling of professionalism and organized preparation.
- The creation of a non-threatening climate of learning.
- The creation of a "learning can be fun" feeling.
- The recognition of the importance of the workshop topic and the seriousness of the learning.
- The foundation for the participants to share their expertise and experience.

End of Example

LEARNING OBJECTIVES = DESIRED OUTCOMES

Writing learning objectives is one of the most important instructing tools for building a course, yet often this is where instructors stumble. The learning objectives must meet the criteria of the desired outcomes. This is limited to those actions of the learner that are observable by others. The skills outcomes from the previous page qualify as well as demonstrations of knowledge and problem solving. This is like having a vision or mission; it keeps the instructor focused on the desired outcome and goals. This allows the participants to temporarily wander off track without losing the desired outcome. The following are some guidelines to assist the instructor with training objectives.:

1. Learning objectives are statements that describe what you expect the learner to be able to **do** at the conclusion of the training.
2. Learning objectives will communicate your **intentions** to the degree you have described:
   a. What the learner will be **doing** when demonstrating that he or she has mastered what you have taught.
   b. How you will judge that the learner has mastered the tasks.
3. Learning objectives **describe** what the learner will be doing upon successful conclusion of the learning event. Good learning objectives will
   a. Identify and name the overall job tasks that will be taught.
   b. State the important conditions under which the tasks occur.
   c. Define the standard of acceptable performance.

4. Learning objectives need to be structured to relatively limited tasks; the more objectives you have, the better chance you have of making clear your intentions for the learning effort. As an option, check against Levels of Learning to make certain you are staying on one or two levels, and not going dramatically up and down the levels of learning scale.

5. Learning objectives need to be given to learners. If you give each learner a copy of the objectives for his or her learning, or at least explain the objectives in detail, the job of instructing will be much easier.

Writing Learning Objectives

1. State what you want the learner to be able to do as the result of the learning.

2. Improve your statement by specifying when and where this task normally occurs.

3. Improve your statement further by specifying how much accomplishment will constitute acceptable performance after he or she has learned the task.

4. Be prepared to defend your improved statement by thinking through why the correct performance of the task is important to the overall operation.

5. Now, write your improved statement in as simple terms as possible to make it perfectly clear.

6. Have several experienced learners read the learning objective you have written and tell you what it means to them. If they do not understand it, then go back and check your what, when, where, how much and why. Chances are, one or more of these key elements is missing.

Examples Of Learning Objectives:

<u>Restaurant Industry</u>

<u>Not So Good</u>

<u>Better</u>

The food server will understand order taking and selling up the menu.

The food server will be able to pleasantly greet the customer, take the order, and suggest a minimum of one higher priced menu selection than the customer selected.

The counter employee will appreciate the importance of making correct change.

The counter employee will be able to make correct change for customer purchases with daily overages and shorts of less than one percent of total sales for their register.

<u>Not So Good</u>

<u>Better</u>

The utility worker will grasp the significance of sanitation regulations for rest-rooms.

The utility worker will be able to clean and sanitize the fixtures, walls, and floor of the bathrooms to achieve no demerits on the Health Department Sanitation Inspection standards form.

The cook will be familiar with the operation of all equipment in the kitchen.

The cook will be able to operate, clean, and describe preventative maintenance procedures for the battery range, the convection oven, the pressure steamer and the overhead broiler.

The following example is a model for a complete job task training breakdown within a specific job situation.

Example A: TASK #06: Preparing Coffee In Urn Equipment

<u>Job Title:</u> **Food Server**   <u>Location:</u> **Dining Room**

<u>**Learning/Training Objective:**</u> Task #06: A food server will be able to prepare coffee in urn equipment in accordance with correct procedures for coffee-water mixture, water temperature, and coffee equipment sanitation. [Standard of Performance: 8 minutes/urn]

<u>**Equipment and Supplies:**</u> <u>Coffee urn, brew-basket filter and rack, one pound of coffee, one gallon container.</u>

What to Do	How to Do It (Important Information)	Remarks
Prepare Coffee in Urn	Check equipment	Be certain urn is clean.
	Measure coffee	Use type specified by supervisor. 1 lb. coffee to 2 1/2 gallons of water.
	Spread coffee evenly over filter. Filters in cabinet below urn	New filter preferred.
	Heat water to 185°F.	Urn will have hot water ready in left half of unit.
	Pour hot water over the coffee.	Use slow circular motion
	Remove filter and and grounds as soon as water has all dripped through.	Usually 4-6 minutes. Discard grounds into garbage
	Draw about one gallon of coffee from urn spigot and pour into the top of the urn to thoroughly mix and blend the liquid coffee.	Coffee strength "layers" in the drip process.
	Hold at 185°F.	Never boil coffee.

The following is a second example of a model for a complete job task training breakdown within a specific job situation.

Example B: TASK #04: PRE-PREPING ICEBERG LETTUCE

Job Title: **Salad Maker**   Location: **Pre-Prep Area**

Training Objective: Task #04: A Salad Maker will be able to pre-prep iceberg lettuce for use as lettuce underliners and salad body, discarding lettuce that is bruised or otherwise damaged and retaining all usable lettuce. [Standard of Performance: 3 cases an hour.]

Equipment and Supplies:
Stainless steel paring knife, lettuce, pre-prep sink, garbage can, large colander, ice, large strainer, sheet pans, cutting board.

What to Do	How to Do It (Important Information)	Remarks
Wash Lettuce	Fill sink with cold water.	Iceberg Lettuce only.
	Add ice to water.	Ice cold water will retain freshness.
	Place lettuce in water, allow to soak.	Do not crowd lettuce. soak 5-10 minutes.
	With knife, remove core from lettuce.	Stainless steel knife will prevent "rust color" formation on lettuce caused by by reaction to carbon knife.
Remove damaged outer leaves	Run water into core hole to help separate leaves. Discard damaged leaves.	Use plastic liners in garbage cans or use garbage disposal unit.
Remove lettuce underliner leaves	Running water will separate leaves. Place in colander to drain	Save heart of lettuce for salad body.
Storing liners	Place liners in sheet pans and cover with plastic wrap. Place in refrigerator.	Cover completely to retain freshness.
Cutting salad body lettuce	Cut hearts saved earlier into approximately one inch cubes of lettuce.	Cut with stainless steel knife on cutting board.
Washing and freshening lettuce	Place cut lettuce pieces back into soak sink full of ice water.	Soak for 5 more minutes.
Drain lettuce	Place lettuce pieces in colander and drain.	Scoop pieces from sink with large strainer to reduce handling.
Store cut lettuce	Spread lettuce pieces on sheet pans and cover with plastic wrap. Place in refrigerator.	Cover completely.

The Following is an Example: From Learning Event Instructor Manual: Beginning and Objectives

 Ripley Institute and Academy: Learning Event T121

Leader and Manager
Both Important, But Different
LET MANUAL # <u>01</u>

© R. E. Ripley and M. Ripley, 5th Rev, March, 2008   Published by: **Carefree Press**

Ripley Learning Event Instructor Manual
Table of Contents for LEADER AND MANAGER

Review CEUs and "Housekeeping"
Their Agenda for the Day

T121 LEADER AND MANAGER Learners Manual's
TABLE OF CONTENTS

RIPLEY INSTITUTE AND ACADEMY

ACKNOWLEDGEMENT

This proprietary, intellectual capital, BPF Learning Event Manager/Trainer Manual was developed by Robert E. Ripley, Ph.D., Marie Ripley, M.A. and Briana Warner, MSCIS. The purpose is to implement a consistent Model for management, instruction, facilitation and evaluation for all Learning Events.

LEARNING EVENT INSTRUCTOR Manuals

Instructor manuals have three primary purposes.

They function as:

- Preparation before the Learning Event begins.
- Instruction aid during learning.
- Standardization to ensure that the Learning Event is delivered as designed.

Before the Learning Event: Overall Learning Event Goals Learner Outcomes

0.1 The learners acquire the skills and knowledge to achieve excellence and succeed in today's complex business environment.

0.2 The learners determine what to do and what not to do as a leader and a manager.

0.3 The learners improve their effectiveness as a manager as well as a leader.

0.4 The learners delegate more effectively, communicating their expected outcomes.

0.5 The learners determine when to purposely use leader and manager skills and processes.

0.6 The learners recognize their opportunities to maintain and increase profitability of their organizations through both their own actions and the behaviors of others.

The course overall goals are related to certain specific modules more than others, as indicated in the next chart.

Learning event Layout and Learning Taxonomy
T121 LEADER AND MANAGER

Course Layout	Bloom's Cognitive Levels		% Attitude*	% Skill	% Knowledge	% Application	
Module I	2		70%	10%	10%	10%	
Module II	1, 3, & 4		20%	15%	50%	15%	
Module III	2, 3, 4 & 6		16%	20%	30%	34%	
Module IV	2, 3, & 4		16%	17%	27%	40%	
Module V	2, 3, 6, & 6		21%	18%	23%	38%	
Module VI	4		10%	10%	40%	40%	
Module VII	3 & 4		10%	20%	40%	30%	
Module VIII	2 & 4		45%	15%	20%	20%	

*Horizontal rows of % add up to 100.

Course Layout The above chart lists the overall goals for the various modules. Then the Learner Outcomes are listed by number. You may have the Ripley course learner outcomes in a separate handout. In this manual these are written out only in each module. Bloom's Cognitive

Levels are listed for each whole module. In the beginning of each module's section in the manual proper, these levels are further broken down by each Learning Outcome.

This same further breakdown is also available for the Attitude, Skill, Knowledge, and Application categories. These first four are expressed as percentages, that horizontally add up to 100%. Each number on this chart is actually an average (mean) of the figures from the Learning Outcomes listed under that module (in the charts in front of each module in the manual proper).

As a quick review or introduction, below is a condensed form of ideas from of Bloom's (1956) *Taxonomy of Educational Objectives: Cognitive Domain.*.

Blooms' Explained

The six levels of Bloom's Taxonomy were used as instructional helps to classify learner's resultant behaviors. These may help to explain the level of complexity of thought or behavior involved in the particular learning event. The levels could be used as categories to group similar types of learning processes.

Level 1 - Knowledge (Bloom)   This level involves the recall of previously learned material. This could range from facts to theories. The following list of verbs is related to this level:

Acquire	Group	Locate	Quote
Choose	Match	Read	Select
Count	Recall	State	Identify
Define	Name	Recite	Tabulate
Draw	Indicate	Trace	Pick
List	Record	Remember	Underline
Label	Point	Repeat	Write
Reproduce	Memorize	Recognize	

Typical tasks are naming, listing, defining, and describing. Using examples, lectures, videos, visuals and illustrations are helpful in instructing at this level.

Level 2 - Comprehension (Bloom) This level involves the grasping of the meaning of material. More than rote memorization is required at this level, one step beyond simple remembering. This may be shown by interpreting material, translating material from one form to another or by estimating consequences or effects of the material. Some related verbs are:

Account for	Discuss	Translate	Generalize
Associate	Draw	Predict	Reword
Restate	Translate	Describe	Recognize
Illustrate	Identify	Explain	Express
Classify	Group	Express	Summarize
Infer	Realize	Target	Interpret
Determine	Acknowledge	Accept	Explain
Change	Rewrite	Show	Suggest

Typical tasks at this level include questions, discussions, reviews, tests, reports, learner presentations, comparisons, contrasts, paraphrasing, and summarizing.

Level 3 - Application (Bloom)   This level includes the ability to use the material in new and concrete situations. The application of rules, methods, concepts, principles, laws and theories. This requires a higher level of understanding than comprehension. Some related verbs are:

Apply	Determine	Generalize	Record
Collect	Accept	Graph	Choose
Discuss	Discover	Interpret	Employ
Present	Use	Demonstrate	Practice
Illustrate	Operate	Schedule	Solve
Predict	Classify	Examine	Graph
Plan	Record	Choose	Construct
Organize	Investigate	Develop	Select

Some tasks typical at this application level are computing, relating, preparing, producing modifying, and classifying. By doing exercises, practices, demonstrations, projects, simulations and role play, this level is put to use.

Level 4 - Analysis (Bloom) The ability to take material and break it down into its component parts is referred to here as analysis. This may expose the organizational structure of the material, or the relationship among the parts. As both understanding of the content and the structural form of the material are required, analysis is seen as intellectual more challenging than previous levels. Some related verbs are:

Analyze	Determine	Examine	Simplify
Break down	Diagram	Formulate	Outlin
Sort	Categorize	Group	Compare
Distinguish	Differentiate	Appraise	Calculate
Experiment	Test	Contrast	Criticize
Diagram	Inspect	Debate	Question
Inventory	Relate	Infer	Formulate
Survey	Anticipate	Acknowledge	Uncover
Transform	Identify	Search	Select

Some typical analysis tasks are problems, exercises, case studies, critical incidents, discussions. questions, and tests.

Note: verbs may appear in more than one level, so staying with the definitions is safest. Also note that Ripley Levels of Learning are doing a slightly different job, categorizing the knowledge material itself, and ways of learning at the various Learning Levels.

Level 5 - Synthesis (Bloom) In synthesis, the parts are put together to form a new whole. This ability or cognitive level may produce a unique plan, proposal or scheme. Creative behaviors or the forming of new patterns or structures may be part of the learning outcomes at this level. Some related verbs are:

Arrange	Compose	Integrate	Propose
Design	Formulate	Organize	Prepare
Collect	Construct	Create	Plan
Categorize	Combine	Derive	Modify
Develop	Explain	Generate	Predict
Synthesize	Rearrange	Reorganize	Revise
Sequence	Prescribe	Generalize	Imagine

Some typical synthesis tasks are projects, problems, case studies, creative exercises, develop plans, constructs and simulations.

Level 6 - Evaluation (Bloom) Judging the value of the material is what is meant by evaluation. The judgments are based on specific criteria, either given to the learner or chosen by the learner. Some of the criteria may be utility, economy, accurateness, effectiveness or satisfaction. The judgments may be qualitative or quantitative. Some related verbs are:

Appraise	Consider	Determine	Interpret
Assess	Judge	Evaluate	Rate
Compare	Value	Revise	Score
Award	Select	Choose	Estimate
Validate	Measure	Conclude	Criticize
Consider	Decide	Defend	Distinguish
Justify	Summarize	Rank	Support

Some typical evaluation tasks are projects, case studies, exercises, critiques, simulations, presenting rationales, and appraisals.

Note: Bloom places all choices in the evaluation level, where as the Ripley Levels of Learning, covered next, distinguishes simple choices as *Multiple Discriminations*, while complex judgments are placed under *Problem Solving*.

Chapter 11
⌈⌉§⌈⌉⌈⌉ RIPLEY LEVELS OF LEARNING ⌈⌉⌈⌉§⌈⌉

Levels of learning (1) is a framework for talking about and solving everyday learning situations, (2) gives a theoretical framework on which to design the training, (3) assists the instructor to get from the beginning to the end of training without missing important steps and ensures starting the training on the right level, and (4) helps to explain why what the instructor is doing works.

The levels of learning explains the naturally occurring phenomenon of acquiring knowledge, skills, understandings and problem solving ability from the simplest to the most complex in a systematic manner.

RIPLEY LEVELS OF LEARNING
Building Blocks

Creative ---------- Higher Order ----------- Strategic
Thinking   Problem Solving   Planning

Level 8   Problem Solving
                          /   \
Level 7   Principle   Principle
                          /   \
Level 6   Concept   Concept
                          /   \
Level 5   Multiple   Multiple
                    Discrimination Discrimination
                          /
Level 4   Verbal   Verbal
Verbal

                    Chaining <---- Chaining <----
Chaining
                          /
Level 3   Chaining <---- Chaining <---- Chaining
                          /
Level 2   Reward the
                   Response
                          /
Level 1   Signal

This section contains brief descriptions of the levels of learning that are distinguishable from each other in terms of the conditions required to bring them about. There are some "old friends" in new clothes, which will be recognized from your previous experiences and learning. There are also some "new characters" who should be quite familiar from common experience, but whose names are presented differently.

LEVEL 1	SIGNAL LEARNING

Definition Linkages

SIGNAL	•A **sign** or gesture giving information or a command, a message made up of such **signs**. •An act or event that immediately produces a general reaction.
Sign	•Something perceived that suggests the existence of a fact or quality or condition, either past, present or future.
STIMULUS	•Something (a signal) that **rouses** a person to activity or energy or that produces a **reaction**.
Rouse	•To cause to awake •To cause to become active or excited
Reaction	•**Response** to a **stimulus** or **act** or situation
RESPONSE	•An **act** or feeling or movement produced by a **stimulus** or by another person's **action**
Act	•To produce an effect, to perform a specified function

Source: American Oxford, American Heritage and Webster's New Collegiate Dictionaries

Learning to respond to a signal is a kind of learning quite familiar to everyone.   It is when two stimuli occur together, purposefully or inadvertently. Usually one stimulus is verbal, one is not. Signal learning is a reactive type of learning (even at times accidental) compared to other levels which are more purposefully rewarded or acquired. Signal learning is a reaction established because two stimuli happened to occur together.   The resulting reaction is the response and this can be "generalized" to new situation. The classic example in psychology is the baby who was presented with a sudden loud noise and a furry white rabbit at the same time. The result was to create a fear which generalized to all furry white objects and then even to an adult dressed up as Santa Claus with a white beard.

Another example is this classic story:
Two small country boys who lived before the day of the motor cars had their Friday afternoons made dreary by the regular visit of their pastor, whose horse they were supposed to unharness, groom, feed, and water and then harness again on his departure. Their gloom was lightened finally by a course of action which one of them conceived. They took to spending the afternoon of the visit re-training the horse. One of them stood behind the horse with a hay-fork and periodically shouted "Whoa" and followed this with a sharp jab with the fork. Unfortunately no exact records of this experiment were preserved save that the boys were quite satisfied with the results.

This is, of course, a description of a set of circumstances appropriate for the establishment of a conditional response. It is customary to represent what has been learned here in the following way:

"Whoa" =   S1----------->**R** =

                                                \

(timed close together)   **Pain Response**

                                                /

Poke =   S2----------->**R** =

Later:
    "Whoa" =   S1---------->**R** = **Anticipated Pain Response**

In other words, a response behavior or capability had been acquired by the horse that was not previously present: making a response to the sound of "Whoa!" typical of that to pain (including struggling, running, shying, etc.). It was as if the horse had learned to anticipate the painful stimulus; the verbal command had become a signal for pain, or the expectation of pain. Fear may be the anticipation of possible pain.

Conditions for the establishment of this form of signal learning:
There must be nearly simultaneous presentation of the two forms of stimulation:
  a. The stimulus (S1 - "Whoa"), initially only paired with stopping (previous learning) is capable of producing a generalized reaction of the sort one is interested in establishing.
  b. The stimulus (S2 - Poke) provides the paired association of "Whoa" with pain or anticipation of pain, as long as the signal comes simultaneously (in this case) with the painful stimulus (S2). The S1 ("Whoa") cannot become a signal if it comes too many seconds before or after the painful stimulus (S2 - Poke).

The number of times this pairing of a stimulus must occur is a question that has no single answer. This could occur in one trial or take many pairings, depending on the internal previous conditioning, the external environment, and the purpose of the learning. The adult who has peeled many onions may feel tears at the sight of one. The military command, "Attention!" is designed to signal a condition of alertness and a physical positioning of the body. Involuntary fears of many sorts, such as fear of the water and fear of heights, may be engendered in people when these signals have been accompanied by painful or frightening stimulation. Presumably, pleasant emotions may just as well be involved in signal learning. The sight of a mother's face may become a learned signal to the person at any age for various pleasurable events associated with the presence of his or her mother. The sight of one's old high school after many years of absence may evoke pleasant feelings of nostalgia that are quite independent of the recall of any specific events.

Signal learning has a truly involuntary character, and applies to responses that are not typically under voluntary control. A fear response, involving general and diffuse activity including speeded heartbeat, constriction of blood vessels, and other internal involuntary behavior, may readily acquire a connection with a signal under the conditions we have described.

This relates to Pavlov's classical conditioning where the paired stimuli were food and a bell. There is much evidence to indicate that there are marked individual differences in the rapidity with which people acquire stimulus-response connections. Such differences are not related to intelligence, but are significantly related to the level of anxiety in the adult when typically facing life's problems and decisions. Adults who tend to be anxious acquire conditioned responses more rapidly than do non-anxious adults.

Learning occurs dependably when the conditioned stimulus ("Whoa") precedes the unconditioned stimulus (Poke) by an interval between 0 and 1.5 seconds, and most readily when the interval is about 0.5 seconds or less. Repetition is usually required, however learning may occur as a one-time learning, i.e. post-traumatic stress syndrome where one traumatic incident is sufficient. Think about when this happens on the job i.e. in the form of sexual harassment, crossed signals, verbal statement, fear of loss of job, etc.

Extinction is the kind of *unlearning* that results in the disappearance of the previously learned connection. When S1 ("Whoa") occurs alone a significant number of times without the S2 (Poke), these events result in the disappearance of a previously learned connection, i.e. no more physical or mental reaction when "whoa" is heard. However, any renewed pairing of S1 ("Whoa") and S2 (Poke) will re-establish the connection for at least another 100 times.

But "precise voluntary responses", such as kicking a football or writing one's name cannot be acquired in this way.

Signal Learning is sometimes used by instructors to establish a state of alertness on the part of their learners. An instructor may deliberately us a clap of the hands, for example, as a signal for "paying attention." Such learning might be accomplished initially by making the hand clap a fairly loud and startling stimulus. After a few repetitions, the instructor finds it possible to generate a similar state of alertness by means of a much gentler hand clap. This is an example of stimulus generalization.

LEVEL 2:   REWARDING THE RESPONSE LEARNING   (SHAPING)

Dictionary Linkages

> **REWARD**   •Something given or received in return for what is done

In this level of learning, the learner also responds to a signal. Level 2 is more important than Level 1 because it involves making very precise movements of the skeletal muscles in response to very specific stimuli or combinations of stimuli. The resulting voluntary responses make up the observed output. In other words, this kind of learning makes it possible for an adult to perform an action when he or she wants to.

A simple and well-known example of such learning occurs when a dog learns to "shake hands" in response to a vocal stimulus supplied by the owner or by another friendly person. While playing with the puppy, the owner says, "Shake hands!" At the same time, the owner gently raises the dog's paw and shakes it, then pats the dog's head, or gives the dog a piece of a dog biscuit. The owner then repeats this entire procedure on several subsequent occasions, perhaps using progressively lighter force to raise the paw. After several occasions of this sort, the dog raises the paw when the owner says, "Shake hands," and is patted or fed as usual. Eventually, the dog comes to perform this act promptly and more or less precisely whenever the proper signal is given. It can then be said that the dog has learned what may be called a stimulus-response capability

This kind of learning is distinguishable from Signal Learning in terms of its outcome.

The response acquired by this means is a fairly precise, circumscribed, skeletal muscular act, far different from the generalized emotional response that characterizes the Pavlovian kind of signal-responding of level 1.

Certain other conditions are necessary for the acquisition of this kind of capability.

1. There appears to be a typical gradualness of the learning of this act. At least a few occasions of repetition appear to be necessary.
2. The response that is made becomes more and more precise throughout these several occasions, in other words: *Shaping*. Shaping or Successive Approximation is rewarding the action or behavior that is progressively closer to the desired performance.
3. The controlling stimulus also becomes more and more precise. Whereas initially the dog may respond to other commands than "Shake hands!" other vocalizations eventually lose their control over the outcome.
4. There is a reward or reinforcement.- *Rewarding the Response.* The adult learner is rewarded for responses that are "correct" or that approach being so in the trainer's view, and he or she is not rewarded for those that are incorrect.

Rewarding the response learning appears to govern the acquisition of a new vocalization habit by a person and can be employed to teach an adult the pronunciation of an unfamiliar foreign word. It is also primarily for physical skills, such as golf swing, swimming stroke, batting swing, etc..

Shaping and Rewarding of Response : Effectiveness in the training of adults started when that adult was a child. The parent may frequently introduce the desired signal, such as, "Say mama," and eventually the child does say, "Mama," more or less by chance, immediately following this signal. Suitable reinforcement follows, and the learning of this new capability is then well launched.

Of course, training an adult to perform a new task is a somewhat easier process, although much the same set of events is involved. The trainer begins with an approximate capability already established. When the signal is given, "Do a back stroke," the learner can immediately do something that is almost correct. Subsequent trials then, are largely a matter of bringing about discrimination. The learner must receive reinforcement for responding to a narrow range of correct external movements of a backstroke, and also for a narrow range of internal stimuli from his or her muscles in performing the body movement. The adult learner also reinforces him or her self by recognizing a match between personal body movements of the backstroke and the movements of the swimming instructor. If the trainer is going to do this effectively, the trainer must have previously adopted a suitably precise set of matching criteria.

To illustrate this concept we can use the example of a National Sales Manager and the three reporting Regional Sales Managers. The National Sales Manager required a report from each of the Regional Sales Managers weekly by 10:00 a.m. on Monday, which she then consolidated and presented to the Senior Staff Monday afternoon at 2:00 p.m.. The

National Sales Manager came to us because her best Regional Manager for the first time had let her down. We asked her to describe the reporting behavior of all three of the Regional Managers reporting behaviors. She said that her best Regional had always submitted his report by late Friday Afternoon, the second Regional's report was there the first thing Monday morning, and the third Regional was always at the last minute or even late. She said she "chewed out" the third regional in front of the other two and would turn in an extrapolated projected results report based on the results of the two submitted reports. "But now," she said, "even my best Regional was late and I didn't have adequate data to really make any report." We asked her to analyze what *response* was getting *rewarded* and who was she giving her attention too. She discovered she had been rewarding *turning in late report behavior*. The Regional who was always the latest and caused the most trouble was "chewed out" and received a lot of attention, even if it was negative. She analyzed that she never had to say any thing to her best Regional because he just was so reliable and always complied. We suggested that for the next week she should report to the Senior Staff only the data of the Regionals who had turned in their reports. She was to let them know she had only received the one report and to name the other Regionals that didn't have a report. She then was to give recognition to the Regionals who got their report in on time, complete and correct. She was not to say anything to the other Regionals other than that she had informed the Senior Staff that their report wasn't in and ready. In three weeks all three reports were turned in complete and ready on Friday evening. She was *Rewarding the Response* she wished to create.

So often people think they are punishing when they are actually rewarding.

In Level 1 Learning, the extinction of behavior occurs when the reinforcement that follows the learned response is omitted.

In Level 2 Learning, the extinction of behavior also occurs when the learner has in fact been unsuccessful in bringing about reinforcement. This may be a sort of trial-and-error learning. Those particular behaviors that are reinforced, on the other hand, become selected and continue to appear (on the next repetition of the stimulus situation).

Level 2 learning appears to be quite resistant to forgetting. The learning, if learned correctly in the beginning, tends to be retained for many years without appreciable loss as these tend to be relatively isolated acts having few activities to exhibit interference with them, (in contrast with Level 4 - verbal chainings which have many interferences). After several years of not performing a physical function you can have *spontaneous recovery* of that activity to a very high level close to your original level for a short period of time. For instance, tennis, basketball, or golf skills can resurface. However, the second repetition of the old non-performed activity will have a much lower performance level, but not as far down as when you first begin the learning. The eventual recovery of the function to a higher level of performance will also be much quicker than it was when originally learned.

If suitable conditions for reinforcement are present both within and outside the learner, the establishment of reward-the-response learning becomes primarily a matter of arranging conditions for the desired stimulus discrimination to occur most readily. Anything that is done to make the recognition of a correct stimulus easier than it would otherwise be, will speed up the learning, and thereby decrease the number of repetitions required for learning. In other words, seek to arrange the stimulus situation so as to reduce the amount of repetition required for learning. If the stimuli are vivid and distinct, learning will be rapid.

When an increase of hope or a reduction in fear is brought about by a response made by the human, the reinforcement conditions of the **rewarding the response** learning - Level 2, are in effect.   Level 2 learning is a basic therapeutic technique.

Level 2 learning leads directly to level 3 and 4.   One cannot acquire Level 3 - chains, or Level 4 - verbal chains, unless more basic capabilities have been learned first.   The prerequisites are essential to all higher orders of learning.   The individual truly cannot write before they have learned to hold a pencil.   The individual cannot calculate before they can identify numerals and they cannot read until they have learned to discriminate printed symbols.

LEVEL 3   CHAINING

Dictionary Linkages

CHAIN	•A **connected series** or **sequence** •A **series** of events, each of which causes or **influences** the next
<u>Connect</u>	•To join or be joined •To think of things or persons being associated with each other
<u>Sequence</u>	•The following of one thing after another in an orderly or continuous way •A **series** without gaps, a set of things that belong next to each other in a **particular order**
<u>Influence</u>	•The power to produce an effect
<u>Series</u>	•A number of things of the same kind or related to each other in a similar way, occurring or arranged or produced in **order**.
<u>Order</u>	•The way in which things are placed in relation to one another •A proper or customary sequence •A condition in which every part or unit is in its right place or in a **normal** or efficient state
<u>Normal</u>	•Conforming to what is **standard** or usual
<u>Standard</u>	•A thing or **quality** or specification by which something may be tested or measured •A higher level of **quality**
<u>Quality</u>	•A degree or level of excellence

Chaining is a relatively simple and widely occurring learning situation. Chaining is a matter of connecting together in sequence two or more previously learned stimulus and responses. By chaining is meant the connection of a set of individual S's-->R's in a sequence: Sl->R1->.S2->R2->S3->R3->S4->R4.

Chaining sequences can be made up of motor responses, like that of turning on a television set or a washing machine.

There are also sequences that are entirely verbal, like the greeting, "How have you been?" or the pledge of allegiance to the flag.

A young girl had acquired the habit of dropping her coat on the floor when she entered the house. Being annoyed with this practice, her mother had many times scolded her daughter and required her to go back and pick up the coat. But this was quite ineffective in overcoming the unwanted behavior. The mother, however, discovered an effective procedure: she made the girl go out of the house again with her coat on, then come in and hang the coat up properly. This illustration shows the importance of correct sequencing of the events in a chain.

The original chain that was troubling the mother was:

enter house--> drop coat --> see mother --> mother says, "Pick up coat" --> pick up coat --> hang up coat.

But what had to be established was a shorter chain with quite a different sequence, namely:

enter house --> keep coat on --> approach closet --> hang up coat.

The important thing to note is that the second chain could not be learned by simply adding links to the first one. What is necessary is the institution of the desired chain with correct links from start to finish.

Another example: **Unlocking a door and entering a room.**

Descriptively, what must be learned is a sequence like the following. Having the key in your hand, and facing the lock, you first check to see that the key is right side up. Then you insert the key into the lock until the stop is reached, you then turn it until another stop is reached, and you push the door open and step into the room. Obviously, each part of this sequence must be performed correctly, and in the proper order, or the performance of opening the door will be unsuccessful. If the key is not right side up it cannot be inserted; if the insertion is not complete it cannot be turned, and so on. The point is, the chain as a chain cannot be learned unless the individual is capable of performing the individual links.

Key in hand --> key positioning --> key up --> inserting key --> key pushed stopping point --> turning key --> key turned to stopping point --> turn handle --> push door open --> step into room.

The opening of the door constitutes a completion act providing reinforcement for the final link and also for the entire chain.

With an adult learner who did not know how to do this act, you could use verbal instructions to guide the sequencing. This is a major function of the adult trainer. The most important purpose is to provide external cues to the learner for the selection of exactly the right links for the chain. Of course, additional external cues will increase the probability that the adult reinstates the correct response and rejects others. For instance, adding the links "have the serrated edge up" and "push the key all the way in" could make the chain more complete.

It is important not to overload with more and more links initially because then *information overload* (resistance and loss of sequence retention) takes over. It is better to get the basic sequence down and then use verbal and illustrative corrections and selective reinforcement to correct mistakes in the next repetition. This combines whole and part learning for the adult. The adult wants to first see the whole picture and then to get more precise in the sequence of the parts.

After the first or second trial, the instruction may be self-administered until eventually the chain may be below the individual's threshold of awareness and just become a habit. The self-administered instructions are part of the conditions of learning, but not a part of what is learned. *Practice* then is used to permit the extinction of residual incorrect connections, rather than to establish new ones.

The important factor in chaining is that the terminal link must lead to a satisfying state of affairs for the adult learner - the door must open, the engine must start, the water must come out of the hose, etc.

The occurrence of some terminal satisfaction appears to be essential to the establishment of chains. If someone learns to just unlock the lock without pushing the door open, the whole sequence can be forgotten because there is no rewarding action following the terminal part in the sequence. If the reinforcement is omitted, extinction of the final link occurs, and the chain as a whole then disappears. It has been found that the reinforcement needs to be immediate in order for chain learning to occur most readily. The introduction of a delay in reinforcement markedly increases the delay in learning.

Forgetting -- should an adult forget a link in the chain of events, of course this disrupts the entire chain and the individual may get the impression that the whole has been lost. However, when the link is restored the whole chain may and usually does appear in its entirety. For instance, take bicycling, skating, swimming or a long unpracticed musical piece. The chain is returning quickly when the links in the chain are again restored in sequence and result in a satisfying experience after the completion of the terminal link. This then becomes an internal self-reinforcing activity.

Take the adult back to the child to identify one of the simplest human examples. The child is learning to ask for a specific object by name. The parent has attempted to teach the young child to call for an object, say a doll, by its name. After a number of parental tries at presenting the doll and saying "doll," distributed perhaps over several days, weeks or months, the child eventually achieves success. In fact, the child appears to acquire such a capability "suddenly" and without there being any entirely clear relationship between calling for a doll and the events that have gone before.

Once this chain is connected this chain can be linked in sequence or associated to another chain. Now having this doll can be linked to lying down, etc. This chaining activity can go on in the same way with adults learning the chaining in sequence. When the whole desired responses are learned, it appears that the chaining was not a gradual process but one which occurred on a single occasion. The whole is the sum of the parts.

In designing training for Level 3 - Chaining it is important to identify every link and then to precisely sequence them. Too often in training, trainers take shortcuts which can later lead to "chain" failure. Level 3 - Chaining can be as varied as opening a door to starting a jet airplane.

LEVEL 4	**VERBAL CHAINING**

Dictionary Linkages

    CHAIN   •Same as Level 3, except only **verbal input** and **output**

Verbal Chaining might well be classified as only a variety of chaining. But because these chains are verbal, and therefore exploit the remarkable versatility of human processes, verbal chaining has some unique characteristics.

One learns to translate an English word into a foreign one by acquiring a chain. For example, the French word for "match" is "alumette." In order to learn this equivalent most expeditiously, something like the following set of events occurs. One examines the combination "match-alumette" and notices that something already known connects the two: the syllable "lum" which occurs in the "illuminate." One then runs through the sequence, not necessarily out loud, "a match illuminates; lum" alumette." For many people the chain is most readily established by means of an image of a match bursting into flame to illuminate the area --"alumette".

If a person doesn't know the word "illuminate," it is obvious that the chain he or she acquires must be an entirely different one. It may be a longer one, or a shorter one; and it may involve a visual image, or some other kind of internal representation.

The conditions for the learning of verbal chains of this sort would appear to be as follows:
1. The individual must know what a match is.
2. The individual must know how to say the word "alumette" with sufficient accuracy to be considered correct so as to be tied to the key syllable lum.
3. A "coding connection" must also be available, that is, it must have been previously learned, if the chain is to be established with ease. In this case, the code is represented by the association of the image of the flaming match and the word "illumination." The selection of this code by the individual depends on their own previous history. A highly verbal adult may have many codes available, whereas an adults who ranks low in such ability may have very few. Probably, the code we have depicted here would serve adequately for a large portion of the adult population.
4. The chain must be "reeled off" in a sequence, so that each stimulus-response is contiguous in time with the next; in other words, links of the chain must follow quickly in order for learning to occur. Under these circumstances the chain, like other learned behavior chains, is probably acquired on a single occasion.

Our language is filled with such chains of sequences as is revealed by word associations. Salt and -----, Horse and -----, Night and -----, Before and ----, now and then, a penny saved is -- ---- -----, it is darkest ---- ----- --- ----, a stitch in time ---- ----, just to mention a few of the hundreds of chainings. The first member of the sequence seems firmly tied to the second. These then become strong culturally chained responses.

It appears that a verbal chain of about seven links (plus or minus 2) represents the limit of what can be learned as single event. Verbal chains longer than this must be broken up into parts in order for learning to occur most efficiently.

If presented with an entire verse of poetry to learn, the adult learner may break it up into various pieces, and put the pieces together in various ways.   On the whole, the evidence suggests that under many circumstances the most efficient procedure is what is called the Progressive Part method. Here the learner adds a new part (like a line of the poem) as they continue to rehearse the older parts. On the first try, the adult learner may attempt to say line 1; on the next, lines 1 and 2; on the next, lines 1, 2, and 3; and so on.

This procedure not only ensures that parts are chosen which are within the span of immediate memory, but also allows for the continued practice of earlier learned parts that are subject to forgetting through interference.

The most important condition for the prevention of forgetting of verbal sequences is repetition - overlearning. When the adult acquires a chain that makes it possible for them to say "alumette" to "match," and then goes on to learn to say "fromage" for "cheese," he or she may by so doing weaken the first chain. Now the adult may forget the French word for "match" and may also find it harder to remember "fromage" for "cheese" than it would have been had the adult not first learned alumette for "match." If the adult tries to learn four French words at once, rather than a set of two, this will be more than twice as difficult; six at once will be more than three times as difficult; and so on. A new learning process has entered the picture.

Short chains are easy to learn but hard to retain. Increasing the number of chains to be learned does not change the basic nature of the learning process--but--highlights the effects of another process -- Forgetting.

All learning above level 2 is discrimination learning. That is, being able to recognize or draw distinctions and separate into distinct parts or components; analytical.   Being analytical and perceiving the distinguishing or peculiar features that differentiate or make unique into categories or classes or one stimuli from another. In discrimination learning, it does not make any difference what sort of prompt is used, just so long as it serves to bring forth the required response, and thus to establish the chain.

LEVEL 5   MULTIPLE DISCRIMINATION

Dictionary Linkages

Discrimination
- To select out of a greater number of things
- To decide, to prefer
- To have good **judgment**
- To make a **distinction**

Distinction
- Seeing or making a difference between things
- To see or point out a **difference**

Different
- Unlike other nature or form or quality
- Separate, **distinct**

Distinct
- Able to be perceived clearly by the senses or mind, definite or unmistakable
- **Different** in kind, separate

Judgment
- To be able to give an authoritative opinion on the merits of something
- To form or give an expert opinion, comment, or judgment based on a **discrimination**

Decision
- Making reasoned **judgment** about something

Decide
- To **think** about or make a choice or judgment to come to a conclusion

Thinking
- Exercise of the mind in an active way to form connecting ideas
- To take into consideration
- To call to mind, to remember
- To be of the opinion or **judge**
- To form an intention or plan

Reason
- The capability to **think** and **understand** and draw conclusions
- Good sense or **judgment**

Understand
- To perceive the meaning or importance or nature of
- **Know** the ways or workings of
- To **know** how to deal with (i.e. machine)
- To **know** the explanation
- To become aware from information received to draw a **conclusion**

Know	• to have in one's mind or memory as the result of learning or experience or information
	•to feel certain
	•To **recognize**
	•To **recognize** with certainty
	•To **understand** and be able to use
Recognize	•To identify from one's previous knowledge or experience
	•To **know** again
Conclusion	•A **belief** or expert opinion based on **reasoning**
Belief	•Something accepted as true
Authority	•Someone with special knowledge

It is the choice or judgment from among what is and isn't available. It is making distinctions and recognizing with certainty what you know so you can draw appropriate conclusions.

Many young Americans undertake to learn to identify by names all the new models of automobiles products in any given year. They do not learn this in school, but it is surely as marvelous an accomplishment as many that do take place there. Each year there are new model names, as well as old ones, and these in turn are but subordinate categories of larger classes of names for major automobile manufacturers. Within a few weeks after all the new cars appear, a young person may be able to identify correctly the scores of new models that are adding to road congestion, as well as the ones learned last year or the year before. The adult, in contrast, may never get them straightened out and he or she has given this up long ago. This is one of those growth factors. You lose this capability as you grow older and increasingly in the higher order Levels of Learning.

What the young person has acquired is a set of ***multiple discriminations***. Each single identifying connection learned is a chain. As a stimulus, each automobile must be discriminated from other stimuli, like trucks and business. As an individual chain, each is learned rather easily. Each individual model, with its distinctive appearance must be connected with its own model name and with no other. Now the new chains interfere with the retention of those already learned, and vice versa. The phenomenon of interference, which presumably is the basic mechanism for forgetting, is therefore a prominent characteristic of the learning of multiple discriminations. The question then becomes how to arrange the conditions for the learning of multiple discriminations to mainly reduce or prevent interference.

Up to this point each learning level seems easy, and in fact is easy, just so long as each instance of learning is carefully distinguished and insulated from other instances that may tend to occur at the same time, or from other instances of a similar sort occurring at different times in the same individual. But we also know that, practically speaking, making a permanent change in behavior and attitude by means of learning is not always so easy. The reason at once comes to mind: people readily forget what they have learned. The marvelous plasticity that characterizes the nervous system and makes possible these fundamental varieties of modification is counterbalanced by another characteristic: what has been learned and stored is readily weakened or obliterated by other activities.

The conditions for learning multiple discriminations are as follows:
1. Individual chains connecting each distinctive stimulus with each identifying response must be learned.
2. The learner learns to distinguish between stimuli. They decide that something belongs and something does not. They make judgments

and are trying to draw conclusions based on previous learning. The learner is making decisions based on what they know and recognize so as to make sequential distinctions. By learning verbal chainings, we have correct sequences from the beginning to the end. In multiple-discimations one chooses among chainings. In chain learning, one may learn a route driving from home to the mall. After more than one route is learned, the choice between two or more routes involves multiple discrimination.

3. In order to ensure retention, measures must be taken to reduce interference. Generally speaking, you attempt to make the stimuli as highly distinctive as possible. A highly distinctive appearance of a car model virtually ensures that its name be easily remembered, i.e. the Ford Mustang.

Multiple discrimination is the type of learning the trainer undertakes in order to be able to call each of the adult learners by their correct name. It is the type that applies when you learn to distinguish plants, animals, chemical elements, rocks, and to call them correctly by their individual names. It is the kind of learning that is remarkably prevalent in all of formal education.

Take for instance, the auto mechanic - who people think is problem solving. The form of the work is trouble shooting with multiple discrimination as the mechanic tries out a chain of ideas and does multiple discriminations. Very often the trouble is not correctly found because the mechanic does not have a long enough learning chain to get to the primary dysfunction. What we often pay people for is their learned collection of multiple discriminations and learned chainings. A large portion of what is taught in adult training is multiple discrimination. This is why 75% of all jobs in the America can be taught in 30 days or less.

This is not rote learning. The prominent characteristic of multiple discrimination is not the acquiring of new entities as such, since these are simply chains, each of which is readily acquired in isolation. The important factor in multiple discrimination is the interference that must be overcome if retention is to be assured. Rote implies repeated practice as an optimal method of learning and this is not necessarily the case.

Just remember the older the person gets, the less this learning type is effective or possibly even useful. The older we get, the more we can effectively use the higher learning types which the younger persons seldom has enough experience yet to use.

Multiple-discrimination between a screw and a bolt is possible by visual recognition of characteristics. But to understand the concept screw or the concept of bolt requires the understanding of the value of inclined plane, etc. via physics. So one may or may not have the concept of screw and yet be able to recognize and discriminate one when presented.

LEVEL 6   CONCEPT LEARNING

Dictionary Linkages

CONCEPT

- An <u>idea</u>, a general notion
- Something conceived in the mind, thought, notion
- An **abstract** or generic idea generalized from particular instances

<u>Idea</u>

- A plan, etc, formed in the mind by thinking
- A mental impression
- An opinion for a vague belief or fancy
- A visible representation of a **conception**
- A **formulate** thought or opinion

<u>Plan</u>

- A **method** or proceeding thought out in advance

<u>Method</u>

- A **procedure** or way of doing something
- **Orderliness**

<u>Proceed</u>

- To continue, to carry on an activity
- To come forth to **originate**

<u>Orderly</u>

- Methodical
- Obedient to a discipline
- Well arranged in good order

<u>Originate</u>

- To give **origin** to, to cause to begin

<u>Origin</u>

- The point, or source, or cause from which a thing begins its existence

<u>Formulate</u>

- To put into a systematized statement or expression

<u>Formula</u>

- A conventionalized statement intended to express some fundamental truth or principle
- A prescribed or set form or method: an established **rule** or custom

<u>Rule</u>

- A statement of what can or must or should be done in a certain set of circumstances
- Customary or normal state of things or course of action

<u>**Conception**</u>	•A general idea concept, a complex product of **abstract** or reflective thinking •The sum of a person's ideas concerning something
<u>**Abstract**</u>	•Dissociates from any specific incident •Expressing a quality apart from an object •To consider apart from application to a particular instance, to **summarize**
<u>**Summary**</u>	•A statement giving the main points of something briefly •Comprehensive, covering the main points **succinctly**
<u>**Succinctly**</u>	•Conceived, expressed briefly and clearly •Marked by compact, precise expressions without wasted words •Comes from the word - to **gird**
<u>**Gird**</u>	•To put a band around - boundaries

We now turn our attention to the kind of learning that appears to be critically dependent on mental representation for its very existence. By this we mean the capacity to make internal pictures of your environments. In the human, this function is served by language. Adults employ this capacity freely and prodigally and are highly inclined to internalize their environment. They "manipulate" it symbolically, thinking about it in endless ways.

The adult finds a method or procedure or a way to do things. They are trying to surround their ideas with boundaries at an abstract level where there are formulas and rules. If they follow these rules they will get a particular outcome.

Learning a *concept* means learning to respond to stimuli in terms of *abstracted properties* like colors, shape, positions, number, as opposed to concrete physical properties like specific voltages or exact dimensions.

Take the word "cube". There are a great variety of physical stimulation that may correctly be identified as "cubical." However to define what is meant by "cube," a geometer requires some very precise language. But, of course, a person does not have to understand such a definition in order to identify correctly a cube under most ordinary conditions of their existence. The individual identifies a cube "intuitively," that is, on the basis of an internalized representation that does not employ the words of the geometer's definition.

Whatever the internal process is, there can be little doubt that a concept like cube is learned, and that its possession enables the individual to classify objects of widely differing physical appearance. The adult's behavior comes to be controlled not by particular stimuli that can be identified in specific physical terms, but by abstract properties of such stimuli.

How does a human being learn a concept?

Let's suppose that an adult capable of using language does not know the concept EDGE. Assume it is desired that the adult exhibit the capability of identifying an edge by name, and more importantly, by identifying any one of a class of things called edges in novel situations.

How can such learning take place?

The first step might be for the adult to acquire the word as a self-generated connection (Reward the Response - Level 2 Learning), so that when the trainer says "edge" and then asks that the word be repeated, the learner says "edge." Next, the learner will learn to identify two or three specific edges, by saying "edge" whenever an actual edge is pointed to. By this means the learner acquires individual verbal associates (Verbal Chaining - Level 4 Learning). Following this, there needs to be several occurrences of Multiple-Discrimination learning (Level 5) in which discriminations are established between each edge and a variety of stimulus situations that are not edges. The side of a three-dimensional object, the top, the corner, the curved surface -- all end to be distinguished from the edge. Requiring the learner to make these distinctions by means of words is not essential but might readily be done. The important event is the firm and precise attainment of the edge discrimination. A similar multiple discrimination may be learned for a flat-surfaced object such as a piece of paper, involving distinctions between edge and surface and corner; still another for a drawn two-dimensional figure, which may show shading as well as clear edges.

The learner needs to know what an edge is in a three-dimensional object, in a flat thin object like a piece of paper, and in a drawn two-dimensional picture.

At this point, all the prerequisite learning has been accomplished. The learner can now say "edge" to three different and specific stimulus situations. The adult learner is now ready for that particular event called *Concept Learning.* The trainer now uses a verbal communication and shows the learner a new object or drawing which has not previously been associated with the word "edge." The trainer says, "Show me the edge?" The learner points to it. A Concept has been acquired.

When the learner can immediately and without hesitation identify an edge to a roof, a cliff, an automobile fender, a lampshade, or any of a great variety of situations, the person must have an internalized individual representation of the concept - verbally and pictorially. When the learner can correctly express edge in a novel situation the concept "edge" has been acquired.

Just having a visual picture and one word is fine for multiple-discrimination.   But concept learning needs verbal description, explanation and an orderliness of understanding so that the person can generalize on how to use in a new situation.

The effect of concept learning is to free the individual from control by specific stimuli. This kind of learning then is of tremendous importance for most kinds of intellectual activity engaged in by the human individual. The adult reads in terms of concepts, they communicate with concepts and they think with concepts.

The learner does not have to see the stimuli of edge to respond or explain edge. The test for the presence of a concept is a matter of demonstrating that generalizing can occur.

There must be a demonstration that the learner can generalize the concept to a variety of specific instances of the class that have not been used in learning.   Otherwise, it is not a concept, but merely a collection of specific chains.

The world experienced by the adult is largely organized by means of concepts.   The adult thinks of his or her environment, as well as themselves, primarily in terms of concepts of objects, places and events. He or she communicates with other people, and other people communicate with them, to an overwhelming degree by means of concepts. There are concepts of data, things, places and people.

The adult is freed from the control of specific stimuli in their environment, and can thereafter learn by means of verbal instruction, presented orally, visually, or in printed form.   Adults can also communicate their intentions, their actions, and their thoughts to other people, again because the specific words the adults employ arouse concepts in the hearers that function just as his or hers does.

The learning can become over verbalized, which means that the concepts learned are highly inadequate in their references to actual situations. Concepts to be learned must have concrete references. This is where language jumps from the concrete to the abstract. A lot of concrete examples of edge have been combined and a new internal reality is formed.

The great value of concepts as means for thought and for application is the fact that they have concrete references. The importance here to adult learning is learning by doing, using the laboratory or discovery methods, demonstration of the concept and group functioning to share and correct with their multiple experiences.   This is the value of experiential learning.

Once concepts have been mastered, the individual is ready to learn an amount of knowledge that is virtually without limit. This is the key to learning your trade and becoming the master to the point of appearing artful and beyond just having the skills.

As another example, consider learning the concept **MIDDLE.**   Initially, you may have been present with a set of apples arranged like this: ☐ ☐ ☐   You can readily learn to pick up the middle apple when someone asks you to give them the middle one. Through reinforcement you learn this very quickly. Similar chains can then be established with other objects, such as sticks | | | or numbers 7 8 9.   You can mix up the chains and just ask for the middle one: | ☐ 8   of this more abstracted learning and you will give them the ☐.

Thus you have come to respond correctly to **MIDDLE** as a *concept* meaning "an object between two others."

The conditions for concept learning contained in the preceding example are presented in the following statements.

1. The stimulus portion of the chain, by means of which a middle apple is differentiated from the two others in the set, must have been previously learned. Likewise, the internal coding portion of the chain must have been previously acquired, which enable the individual to verbalize the word "middle" (some other word could serve the same function). And the response portion must also be available (saying "Middle," or pointing to it).

2. A variety of these situations must be presented incorporating the conceptual property (In this case middle) to be learned, in order that this property can become discriminated in its internally represented form.

3. Because of the necessity for this internal process of discrimination taking place in a variety of different stimulus situations, the learning of a brand-new concept may in some circumstances be a gradual process.

Initially the mistakes the child makes, in correctly identifying, for instance a saucer as circular, but not a dime, results from their having responded to an inadequate variety of stimulus situations. The concept may become more nearly adequate when the individual has a greater number of experiences in the course of everyday existence. This is what is usually behind the words: "You're not dry behind the ears yet," or "You haven't lived long enough." This illustrates the advantage the adult has by having had so many experiences.

Concepts are what give verbal chains meaning - otherwise they are just auditory sounds linked together. However, concepts may become equally comprehensive as a result of a deliberate instructional process carried out over a much shorter period of time. This way you don't have to grow so old to get so wise. This is why we say go an get some experiences.

It is quite important to note, however that adults do not always, or even frequently, learn new concepts in the manner just described. Adults can take shortcuts because they have a greater storehouse of language. If an adult does not happen to know what middle means, they can learn it by acquiring a chain linking this word with another concept they already know, such as "in-between".

Suppose an adult were presented with the situation of three apples in a row: ☐ ☐ ☐ . The adult is told "Give me the middle one." Now suppose the adult respond incorrectly. Assume also that the adult possesses the concept "in-between" from previous learning. In order to learn this new and strange concept middle, it is simply necessary for another person to say, "Middle means in-between". As a result of this communication, the adult acquires a Verbal Chain (Type 4 learning) that becomes a part of the longer chain leading to the correct response.

This example of adult concept acquisition is important for two reasons.
1. It illustrates how *verbal instruction* can function to remove the necessity for the gradual process of experience with a variety of stimulus situations necessary for concept learning in the child. By means of this *verbal chaining* an adult can acquire a new concept, at least a fairly adequate one, in a single trial.
2. The apple example emphasizes the difference between the genuine learning of a *truly novel concept*, as in a child, and the *verbal generalization* of an *already learned concept*, as in an adult.

LEVEL 7	PRINCIPLE LEARNING

Dictionary Linkages

PRINCIPLE
- A comprehensive and fundamental **law**, **doctrine** or assumption
- Facts of nature, underlying the workings of an artificial device
- A primary source: **origin**
- An underlying faculty or endowment: an ingredient
   that exhibits or imparts a characteristic quality
- Often used in combination
- Basic **truth** or a **general law** or **doctrine** that is used as
   a basis of reasoning or a guide to action or behavior

Law
- A rule established among a community by authority or custom
- A factual statement of what always happens in
   certain circumstances, as of regular natural occurrences

Doctrine
- A **principle** or **set of principles** held by a group
- Ancient meaning: Teaching or Instruction
- **A principle** or position or the **body of principles**
   in a branch of knowledge

Truth
- The quality of being **true**
- The state of being the case, fact
- The body of real things, events and facts: actuality
- A transcendental fundamental reality
- A judgment, proposition, or idea that is **true** or accepted as true
- The property of being in accord with fact or reality
- Fidelity to an original or a standard
- The quality or property of keeping close to fact or
   avoiding distortion or misrepresentation

True
- Being in accordance with the actual state of affairs - fact or reality
- Conformable to an essential reality, ideal
- Being that which is the case rather than what is manifest or
   assumed
- Consistent
- Accurate
- Corrected for error

INDUCTIVE <u>**Induction**</u>	•Of or using **induction** - Ex: Inductive Reasoning •Logical reasoning that a general law exists because particular cases that seem to examples of it exist •The act, process or result, or an instance of reasoning from a particular to a whole, from **particulars** to generals, or from the individual to the universal
DEDUCTIVE <u>**Deduction**</u>	•Reasoning by **deduction** •Logical reasoning that something must be **true** because it is a **particular** case of a general **law** that is known to be **true**
<u>**Particular**</u>	•Relating to one person or thing as distinct from others, individual •A detail, a piece of information •Ancient meaning: A separate part of the whole •An individual fact, point, circumstance or detail •A specific item or detail of information

It should be emphasized that these higher levels of learning seldom occur by chance or in the everyday experience. Each of them builds on learnings that have preceded them. Although the learning of *principles* and the *solving of problems*   may well represent some ultimate goals of a formal training process, it would be mistaken to believe that these goals can be reached by simply ignoring all other forms of learning. The varieties of learning described here are possible only because they have been preceded by the acquisition of a set of prerequisite capabilities that extend down to the simplest **reward the response** connection.

Principles   are chains of concepts that make up what is generally called knowledge. Principles are stated as sentences that contain at least two concepts. The core of a principle is a fundamental law, doctrine or truth. An example is: all adults have at some time exhibited neurotic behavior.

The simplest kinds of principles are naturally those that the young child learns. The child is not able to learn the complex principles of which adults are capable. First, because the child may not have acquired all the prerequisite *concepts*, and second because the child has perhaps not yet acquired the subtle *multiple discriminations* that underlie certain complex *principles*. They haven't lived long enough or had enough experiences to draw on.

Since principles are chains of concepts, they can accordingly vary in length. A simple principle like "birds fly" can be expanded to birds fly south in the winter, containing four concepts rather than two. Or they can be in the form of a definition which can sometimes be very lengthy. For instance: "Mass is that property of an object which determines how much acceleration will be imparted to the object by the action of a given force." Usually, such principles as these are stated at the end of a sequence of training, rather than at the beginning. To learn these long *concept chains* requires breaking them up into simpler parts, which are then finally put together as a total principle.

Of course, the adult learner may know them as *principles* without necessarily being able to state them in an exact verbal form. ***Knowing them*** means being able to demonstrate their use in specific situations, whether or not they can be repeated as verbal sequences.

As previously emphasized, knowing the concepts means being able to identify any members of that concept's class. It is only when such prerequisite concepts have been mastered that a principle can be learned with full adequacy. Otherwise there is the danger that the *conceptual chain,* or some part of it, will become merely a *verbal chain*, without the full meaning that is inherent in a well established principle.

The conditions of principle learning often begin with a statement of the general nature of the performance to be expected when learning is complete.   The trainer says, "I want you to answer the question, What kinds of things roll?"   Rather than stating the principle outright - increased friction restricts the ability of an object to roll. Why does the trainer say this? Isn't the trainer simply stating the principle, giving it away, so to speak? The main reason for making such a statement, which the adult learner holds in their mind during the learning, is that it provides the learner with a means for obtaining immediate reinforcement when he or she has reached the terminal act. Having this statement for a model, the learner will be able to know when he or she has finished learning. Through their discovery learning process of combining concepts they come to the over-riding principle.

Finally, a verbal question asks the learner to demonstrate the principle. The trainer says, "Show me." The exact form is not of great importance so long as it truly requires the learner to demonstrate the principle in its full sense.

Repetition has not been shown to be an important condition for this kind of learning, nor for its retention.   However, the possible need for repetition in the form of review exercise to overcome the effects of interference should not be discounted.

The capability acquired when a principle is learned is usually somewhat abstractly represented, since by its nature it may not be related to specific stimuli, but only to the classes of stimuli that arouse its component concepts.   Sometimes you can physically touch an example of the concept i.e. bird ,but you cannot touch all birds so one stimulus must be generalized to the stimuli that makes up the concept.

The instructional sequence for principle learning
1. Inform the adult learner about the form of the performance to be expected when learning is completed.
2. Question the learner in a way than requires the reinstatement (recall) of the previously learned concepts that make up the principle.
3. Use verbal statements (cues) that will lead the learner to put the principle together, as a chain of concepts, in the proper order. (see chapters 10 and 17)
4. By means of a question, ask the learner to "demonstrate" one or more concrete instances of the principle.
5. (Optional, but useful for later instruction) By a suitable question, require the learner to make a verbal statement of the principle.

The organization of knowledge may be represented as a hierarchy of principles. Two or more principles may be prerequisite to the learning of a superordinate principle. Once the latter is learned, it may combine with another principle to support the learning of still another higher-level principle, and so on. The entire set of principles, organized in this way, forms a hierarchy that may be called the structure of organized knowledge about a topic.

Higher level principles are dependent on the mastery of prerequisite lower level principles. Determining the prerequisites for any given principle may be accomplished by asking the question, "What would the learner have to know how to do or understand in order to be instructed in this principle?"

If all the prerequisite principles are known, does this mean that the higher order principle is immediately known also?

No, this is not enough.

It has to be learned. There must be some training, which includes the steps of informing the learner about the expected form of the performance expected, encouraging recall, and cueing the proper sequence of acts, as described in the instructional sequence.

Most topics learned in business, industry, government agencies and educational institutions have the character of organized knowledge and may be represented as hierarchies of principles. The obvious ones, all the sciences, as well as mathematics, are composed of sets of principles that build on each other. However, the principle level of learning also can relate to topics like Total Quality Management, Participative Management or Area 4 - Human Resources of the Malcolm Baldrige National Quality Award and including such principles as: Self-Managing Teams improving the efficiency and quality of life of the work place.

The organized nature of principles appears to resist the effects of interference and to maintain retention at high levels. Since principles are built on the primary laws, facts, truths, there is little interference for retention because seldom do these laws, facts and truths contradict each other. They become the framework for understanding the concrete reality around them. The practical implications are quite clear. Learning principles not only produces a capability commonly referred to as understanding but at the same time it establishes a capability that is retained well for relatively long periods of time.

Principle Learning has some well-known conditions for its establishment. The different varieties of learning can be distinguished by the conditions required to bring them about. This is a more complex form of learning, building on the combining of Concepts - Level 6 Learning. Therefore to understand, participate or train this form of learning, the applicable concepts must be learned first or be already present. You may have been to seminars where the training seemed to go right "over everyone's head". The reason was probably because Principles were presented without clarifying or building on the underlying concepts.

The most ideal training starts at the present level of the learners (i.e. Level 5 - Multiple Discrimination, etc.) and brings the learners through the levels of learning in order, to the appropriate level for the desired performance outcome (i.e. Level 8 - Problem Solving, etc.).

Principle Learning may be exemplified by the acquisition of the fundamental contained in such propositions as "gases expand when heated;" "the pronoun each takes a singular verb;" "salt is composed of the elements Na and Cl;" "the definite article "die" goes with the feminine (German) noun," etc., etc. Surely there can be little doubt than human beings must learn large numbers of such principles, some interconnecting, some not, along the road to attaining the status of being considered educated adults.

You may say, "Why, these are simply verbal facts to be memorized!" Not so: and that is why the word fundamental has been employed to describe these principles, inexact as that word may be. From the previous discussion, it is apparent that each of these statements can be learned as a verbal chain. Yes, you can teach a five year old to memorize them but they would not understand them or be able to use them in generalizations or other novel, or unique situations.   If an individual is able to demonstrate this capability in a number of instances, one is justified in concluding that the person has learned a principle.

The conditions for the learning of principles appear to be these:
1. The *concepts* to be linked must have been previously learned. When a principle is to be learned, the adult must already understand the concepts being chained.
2. Assuming that the first condition has been fulfilled, the process of chaining is a very simple matter. Usually, one simply states the principle verbally, as "The pronoun each takes a singular verb."
3. Under these circumstances, the learning of a principle takes place on a single occasion.

Adults have discovered principles on their own. What happens is that the individual selects their own idiosyncratic representations of the concepts to be chained.   Out of one's experience, people create their own combinations of concepts to formulate their unique principles. Some of these may have limited generalization or be situation specific. So when such a person enters a specialized training course, these may need to be reorganized and reconnected, creating for the person a *new field of experience*. If you investigate you can always understand how they got there.

> "The behavior exhibited always makes sense to the person doing the behaving." – Ripley & Ripley

The danger in using verbal statements as a kind of shortcut to learning lies mainly in the possibility that sheer *verbal chains* will be acquired rather than truly *conceptual chains*.   All trainers are acquainted with the adult learner who can say the principle without being able to do it. This is really an example of ineffective instruction. What it implies is that the adult learner has not previously acquired the concepts (condition #1, above); therefore, the adult learner reacts to the verbal statement as a verbal chain to be memorized. If one makes certain that the concept "each" is known, as well as the concept "singular verb", as well as the concept "takes", the statement "*each* takes a *singular verb* " should in fact represent an optimal condition for learning. Of course, to test this, the trainer must determine whether the adult learner can use the principle. (The verb takes could also be "needs", "requires", "uses", etc. - so restating the principle in slightly different words while not changing the essential meaning may help some learners to understand the principle better - a useful learning technique.)

LEVEL 8	**PROBLEM SOLVING**

Dictionary Linkages

PROBLEM
- Something **difficult** to deal with or understand
- Something difficult that has to be accomplished or answered or dealt with

    Difficult
- Needing much effort or skill, not to easy to do or practice
- A difficult problem or thing, a hindrance to action

SOLVE
- To find the answer to, (a problem or puzzle) or the way out of a **difficulty**

    Skill
- The capability to do something well

Broader Order Problem Solving:

STRATEGY
- The planning and directing of the whole operation
- A plan or **policy** of this kind, or to achieve something

    Policy
- The course or general plan or action
- A definite course or method of action selected from among alternatives and in the light of given conditions to guide and determine present and future decisions
- A high level overall plan embracing the general goals and acceptable **procedures** of a group

CREATIVE	•Having the power or capability to create things •Showing imagination and originality as well as routine skill (Knowing how to do something very well)
Create	•To bring into existence, to **originate** •To give rise to, to produce by what one does •Having the quality of something created rather than imitated •To bring into existence, to invest with a new form •To produce or bring about a course of action or behavior

Usual discussion about problem solving focuses on the various methods and their various merits. Some of the many methods of problem solving include: American scientific methods, deductive reasoning, inductive reasoning, statistical analysis methods and Eastern philosophy methods.

Before these can be applied, one must realize that problem solving is founded on previously learned capabilities, i.e. Levels 2 - 7 and does not take place in a vacuum devoid of content knowledge. Often others have no foundation to build on as they are not aware of the underlying basis of Levels of Learning. Most new discoveries come to the prepared mind, i.e. Fleming and penicillin, Salk and polio vaccine.

Problem solving involves many different processes and analysis rather than just multiple discriminations, chaining or combining into concepts and principles. Once the adult learner has acquired some principles, they can be used for many purposes in dealing with and controlling the adult's environment.

Analysis refers to the separation of an intellectual or substantial whole into its constituent parts for individual study. In chemistry it is the separation of a substance into its constituent elements to determine either their nature (qualitative analysis) or their proportions (quantitative analysis). In mathematics it involves differential and integral calculus, sequences, and series and is concerned with limits and convergence. It is also the method of proof in which a known truth is sought as a consequence of a series of deductions from that which is the thing to be proved. In linguistics it is the use of function words such as prepositions, pronouns, or auxiliary verbs instead of inflectional endings to express a grammatical relationship; for example, the cover of the dictionary instead of the dictionary's cover. In philosophy it is the resolving of complex expressions into simpler or more basic one. In other words, analysis is the separation of a whole into its parts for study - resolution, breakdown, dissection.   Analysis is a systematic study, investigation, review, examination or inspection.

Thinking And Combining Past Levels Of Learning
Besides analysis the adult learner can also do something else that is most important: he or she can think through difficult things or situations based on their past learning. Basically, this means he or she is able to combine the principles they have already learned into a great variety of novel higher order principles.   The adults may do this by stimulating themselves and also by responding to various forms of stimulation from their environment.

By means of the process of combining old principles into a new one, the adults solves problems that are new and difficult for them, and thus, acquires still a greater store of new capabilities. The problems they solve are new to them, but they may not be new at all to other people. By combining all the "building blocks" of previous learning levels, the adult can apply these to solutions for new problems presented that have never before been encountered by the person.

Problem Solving - the thinking out of a new principle that combines previously learned principles, is a process that is very familiar to most adults. People often believe there is nothing very special about such events. There is a difference between Level 5 - Multiple Discrimination *choices* and Level 8 - Problem Solving *solutions*. Who to have lunch with is a *choice*. Learning about a time management plan in response to controlling stress is *problem solving*. The dictionary appropriately defines "problem" as "something difficult" - these are not just choosing an item from a menu. This is drawing up the menu.

The act of problem solving actually results in some very substantial learning. The change in the individual's capability is just as clear and unambiguous as any other level and is as retainable as the principle level. The major condition for encouraging the adult learner to think, is to be certain they already have something to think about. Learning problem solving leads to new capabilities for further thinking.

A number of conditions can be identified as essential for this problem solving act of learning.
1. The adult learner must be able to identify the essential features of the response that will be the solution, before they arrive at it. (Some writers on problem solving have said the learner must have a goal.) This particular condition appears to be important because of the lengthy chains involved, and the steplike character of the problem-solving act. Some analysis processes may be used.

2. Recall relevant principles (Level 7), which processes previously have been learned and select (Level 5) which ones are usable.

3. The recalled principles are combined so that a new principle emerges and is learned. However, it must be admitted that little is known about the nature of this combining event, and it cannot now be described with any degree of completeness. Simply writing down in a sequence the logical steps followed in the thinking does not answer this question. These steps are the intermediate responses made by the learner, that is, they are the outcomes of the adult's thinking. But they provide few clues as to the nature of the combining process itself.

4. The individual steps involved in problem solving may be many, and therefore the entire act may take some time. Nevertheless, the solution is arrived at suddenly, in a flash of insight. Repetition has little to do with it. Nor is repetition a very powerful factor in the prevention of interference, or forgetting, as in the case with multiple discrimination learning. A higher-order principle resulting from an act of thinking appears to be remarkably resistant to forgetting.

5. Next, analysis of all the alternatives, all flashes of insight. This allows the person to look mentally at possible outcomes, imagine what will happen next - the possible repercussions and chain reactions set in motion (i.e. law suit from firing a troubling employee.) This may entail a comparison of possible solutions, or testing out the results of the person's one single new solution.

Problem solving results in the acquisition of new ideas that multiply the applicability of principles previously learned.

The kinds of events called ***problem solving*** are of infinite variety; yet they appear to have several formal characteristics in common. A business owner may have the problem of figuring out why revenue is down by 12%. A self-managing team determining what to do with a troubling employee. A scientist may have a problem of accounting for a discrepancy in the predicted and measured velocity of a type of nuclear particle. All these situations imply the existence of problems that are to be brought to some successful termination by thinking. All these problems are solved by the use of principles, simple or complex. Principles are the stuff of thinking.

You might conclude now that ***problem solving*** is a set of events in which human beings use principles to achieve some goal. This is quite true but is not the whole story. The results of using principles in problem solving are not confined to achieving a goal, satisfying as that may be to the thinker. *When a problem solution is achieved, something is also learned, in the sense that the individual's capability is more or less permanently changed.* The individual hasn't just chosen an answer. What emerges from problem solving is a new principle, which thereupon becomes a part of the individual's repertoire.

The same class of situation, when encountered again, may be responded to with greater facility by means of recall, and is no longer looked on as a problem. Problem solving, then, must be considered a form of learning.

A good example of problem solving using **problem solving strategies** and **creativity** was demonstrated while the authors were working as consultants for Motorola.

Presenting Problem in the Semi-Conductor Sector: There was a potential lay-off of employees due to a downturn in the economy which was being termed as a recession. The company did not want to lay off any highly skilled multiple discriminating workers if it could be avoided.

Goal: Maintain full employment with no lay-offs
Solution: Obtain enough orders to maintain production.
Customer Problem Analysis: Customers have fear of downturn and do not want to place large orders because of potential inventory storage problems and a "cash crunch."

The Motorola Vice-President in charge (Henri Jarrat) of the semi-conductor plant met with his staff and explained the situation. The staff voted not to join the recession.

Solution: Offer customers the opportunity to make a number of successive small orders, with payment for each small order when delivered, on a guaranteed delivery date so the inventory would be received Just-In-Time with little to no storage.

The Vice-President then booked flights to all of their customers and personally presented this problem solving idea. He came back to the production plant with enough orders to fill production for the next six months.

The result had a positive lasting effect because they did the process right. This also created a future positive business procedure and added to the business vocabulary: Just-In-Time delivery.

Problem solving is not just choosing the immediate best answer - that is Level 4 - Multiple Discrimination. In problem solving you take into account the underlying principles and concepts by viewing both the horizontal and vertical levels of learning interactions. If you just pick what seems to be the best answer for you at the moment, then expediency is the problem solver. In problem solving you need to be concerned with what will be caused in the future by such a choice and the effect on others that will ultimately come back and in turn again effect you. You must look at the past, the present and the future implications. The best type of problem solving looks *creatively* at *strategies*.

Creativity And Problem Solving

No one can fail to stand in awed admiration of the great intellectual discoveries of history -- Newton's laws of motions, Kepler's principles of planetary movement, Einstein's general theory of relativity. Equally awe-inspiring are artistic creations in painting, sculpture, music and literature, which have also been generated by individual discovery. What do these remarkable achievements of genius have to do with problem solving as described here?

A great scientific discovery or a great work of art is surely the result of creative problem-solving activity. The solution to a problem, we are told, often comes to the thinker in a "flash of insight," although he or she may have been turning the problem over in the mind for some time.

As problem-solving behavior, these creative acts are based on a tremendous amount of previously acquired knowledge, whether this be of the "public" sort known to science, or of the "private" sort known to the artist. Many creative thinkers testify that they have previously immersed themselves deeply in the subject matter of the problem, *often over considerable periods of time*. Indeed, it would be strange if they had not done this. Nothing in such testimony supports the idea that there is anything very different about the problem solving that leads to discoveries of great social impact. The act of discovery, even in the relatively predictable sense that it occurs in everyday learning, involves a "sudden insight" which transforms the problem situation into a solution situation. As we have seen, it too requires that the learner has previous knowledge of the principles and concepts, etc. involved in the solution.

The major creative discovery, in contrast to the common garden variety, involves a feat of generalizing that goes far beyond what may be expected in the usual learning situation. There is an **"inductive leap,"** a combining of ideas that come from widely separated knowledge systems, a bold use of analogy that transcends what is usually meant by generalizing within a class of problem situations.

What has learning to do with the great creative discovery? The most obvious and dependable answer is that discoveries of great social importance have been made by men and women with a great deal of knowledge. They are men and women who have acquired many kinds of hierarchies of principles. They have been deeply immersed in the principles of the discipline within which they work, and, often, in the principles of other disciplines also.

How did they learn these principles? Just as everyone else does -- by combining sets of subordinate principles and concepts, partly perhaps with the aid of verbal instructions, and partly by making the "small" discoveries that are involved in the acquiring of all the levels of learning of any particular topic or knowledge system.

Creativity as a concept is sometimes confused with the simpler concept of expression or with the physical occurrence of something later labeled aesthetic. Level 1 - Signal Learning can result in physical movement and the expressions resulting in works of "art". If a child is allowed to keep their expressive channel open through out all their childhood to adulthood, they will have developed through to the process of creativity (Level 8) and still have it intact to use as an adult. This however is extremely rare and usually creativity needs to be rediscovered at a later date.

Modern art has been plagued with comparisons of "art" by monkeys and even elephants to the adult or child. Art is usually judged and critiqued at level 5 - Multiple Discrimination, on the basis of aesthetic results. Any particular "result" may or may not be the result of creativity. It may just be an aesthetic event not purposefully created, i.e. a paint splashing accident by a monkey or the way nature grew a particular tree. The creative event is what we are concerned with here. A better critique is at level 8: What was the problem the artist or whoever was trying to solve.

Strategies And Problem Solving

Strategy is the science and art of using all the forces available to execute approved plans as effectively as possible. It is the plan of action resulting from the strategy or intended to accomplish a specific goal.

Strategy is a careful plan or method for making, doing, or accomplishing something - idea, plan, project, design, scheme, layout, schema, blueprint. Tactics and logistics are thought through for the foreseeable barriers to successfully accomplishing the goal. Tactics is the art or skill of employing available means to accomplish an end. Logistics is the handling of details in an operation, such as procurement of materials, personnel, transportation, equipment and facilities. The tactics is the overall plan and the logistics is how to carry it out. A strategy then is using the best plans, which can be a sequence of plans with back-up plans to most efficiently and economically arrive at the desired solutions. Strategy is the development and implementation of simultaneous alternate tactical plans or methods to uncover a here-to-fore undiscovered solution and logistical procedures to make it happen effectively. This is best accomplished in teams or with two or more people collaborating. There is no way of knowing how many strategies there are. Corporate strategies fill whole books.

In the Motorola problem solving example, once the Motorola Vice-President (Henri Jarrat) used his and his staffs creativity, they then carefully devised the plan to accomplish the specific goal, i.e. obtain enough orders to maintain production in order to maintain full employment with no lay-offs. Here as in most problem solving situations, the person starts with the goal and moves back to the current state, analyzes the situation and then devises strategies for moving from the now to the desired outcome. At the same time, the problem solving person does an analysis of the potential repercussions, or what comes next and what will be the new problems as the result of achieving the desired results.

To summarize, *problem solving* involves the combining of previously learned *principles* into a new higher-order principle that "solves" the problem and generalizes to an entire new class of situations embodying other problems of the same type. Problem solving learning occurs when the instructions provided the learner do not include a verbally stated "solution," but require the learner to construct such a solution "on their own." When this happens the individually constructed new principle is effective in generalizing to many situations and is at the same time highly resistant to forgetting.

LEARNING WAVES

Learning waves is a graphic method for diagramming at what levels of learning a training or education task is being performed.

Plotting learning waves is a way to design and track training to ensure no level has been left out, resulting in better clarity and retention of learning. Because so little learning is properly designed, it is easily understood why so many children hate most schools and many adults don't seek new learning.

LEARNING WAVES
Hypothetical: Graphic plotting of steps in a particular learning sequence

Learning Level

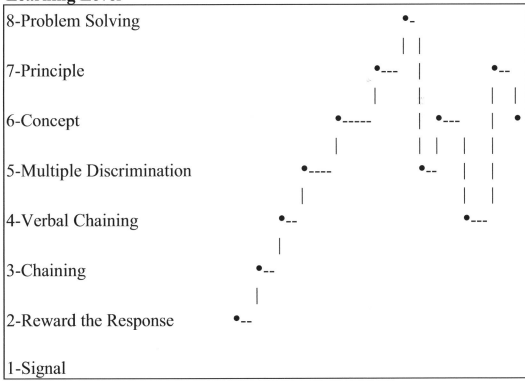

Learning Level
8-Problem Solving
7-Principle
6-Concept
5-Multiple Discrimination
4-Verbal Chaining
3-Chaining
2-Reward the Response
1-Signal

In this graphic presentation the material is being acquired by all the learners. The top 10% of the learners will want to move more quickly and may give indications of boredom. A typical learning sequence will aim only at the top 10% of the learners and start the learning at level 5 - multiple discrimination and then jump directly to problem solving without going through concept or principle learning and then jump down to level 2 - rewarding the response and call this the complete learning. Other trainers will start with level 2-reward the response, then immediately jump to level 5-multiple discrimination without determining the chaining of the materials and then jump to level 8-problem solving with no explanation or testing out of understanding of concepts or principles. Again it is nothing wrong with the levels of learning but the people using them. Graphically plotting the learning at each level provides a check and balance to ensure that nothing has been left out, overlooked and that everything is done in a proper sequence.

In the graphed example this could be the sequential training of a firefighter. First when the firefighter is in initial training to learn to handle a hose, they are given a positive response by the trainer when they pick up a hose off the truck correctly. Then the trainer combines level 3 and 4 together and explains the physical movements, in sequence in properly handling a hose. They physically practice the sequence chaining of level 3 aided by the verbal chaining of level 4. Next the trainer presents a level 5 situation with several hose sizes and situations in which to use each. Then the firefighter learns to discriminate the hoses and nozzles to fit the fire situation type (level 5-multiple discrimination). Now they study the concept "fire" and procedures, ideas and methods for using hoses on different fires (level 6-concept). Then they learn the laws of fire - if they do A, B will happen. By using inductive reasoning of what they know about specific hoses and nozzles, they can predict what will happen in a particular situation. In the next stage of their learning, the firefighter is presented with a novel situation, using a "live burn" or a simulation. Here they are learning "fire ground" strategy. As a team, they approach and control the problem situation (level 8-Problem Solving).

The firefighters return to level 5-multiple discrimination to distinguish different types of fire situations, i.e. automobile fires, open range fires and high rise fires. Then they learn about Hazardous Materials - level 6-concept - what is and is not a hazardous material. By going back to level 4-multiple discrimination, they learn the sequence of identification of the particular hazardous material. By knowing about hazardous material, the next learning is at level 7-principle - where deductive reasoning is used to look at the general laws known to be true in the hazardous materials case. The firefighters then select the method or procedure (from level 6-concept) to fulfill and control the hazardous materials. (Thanks to the Phoenix Fire Department, especially Chief Brunacini, Chief Storment and Chief Summers.)

SUMMARY OF THE EIGHT LEVELS OF LEARNING
Eight different classes of situations in which human beings learn have been distinguished -- eight sets of conditions under which changes in capabilities of the human learner are brought about. In brief, the eight levels of learning that can currently be distinguished are as follows:

Level 1   Signal Learning
The individual learns to make a specific or general, diffuse response to a signal. This is the classical conditioned response. Starting with paired stimuli, the S1 now rouses the individual to act even though S2 is no longer there.

Level 2   Reward the Response Learning
The learner is rewarded for making a specific desired response or sometimes called an instrumental response. The learner acquires a shaping of a precise response by receiving a reward for what is done.

Level 3   Chaining
What is acquired is a chain of two or more stimulus-response connections. The connection is in a sequence or series in a particular order. The learning is dependent upon all the links being acquired in sequence and must have a completion action providing a reinforcement.

Level 4   Verbal Chaining
Verbal Chaining is the learning of chains that are verbal. Basically, the conditions resemble those for other motor chains. However, the presence of language in the human being makes this a special type because internal links may be selected from the individual's previously learned repertoire of language.

Level 5   Multiple Discrimination

The individual learns to make several different identifying responses to as many different stimuli, which may resemble each other in physical appearance to a greater or lesser degree. Although the learning of each stimulus-response connection is a simple Level 2 occurrence, the connections tend to interfere with each other's retention. The learner learns to know, understand, recognize, reason and make distinctions and judgments between two or more things.

Level 6   Concept Learning

The learner acquires a capability of making a common response to a class of stimuli that may differ from each other widely in physical appearance. The learner is able to make a response that describes an entire class of objects or events. The learner abstracts out from lower level learning. The concept can include procedures, ideas, formulas and a method conceived in the mind.

Level 7   Principle Learning

In simplest terms, a principle is a chain of two or more concepts. It functions to control behavior in the manner suggested by a verbalized rule of the form "If A, then B," where A and B are concepts. However, it must be carefully distinguished from the mere verbal sequence learned as Level 4. The principle combines truth, deductive and inductive thinking, general laws or a doctrine that is used as a guide to action or behavior.

Level 8   Problem Solving

Problem solving is a kind of learning that requires the internal events usually called thinking. Two or more previously acquired principles are somehow combined to produce a new capability. Problem solving includes finding answers to difficulties and includes the developed skills to do something well. Higher order problem solving involves strategies, and creativity.

Chapter 12
// • # • > Instruction Methods and Media < • # • //

Interesting and worthwhile training hinges almost entirely on the variety and usefulness of the training methods. The more useful to the adult learner the better. Results oriented learning requires utilization of old and new training methods.

The Lecture

General Considerations

You have learned many of the things You know from listening to lectures. People will always learn by listening to others. The lecture is a quick way to cover a lot of ground, and can save valuable time. This is especially true if the presenter who is talking knows the important points that will assist others to dig into the subject more easily. The following rules of moderation will enhance a presentation by making them more interesting and effective:

1. Have a specific reason for using the lecture, that is known and acceptable to your learners.
2. Make definite provisions for combining other methods along with the lecture.

3. Organize your lecture according to a definite plan, so it will be certain to interest the group. Also try not to belabor points over and over or be too elementary.

4. Keep to the subject, and avoid talking over the head of the group in language that is too technical.

5. Develop a sensitivity to the responsiveness of the class. What are they doing while you are lecturing - attentive, talking, writing, sleeping?

6. Be prepared to alter the plan according to the requirements of the situation.
   (Suppose the organization announced in the morning bulletin that they are beginning to use a new piece of equipment that is in variance with the prepared lecture.)

7. Be as brief as possible, then turn to other methods. Don't lecture all the time; use the lecture method only when the occasion really calls for it.

8. Make the lecture fit your own personal style. Be yourself!

9. Know the Goal: To **inform**, **persuade** or **entertain**.

Lecture Methods

It is possible to combine various resources and methods involvement with the lecture such as:

1. **Demonstration** - The illustration of a process by the presenter or a learner helps the learner to visualize something which may be difficult to understand completely by description alone. It is particularly effective when learners have the opportunity to

perform the operation under the observation of the trainer (maps, charts, technical processes, etc.,)

2. **Dry Erase Board**, **Flip Chart** - The presenter in presenting lists, statements, or problems, pictures, graphs, maps, etc., centers the attention of the entire group on a specific point or issue. Having learners go to the dry erasable board to record notes, work out problems, draw graphs or pictures to give them the kind of action that helps them tie learning to behavior.

3. **Films, VHS Cassettes, Slides, Computer Generated Slides (PPTs) Powerpoints, etc**. - Coordinate audio-visual with the lecture. The amount an audience learns from an audio-visual aid is directly affected by how it is used. Some suggestions are:

    a. Select aids on the basis of the purpose and interests of both the group and the presenteer.

    b. Always preview before using.

    c. Discuss with the learning group beforehand on what to look for, facts, problems, new concepts, etc.

    d. Discuss afterwards to answer questions and gain new learning.

    e. Engage in follow-up activities such as related reading, written reports, trips, observation of other trained adults, etc.

4. **Handouts** - Provide such materials as pamphlets, excerpts from magazines, newspaper articles, condensed technical material, outlines of lecture or course, etc. to provide knowledge in special areas in condensed form.

5. **Study and Discussion Guides** -Provide progressive learning experiences toward predetermined goals, and enable inexperienced adult learners to move their thinking in directions set by others.

6. **Guest Speakers** - Can present knowledge and experiences with a personal touch that can add interest and a change of pace. Proper preparation is needed, such as, purpose of having a speaker, ensuring subject is related to learning goals and objectives, prior communication with speaker to make certain subject is meaningful and relevant, possible questions to be asked, etc.). Make certain there is proper follow-up (evaluation, discussion of new ideas or knowledge gained).

7. **Overhead Projector** - Presentation of material in this manner allows for use of sight in addition to listening and thus increases the intake potential and retention of the adult learner. Transparencies can be made in advance. They should always be clear, well organized and to the point.

Discussion

Purposes

Discussion, particularly in its problem solving and discovery aspects, has been called the learning method of democracy.

Discussion is used in every type of organization and training. People discuss whenever they form into any kind of group. It is natural, then, that the discussion method has become a basic method of adult learning, and that mastery of this method is among the most essential requirements for trainers of adults.

As a learning method, discussion is used for the following purposes:

1. To reach decisions or solve problems.

2. To internalize or reinforce ideas and concepts.
3. To progress from known toward the unknown by various processes of deductive reasoning.
4. To determine if a particular body of content has been mastered.
5. To share adult varied expertise and experiences and to assist each participant in more effectively understanding and applying the learning.
6. To provide conflict resolution, clarity of ideas, and tentative testing of solutions.
7. To develop cohesiveness, openness and trust.
8. To allow participants to learn from each other.

Exploration For Learning

Exploration allows for alternatives to be expressed and explored. Exploration learning through discussion is done both by problem-solving and internalization. Problem solving is one of the most complex forms of discussion and one requiring great skill on the part of the facilitating trainer because the "answer" is not known by the facilitator in advance and there may not be one single answer.

Examples of this might be: how to handle employee absenteeism, elimination of material damage and waste, etc.

Remember problem solving is the top step of the eight levels of learning and will work better if lower levels of learning precede it: i.e. concept learning. You need to be aware of the attitudes, skills and knowledge uses in the discussion.

Internalization

The purpose of "exploratory learning" is not to impart factual knowledge but to create new ideas, broaden and focus concepts, develop insights, and bring about understanding. In helping these learning processes take place the facilitating trainer stimulates, focuses, guides, clarifies, and summarizes the discussion. As the learning event moves along, individual members will take over these roles at times. The facilitator's task is to enable each individual to contribute more and more of his or her own background and growing field of knowledge. Any level of learning can be internalized and in fact needs to be before the next level can be attempted with understanding.

Internalization, gained through group discussion, allows the adult learner to make understanding a part of self-knowledge which otherwise might never become more than a series of facts presented in a lecture. New concepts need to be internalized and owned by the learner. Discussion helps this to happen.

For example, supervisors, discussing in a group how to choose a course of action based upon ideas presented in a lecture, will develop a feeling for what the lecturer was trying to say by trying to use the information in a concrete work situation.

Note: When the learners are confronting or arguing, what can really be happening is they are really asking for more information - more exploration. They lack knowledge, information or experience. They are really asking for more input to make better judgments. People are ready to change if you can provide them with better reasons for changing. So by presenting more and more relevant information they can better make their choices and judgments.

Acquiring Information

Acquiring Information, the extension and development of factual knowledge, can be accomplished through group discussion.

An illustration of this method of learning would be that of a trainer in a technology class providing training in the structure and function of a diode by asking questions of the class, following a short lecture period. This helps adult learners determine what portions of the content was not clear or fully understood, while providing feedback to the trainer how well various areas of content have been covered.

In addition the trainer can use the information, background, and experience that the learners already have, and though skillful discussion, combine all of this total experience with new knowledge. This helps the unknown to become known. This method of discussion is particularly useful where logical processes of reasoning are involved.

Different Methods of Discussion

The first step in planning a discussion is the same as for any other training method. Decide what your training objectives are to be and then choose the type of discussion that best fits the objective. It is up to the trainer to set the framework for the learning to occur. Leading a group up and down the learning wave can be very stimulating and challenging. This makes the learners explore the roots in concepts and multiple discrimination. They can't hide in abstract principles and ideas.

Some discussion methods are:
1. **<u>Question and Answer Recitation:</u>** An occasional oral review to allow learners to quickly use newly acquired knowledge and therefore internalize the material. Questions need to be determined

largely by your training objective, points to be emphasized, and questions phrased so as to lead to an expansion and clarification of the point. Keep the learners involved in explaining until ideas are clearly expressed and the entire group understands. After asking a question, give time for thinking and reacting to the question. Clarify your question if it is not understood, and try not to embarrass any learner. Learn to read the puzzled expressions, build up to key questions through a series of secondary questions, and remember that the purpose of questions is to stimulate discussion, not merely get answers.

2. **<u>Small Groups Discussion</u>** - This is a very natural technique for increasing learners interaction and may be organized quickly. To organize:

   a. Tell the group briefly what the task is and how they will share in it.
   b. Divide the group into sub-groups of four to seven people
   c. Set up a relative short length of time (around 15 minutes) for each sub-group to discuss the topic
   d. Have one person from each group collect the findings or decisions of the group and then report them back to the entire group
   e. Follow-up with a full group discussion
   f. Ask the group to evaluate its findings or summaries

The value of this technique is that it encourages everyone to feel comfortable in participating, it increases the flow of ideas, each individual within the groups quickly grasps the responsibility to think, and make contributions. The learners work out answers for themselves, therefore making the ideas more meaningful and at the same time building group cohesiveness, openness and trust.

3. **Round-Table - Audience Participation** - With this technique the first part revolves around a discussion of selected participants placed around a table, or on a platform or seated in a semi-circle, etc. with the rest of the assembled group observing. The participants discuss an issue or problem presenting different or opposing views, varying phases of one central issue, or differing methods or solutions concerning an issue. Following the presentations, which need to be kept brief, the observing audience participates, either by asking questions, adding information input, or challenging the roundtable members' comments.

   These roundtable-audience participation training sessions may also be called a forum, a symposium, a panel, a debate, or group interview, depending upon the type of structure selected.

4. **Workshop Techniques** - These center around a specific problem or area of interest. Those involved work intensively over a period of time upon the particular problem they decide upon within the limits of the overall problem or area. Sometimes the discussion remains in the general meeting, although most often the group will break into sub-groups, each group attacking the concern from their unique combinations of expertise and experience. This is one of the best methods for adults.

5. **Case Study Discussions** - This involves participants analyzing and making tentative decisions concerning problems relevant to their experiences and work roles. Breaking into teams and having each team explore the case and then having the teams report back their findings to the total group is very productive for adult learners.

6. **<u>Brainstorming</u>** - This is a well-known and widely used problem identification and problem solving tool. This method encourages the use of the adult learners imagination and creativity.

   Brainstorming also helps elicit numerous solutions to any given problem, i.e., "What shall we name this product?" "What should we do in this situation?" "How can we overcome this obstacle?" This method can be very helpful in eliciting alternatives.

   Some Rules for Brainstorming:
   a. Everyone is encouraged to think up as many wild ideas as possible. It is easier to tame down a wild idea that to pep up a bland idea. In fact, if wild ideas are not forthcoming in a brainstorming session, it is usually evidence that the individual participants are censoring their own ideas. They are thinking twice before they spout out an idea for fear that they may come up with a silly one and sound foolish.
   b. No evaluation of any kind is allowed in the thinking-up part of the session. If you judge and evaluate ideas as they are thought up, people tend to become more concerned with defending their ideas than with thinking up new better ones. Evaluation must be ruled out.
   c. Quantity is encouraged. Quantity eventually breeds quality. When a great number of ideas come pouring out in rapid succession, people are free to give their imaginations wide range, and good ideas result.
   d. Everyone is encouraged to build upon or modify the ideas of others. Combining or modifying previously suggested ideas often leads to new ideas that are superior to those that sparked them. This is consistent with levels of learning from chaining to problem solving.

e. When ideas development are exhausted then the ideas can be combined under major topic areas.

f. The ideas can then be prioritized under each topic area.

g. The ideas can be evaluated for application, practicality, cost and timeliness. (Excerpt from Ripley & Ripley, *Team Skills and Teambuilding*, Carefree Press)

Experiential

Experiential Learning Methods

Learning also results when the adult learner has experienced something rather than just talking about it or listening to someone else talk about it.

Examples of this are simulated games, lab experiences in the classroom or on-site outside the classroom, working on a project, producing a product, role playing, competitive team exercises, or taking a field trip.

1. **<u>Simulation Games</u>** - These provide learners with the opportunity to "try out" a situation before the actual experience might occur at the work site. This allows for identification and correction of potential mistakes or error areas before they occur on the job. This method is excellent in providing fun to the learning, building team cohesiveness and the identification and learning of concepts, principles and problem-solving. These experiential activities are most often what are retained by the adult learner.

2. **Lab Experiences** - This type of learning is accomplished by either bringing hands on equipment into the classroom or by taking the learners on-site to the equipment. This may takes effort in

arranging and preparation time , but this is well worth the learning results.

As a trainer you need to facilitate this whenever possible as **learning-by-doing** is very effective and more permanent as far as retention is concerned.

3. **Producing a Product** - This can be an experiential activity to demonstrate a learning for the desired course outcome or designing a product to be used in the actual work setting. Producing a product that will be used later gives the learner a feeling of having accomplished something usable and meaningful.   Producing a product is good for illustrating what has been learned in the lecture and discussion methods.

4. **Role-Playing** - This enables the group to develop insights into cause and effect relationships and test ideas for producing change in human relationships. This method of training can be an enjoyable and productive way of learning. Two types can be used: The adult learner can act as themselves, or in "roles". This technique is often used in sales training, courses in human relations, or any other activity where the emphasis is on learning more about the ways in which people relate to each other. Role-Playing trains you in the important skill of "putting yourself in someone else's moccasins." Role reversal is excellent for empathizing with and better understanding the other person's position.

   A model for organizing:
   a. Select a particular point of skill, attitude or set of behaviors to illustrate
   b. Describe the characters the learners are to play

    c. Have the class select the participants rather than by trainer assignment

    d. Give participants 10-15 minutes to prepare themselves for the presentation. At the same time ask the rest of the group to choose one or two issues or problems for the role-playing group's interaction forms.

    e. Have the role-playing participants start and continue the action until interest is at a peak; this may vary from 5 to 20 minutes.

    f. Follow-up by providing opportunity for all class members to ask questions of the role-playing participants and visa versa.

    g. Summarize the learning and the applications from the exercise.

5. **Field Trips - On-Site Visits** - These provide first-hand observation of situations and the learners may be taken to various sites within the organization to see processes and procedures in action. Often times the experience of actually seeing an operation can facilitate learning far more than merely hearing about it. This can be used to see a product from design to shipping or delivery to an internal or external customer.

Techniques are to be incorporated in methods. These are what you use to make the methods and materials come alive. Techniques are tools you can use most effectively to impact the learner.

Questioning Techniques

Provide opportunities for questions and reviews.

Make it a ground rule. Pause about every 20 minutes for Q & A.

Use open ended questions to solicit response from participants.

a. Use questions or responses that force a response other than yes, no, or maybe.

b. Use Reflection, Clarification and Abstraction communication skills.

c. Try the double question technique: "Do you have any thoughts on the subject? "What are they?"

Use closed questions to end discussions.

"Do you have any questions before the break?"

"Before we move on, does anyone have a comment?"

Use questions to test for knowledge, skills, and attitudes.

a. Ask participants to summarize lessons or key points.

b.   Ask them to demonstrate the learning related to back on the job.

c. Have them demonstrate the use of the skill by a teach back.

Provide correct and concise answers to questions asked by participants.

a. Go behind the question and come through it with further clarification. Then ask for an understanding back from the participants.

b. Example: "Ellen, explain to me what you just hear me say?" If that person can't answer, go to another person to give the response, but give the first person time to think.

    c. When you don't know - say, "I don't know."

When unable to answer questions asked, research answers and report results back to participants.

Let them know you will find out the answer and report back to them. Make a Do List entry in your Planner.

Answer questions non-defensively.

    a. "If you say so." or

    b. "Help me to understand something specific that you are referring to."

    c. Let them ventilate and then go for understanding.

Refer questions back to participants.

"Who can or would like to answer that question?"

Guide participants to reach answers themselves.

"Tell me which of the ten you already know, Bill, and then we can see which you can't recall." Guide them through answering their own question.

Handle irrelevant questions appropriately.

    a. Keep the response simple - "No" - "Yes" and keep on going, with a smile.

    b. Often the irrelevant questioner is seeking attention or recognition for some reason. (Seek out their thoughts and respond to the behaviors they demonstrate that are desirable) "What are your thoughts on -- whatever the current topic is-.

Typical Steps in the Questioning Process

    •**Ask the question.** Preferably open-ending. Usually starting with a how, when, what and where.

Use the open-ended questions to determine the direction of the discussion. Open-ended questions are questions that ask for more information, but leave the specific content up to the trainee. If the discussion goes astray, refocus the group to the topic at hand.

When you have participants in teams, ask the team the open-ended question and then ask another team to add on to the first team's response.

Open-ended questions are often difficult to ask without preparation before time. When reviewing training unit or module, write down open-ended questions on the side of your notes. Anticipate what questions the trainees might have or that you want to ask to ensure those learning points have been understood and applications made for different situations.

Ask only one question at a time and resist the urge to fill a silence period by rephrasing the question, or by asking another question.

•**Give them time to answer** - pause. Use the silence and time. Let them have enough time to think and formulate a response. Ten seconds is a long time so remember when you say, "Take a minute and think." that this is six times that ten seconds. Time it and you will see just how long one minute is.

The person won't always answer your questions correctly so when this happens redirect the question to his or her team or to the whole group to see if anyone can assist the trainee with the right answer. **Remember** to involve your participants whenever possible to make a learning point. They are adults and have a vast supply of knowledge and experiences from a wide variety of situations.

Give the answer only when no one else can give you the desired response. But then you might want to explore how come this desired answer wasn't available from anyone. Was there something you didn't provide in the explanation or team learning experience? What makes this desired answer so foreign or unique to you in this particular session?

•**Call on a learner by name**, when there is no volunteer response.

•**Acknowledge the person's response and repeat or paraphrase the input.**

After a learner gives an response or input, you need to respond to clarify the meaning of that response. You may need to accurately summarize and paraphrase the learner's inputs to indicate your understanding and clarity of what is meant. This allows both you, the specific learner and other participants the chance to review their thoughts to ensure everyone is on the same track. This also allows the learner, you or another member to clarify more specifically the topic at hand.

•**Ask summarizing questions to bring segment to a close.**

Examples; "Jim, what would you say the key point have been we have covered today?"

"Mona, how would you summarize what we have covered over the past 45 minutes?"

This gives feedback to you as to what the learner received and felt was important. This also gives you an opportunity to ask other participants for additional points that were covered. This also allows you to bring in a point that you feel is very important but they seemed to miss.

Other important Factors In Using Questions

A. **The power of a question lies in the requirement of an answer so that the learners, individually and collectively, are stimulated to think and motivated to discuss.**

B. <u>**Purpose for Asking a Question**</u>
1. To get an answer
2. To obtain learner attention
3. To arouse interest
4. To open a discussion or direct the discussion in a particular way
5. To provoke thinking
6. To accumulate data
7. To distribute discussion
8. To arrive at conclusions
9. To develop a subject
10. To direct observation
11. To discover learner strengths
12. To discover learner unsuccessful areas
13. To check understanding
14. To end or limit discussion
15. To obtain learner participation

C. <u>**Key Characteristics of a Question**</u>
1. Timeliness and in sequence
2. Contributes to achievement of objectives
3. Thought provoking

D. **Factors that affect the level of stimulation and motivation**
   1.   Framing the question
   2.   Choosing the right type of question
   3.   Directing the question
First, let's consider **Framing the Question**
   a. Be brief
   b. Cover a single point
   c. Be directly related to the topic
   d. Develop thinking from a constructive point of view
   e. Use the words that are easy for you to use
   f. Use words that have meaning to the group
   g. In most cases, phrase to avoid "yes" - "no"
Second, **Choosing the Right Type of Question**
   a. The right type of question is dependent upon what the trainer wants.
   b. Several categories of question are:
      1) Factual Questions
         a) Used to get information
         b) Good for discussion starters

         Example: How many employees do you supervise?

      2) Leading Questions
         a) Used to suggest an answer and get group to analyze
         b) Also helps broaden the discussion

         Example: How might your supervisor benefit from this training?

      3) Clarifying Questions
         a) Used to challenge old ideas and develop new ones

b) To avoid snap judgment

c) Helps find real cause to answers

Example: What you're saying then is that you have no trouble with discipline, is that right?

4) Hypothetical Questions

a) Used to suggest or introduce trainer's ideas into the discussion

b) To test a conclusion

Example: What might happen if you were given charge of the department and could plan for the department?

5) Alternative Questions

a) To make a decision between two or more points

b) To comparatively evaluate suggested solutions

Example: Are the best supervisors strict, easy or neither?

6) General Questions

a) Directed at the entire group

b) Used to promote group thinking

Example: So what can be done about it?

7) Re-Direct Questions

a) Directed at trainer but returned to the group

b) Used to promote group activity

Example: That's a good question Sally. How would you answer that in terms of your job, Harry?

E. <u>**Directing the Question**</u>
1. Direct questions to the group as a whole not to individuals
2. If no response, then select individuals to respond
3. Allow sufficient time for a reply
4. Do not hesitate to restate a question if group expression shows confusion
5. Encourage members of the group to question one another

F. <u>**Characteristics of a Good Question**</u>
1. Must have a specific purpose
2. Has a relationship to what is already known
3. Is understood by the group
4. Emphasizes one point
5. Requires a definite answer
6. Discourage guessing
7. Encourages creative thinking
8. Is not threatening to the audience, unless you purposely want it to be

Questioning is really following the Socratic method of teaching. Questioning is a tool for learning, discovering and sharing. Questioning is not to be used to put someone in a corner or belittling them. Instructors who master these questioning techniques will have the attention of the group, keep the group moving in the desired direction. This controlled questioning allows the learner to discover answers themselves and stimulates them to think.

Visual Media: Techniques And Evaluation

An instructor needs to know how to effectively select visual media to illustrate or support the learning. The instructor also needs to know how to prepare a visual aid to best communicate with the learner for understanding and retention.

All four learning modes - attitudes, skills, knowledge, problem solving - can be effectively approached via media. The best media might have parts of all four learning modes. A TV series called Home Improvement involved modes of skill development (handling power drill), knowledge (where to drill the hole to mount the faucet in the counter top), problem solving (how to improve the bathroom) and attitude (I the viewer could actually do something myself - I feel empowered.) Now the viewer has no idea how many "takes" the film crew went through to get that smooth looking process but it makes for popular TV. Most effective TV ads only aim at attitude change and a resulting improved multiple discrimination.

The required conditions for learning can be put into effect in different ways and to differing degrees by each visual medium. Media here are to be considered in a broad and inclusive sense, including such traditional instructional media as oral, printed verbal communication, slides, transparencies, flip charts, motion pictures, videos, interactive video presentations, interactive computer learning. and video feedback.

Some media are much more broadly adaptable for instructional purposes than are others. For example, the concrete objects that may be needed to convey the distinctions among a solid, a liquid and a gas can not be successfully supplanted by a mere verbal description in print. Conversely, though, examples of a solid, a liquid, and a gas, or even pictures of them, have extremely limited function in instruction when compared with verbal communication. By themselves, the objects or pictures cannot instruct in the varieties of solids, liquids, and gases, nor in the principles that relate them to each other. There are, then, some positive characteristics and some limitations of each instructional medium that become evident when they are examined in the light of their learning functions.

These instructional media make up valuable "resources for learning" that a training system can draw on. When these resources are put to use, they are usually placed in some particular arrangement called a mode of instruction. Some of these, like the lecture, are too widely and frequently used, but others, such as simulation and video feedback are used too infrequently.

The various modes of instruction are employed for the purpose of getting the greatest instructional usefulness from media and combinations of media. Thus the choice of modes is also a matter of aiming for optimal functioning in generating the proper conditions for learning.

The choice of media depends on how to best accomplish your training objectives as well as the environment in which the training is taking place. For example, is video equipment useful in the learning and is it available for use? If you are not sure you need to have a back-up media plan.

Guidelines for Visual Media Presentations

General Considerations for the Adult Learner

Words, like styles, have vogues. Every generation introduces new words into our vocabulary. We use a limited number of words to express a limitless number of things. Misunderstanding is a common result. There is little that cannot be communicated in words, but there is some information that can be communicated more effectively if words are supplemented with, or replaced by, graphic representation.

We live in a visual word. We perceive the world around us mostly through our eyes. We notice things before we can identify them. Identification is accomplished through naming or labeling. Then we move from visual object to non-visual things such as ideas or concepts.

Communication then is the attempt of two or more people to exchange their ideas or concepts. What one means and what another understands are frequently not the same thing. Without visualization, learning is limited. We all think in pictures and even use the verb "see" to imply understanding.

We learn approximately:	We generally remember:
•01% through taste	•10% of what we read
•02% through touch	•20% of what we hear
•04% through smell	•30% of what we see
•10% through hearing	•50% of what we hear and see
•83% through sight	•90% of what we hear, see and then do with feedback

Salient Points:

01. Recognize that anything containing quantitative or factual material can be graphically illustrated. Figure out the best way to do it.

02. A good visual is an aid to assist you to **COMMUNICATE**. That means your message must not just be delivered, it must be **RECEIVED** and **RETAINED** as well.

03. Audio-visuals are used to clarify, strengthen and speed up the communication or learning process. Adults learn more quickly and with better retention if they can **"see"** what's being talked about or what they are learning.

04. One of the cardinal rules concerning the preparation and use of audio-visuals, and a rule so frequently violated, is very simple: Synchronize the words in the audio with the visual. Don't make your learner try to listen in one direction as they look in another. When a visual is presented, the audio (your voice) must immediately tie-in with it.

05. Charts and diagrams need to be explained. Attention may be drawn to key points. Printed visuals should be read. Some authorities insist on an immediate verbatim reading of any printed visual. You certainly won't get into any trouble following this rigid rule, but some leeway is allowable. The "audio" can amplify, offer fuller explanation, in greater detail than the visual, but don't verbally wander too far afield. If you leave any part of a visual unexplained and attempt to talk about something else, obviously, your learners will be distracted.

06. Allow ample preparation time. Most of us just procrastinate or just don't want to take the time necessary to prepare the best possible visuals and then to rehearse them thoroughly.

We expect visuals to work wonders for us. When they don't we very often vow never to use visuals again. It is easy to blame the visual.

07. Get clear in your own mind what you want to say. Write it down in a descriptive paragraph first. Describe what you want your adult learner to "see". Be pictorial in your thinking when you plan your visual presentation. Now is the time to let your right brain   assist the left side.

08. Stylized symbols will usually be more effective than elaborate art work. These are adult learners who want to see a clean, clear picture or graph. A rough test of how successful you have been in graphic interpretation is to cover up the type of lettering to see if the symbols can get the basic ideas across by themselves. You'll notice immediately how harmful complexity and ambiguity can be.

09. Make your visuals visible. Use large charts, even for small groups of learners. For big audiences use slides, PPTs, films. Simplify - eliminate details. Be ruthless in eliminating all secondary details. Clarify the "obvious". Key feature should occupy at least half the screen, chart or display. Show all the key points. In the oral presentation include everything necessary to sell through the eyes.

10. Don't take the human out of the play. You can't use audio-visual tools as a crutch to cover up dull, disorganized content or a poor speaker.

11. Make a file copy of your visuals. Use the roughs, or make copies to be kept with your script. This helps in preparation, presentation, and later review.

12. Check on the worst seats. Center your screen or chart for the people on the extreme right and left. Mount the screen or chart

high enough for all to see. Then move it forward, if necessary, to clear the lectern, table, chairs, or other obstructions. Adjust the learners seating as needed.

13. Maintain contact with your learners. Know your visuals so well you can maintain constant learner contact. If you have to fumble with your visuals, peek under charts, etc., you lose your learner. Stick to your presentation like glue. Visuals are produced to emphasize and highlight a prepared presentation. If you depart from that prepared sequenced presentation, you're in trouble because your presentation and you visuals will no longer be coordinated.

14. Never apologize for a visual. If it's that bad, don't use it.

15. Keep the process moving. The eye tends to follow objects that are moving. Every magician knows that and in that knowledge lies the basis of their success. Your eye watches the hand or person who moves. Immobile objects are not noticed. So take a tip from the magician and use movement to attract and hold attention. In using a pointer, walk to the wall screen or chart and point, not on the overhead projector's little screen. This way the learners follow your movement to the point in the visuals.

16. When you're through with a visual, get rid of it. If you leave it around while you go on to a new idea, it will distract your learners. Move to the next visual or move that visual off the screen.

17. When you are through, put your visuals away, in order. Your visuals are priceless to you. To other trainers, they have minimal value. It is your presentation, built around your planned program, presentation, or sequential outline. Other trainers need to build their visuals, so they own the words and own the graphics.

SUGGESTED LETTERING SPECIFICATIONS FOR CHARTS AND PROJECTIONS
These are adults - They need bigger letters

MAXIMUM VIEWING DISTANCE (FEET)	MINIMUM LETTER HEIGHT (INCHES)
10	3/8
20	3/4
40	1 - 1/2
60	2 - 1/4
80	3
100	3 - 3/4

One point or comparison per visual
Maximum of 6 or 7 words per line
Maximum of 6 or 7 lines per visual

Unity: One basic idea or central theme
Simplicity: Avoid the unnecessary and fancy
Organization: Parts arranged for easy utilization and comparisons
Visibility: Every item easily seen by all the learners

Evaluation Of Visual Media

Evaluation of the Most Serviceable Visual Aids

A synoptic evaluation follows on seven visual aid media that are most widely used.

01. Chalkboards and Whiteboards (Dry Erasable Boards)

Availability
- At least one in every classroom or meeting room

Advantages
- Inexpensive visual aid
- Easy to use
- Good for impromptu visualization

Disadvantage
- Material recorded has no permanence
- Drawings tend to be primitive
- Trainer must turn away from the learners

Technique
- Write large, and legibly
- Frequently step aside
- Use as a "point clincher"
- Use a pointer

Cost and Lead Time
- Practically none
- Can be prepared in advance

02. Easel Pads - Flip Charts

Availability
- •Can be purchased in office supply or art store, if not already available.

  Pads and markers are available from the same sources.

Advantages
- •Good control device for discussion
- •Pages can be torn off and hung around the room for reference, or saved.
- •Inexpensive, easy to use
- •Portable
- •Pre-prepared presentations can be used
- •Several groups of learners can work at separate ones at once, working on the same or different topics

Disadvantage
- •Visibility limited to groups of 25 or less
- •Dependent on skill of the instructor
- •Instructor must turn away from the learners

Technique
- •Write large, and legibly
- •Frequently step aside
- •Learn to sift information instantaneously and select what is pertinent.

Cost
- •Inexpensive, cost kept down by keeping spare pads and markers

Lead Time
- •None, when developed during class
- •About one hour per page when prepared ahead of time by the art staff.

03. Board Charts

Availability
- Can be created by art staff, and range in size from 8 1/2 x 11 to about 30 x 40 inches.

Advantages
- Can be pre-drawn by professionals
- Somewhat portable
- Permanent, acetate overlay can be utilized

Disadvantage
- Cannot be mass produced
- Awkward to handle and display

Technique
- Have charts prepared professionally
- Keep charts high for visibility
- Stand beside the chart
- Use a pointer, and speak to the learners, not to the chart
- Do not reveal chart prematurely, and cover after use

Cost
- Depending on the complexity of material and number of charts A couple of charts may not be much expense, 5 or 6 charts and the cost goes up considerably

Lead Time
- Approximately 2 hours per chart

04. PowerPoint - Slide Projection

Availability
- Can be bought or rented from most full service camera shops or audio-video stores.

- Many canned slide presentations are in existence and available for use.
- You can shoot & develop on computer your own presentation.
- PowerPoints easily available with most computers.

Advantages

- Good for large or small groups of learners
- Professional appearance
- Timing controlled by the trainer
- Flexibility of sequence
- Portability
- Easy to store or distribute
- Can create your own with the computer.

Disadvantage

- Requires darkened or shaded room
- Changes require re-shooting/drawing and/or correcting artwork

Technique

- Be your own operator, if possible
- Use a lighted lectern
- Dry run is important
- If possible, never show slides or PowerPoints after lunch

Cost

- Relatively inexpensive, cost of film and exposure, most computers have in programs or can purchase inexpensive software.
- Projector is a one time cost, but remember spare lamps LCD a one-time cost
- Preparation of color artwork can be costly and time consuming, but the results are usually worth it. PowerPoints in color inexpensive
- Once the master set is made, duplicating cost is negligible

Lead Time
- For a presentation of an average complexity, a lead time of 4 - 6 hours per slide or PowerPoint should be allowed for artwork preparation
- Actual slide shooting and processing can be accomplished in one day. Planning the training and tying it to the specific points or areas is what takes the lead time
- PowerPoints require computer and LCD equipment setup and practice. Usually takes twice as long as planned.

05. Overhead Projection

Availability
- Usually available in every meeting room
- Can be bought or rented from an Audio-Video store in most large cities
- Transparencies can be created in the local organization

Advantages
- Can be used in partially, if not fully lighted room
- Instructor faces the learners
- Can make changes or additions directly on the projected image
- Can be computer generated

Disadvantage
- Effective use requires a <u>practiced</u> instructor
- Need to go back and forth to screen, unless you have an assistant changing transparencies
- Overhead sometimes obstructs view

Technique
- Do not illuminate a transparency until you are ready to talk about it

•Turn overhead lamp off or cover while changing
transparencies

•Be certain your material is in proper sequence before starting

•Use a pointer, but point at the screen, not on the transparency
A laser light pointer may be helpful.

•Practice

Cost and Lead Time

•Transparencies, inexpensive - either in color or black and
white

•Cost is in artwork for creative presentations

Lead Time

•Black on clear background can be made in a minute with the
copy machine

•Original artwork for transparencies require a lead time of about
2 to 4 hours each

06. VCR and Monitor and Tapes

Availablility

•Available in almost all organizations

•Can be rented from the local Audio-Video Supply store

•Canned video-tapes available for rental or purchase

Advantages

•Picture and sound

•Monitor(s) can be placed for good visibility

•Trainer can use the pause and rerun or fast forward to specific
point

•Becoming more and more a common general public activity

Disadvantage

•Not easily portable

•Picture quality sometimes varies

Technique

•Doesn't stand by itself. Trainees need to be told what to expect and see in the video.

•If you don't do a small group sharing, then when you only do the large group sharing you need to make certain to relate the points in the video to the learning module being presented

Cost and Lead Time

•Good training videos or example videos are expensive, so they are often kept beyond appropriate usefulness.

•There is a tendency to let video substitute for good training. Trainees can become passive learners and have a low retention.

•Needs training exercise backup for frequent foul-ups of the video, the VCR or the monitor.

Lead Time

•Set-up time about 20 minutes, including checking out the equipment and focusing

•No lead time after checking out equipment. Just turning on the equipment
and inserting the tape in the VCR

07. Closed Circuit Television - Making Your Own Video Tapes

Availability

•Available in many organizations today

•Can be rented from the local Audio-Video Supply store

Advantages

•Instant playback for critiquing

•Monitor(s) can be placed for good visibility

• Can make your own canned presentations
• Instructor can use the pause and the playback for personalization
• Record and replay allow for clarification and reiteration
• Can involve learners with hands-on learning
• Becoming more and more a common general public activity

Disadvantage

• Not easily portable
• Picture quality sometimes varies
• Requires one or more operators
• The operator has to be trained to see the topic through a lens
• Requires operations training time

Technique

When using the video camera and replay equipment

• This is a specialized skill and cost of equipment prohibits operation by anyone other than designated personnel
• Practice being on tape and then observe self before asking others to do it
• Set up the situation, video the learners performing and then play back for critiquing. Point out what they are to see and then replay the tape a second time so that the learners can see what they didn't see
• Excellent for demonstration of typical human relations problem solving back on the job

Cost

• After purchasing the expensive equipment, the cost is only the tapes, which are relatively inexpensive

Lead Time

• Set-up time and placement of equipment usually takes about 20 minutes

None for making the video

The Least Serviceable for Adult Training are:
Each has limited or specialized use only

Displays, Models, or Mock-ups
•Must be realistic, visible to audience

Movies
•Audience contact lost, rapid obsolescence, canned presentation

Flannel Boards
•Limited visibility

Filmstrips
•Sequence unchangeable, audience contact lost, canned presentation

Record Player, Compact Disc and Tape Recorders
•Audio appeal only

TYPE OF MEDIA CONSIDERATIONS

	Chalkboard Dry Eraser	Board Charts	Flip Charts	Overhead Projection	Slides PPTs	Film Video
Audience Size	Small	Small	Small	Large	Large	Large
Production Lead Time	None	Short	Short	Short	Medium	Long
Production Budget	None	Small	Average	Small	Average	High
Handout Copies	None	None	None	Yes	Yes	None
Vehicle Portability	None	Poor	Poor	OK	OK	OK
Sequence Flexibility	Flexible	Flexible	Flexible	Flexible	Flexible	Poor
Audience Contact	Fair	Good	Good	Good	Good	Poor
Controllable Presentation Pace	Yes	Yes	Yes	Yes	Yes	No
Changeability	Good	Good	Good	Good	Good	Poor

Chapter 13
©©©© Distance Learning – On-Line ©©©©
and
Knowledge Management

Distance Learning, On-Line, Distributed Learning, Web Based, Internet, and Cyberspace Instructing

All these topic area words are being used separately and interchangeable. On-line learning and instructing is having an explosive proliferation of courses. Distance learning along with its ever advancing technology may be growing faster than our current ability to effectively understand and manage. There are now thousands of courses and hundreds of public and private accredited and unaccredited institutions offering certificates, diplomas and advanced degrees through the internet.

This has become a several billion dollar industry and an important economic force in many communities. As the President of Grand Canyon College in Arizona said, "We're changing to on-line, it's so lucrative." This is typical today, not what is the best learning model for the adult but what is the best economic type of instruction for the organization. This is becoming the dominant method of providing information dispensing and the providers of this method are printing numerous survey results and semi-scientifically designed reports to protect this "golden goose".

This purpose here is not to say whether it is good or bad, right or wrong, or shoulduv, coulduv, woulduv. Distance learning has been provided to adult learners by colleges and universities for over a hundred years starting with the basic beginning forms of correspondence courses and radio transmissions. The task is to keep building and improving the instruction through the new multiple medias, but not have the technology overshadow and interfere with the learning objectives and desired learning outcomes.

Most of the research and literature supporting or criticizing the process has lacked author or researchers independent objectivity. Many articles read like the authors wrote their desired biased results first and then conducted a study to support what they already personally concluded. We are way past the point of saying whether adult learners can learn through cyberspace. The time now is to conduct different models of instructing with adequate follow-up of the learning outcomes measured at a level III and IV level. (These are covered in Part IV - Evaluating)

The important outcomes must also include what can and cannot effectively be transmitted or transferred through cyberspace. These include human behavior, emotions, tone of voice, nonverbal cues, verbal responding skills in a non-robotic manner, self-managing groups behavior, instructor inflections, classroom motivations, solution thinking time, and effective presentation to the meet the needs of all types of learning styles.

This means an exciting future for new, original kinds of research relating to the adult learners and the optimization of instructing with long-term desired change outcomes. Currently at national and regional conferences on the topic the bulk of the attendees are selling technology equipment, software or new programs. The least amount of attention is on objective research design and results focused on the hundreds of thousands of adult learners.

Instead of focusing on the technology, electronic environment for instructing and learning we are presenting a new synergistic way of looking at the adult learner situation. In the bibliography we have provided some excellent sources for reviewing the history, pros and cons of all aspects of distance learning, and sources on how to understand the terminology and "how too" of building and conducting an on-line course. Our approach is to present the now and the future of the need for knowledge management in this exploding discipline of adult learners.

What is this activity called knowledge management, and why is it so important to adult learning?

We learn by connecting new information to patterns that we already understand. In doing so, we extend the patterns. So, in our effort to make sense, we search for something to connect information to, something that already makes sense

When we first became interested in knowledge as a concept, and then knowledge management, it was because of the connections we made between our organization system studies and the vast amount of recent published information on data (data warehousing), information (information overload), knowledge (Intellectual Capital) and knowledge management descriptions. Saying that we became interested is a bit of an understatement, as we are generally either interested primarily as to how the new buzz words areas tie to the building blocks that came before or intensely involved to find out everything we can about the new concepts present and future use and attempt to build and go beyond where it is at, and seldom anywhere in between. Our study of knowledge management went toward the 'intensely involved', and 'what is beyond it' side.

We managed to survive the Formula Fifties, the Sensitive Sixties, the Strategic Seventies, and the Excellent Eighties to exist in the Techie Nineties, and for a time we thought headed for the Learning Organization, Intellectual Capital or Customer Relationship Management for this twenty-first century   However, what we got caught up in was a focus on Knowledge Management, not as a means, but as an end in itself. Yes, knowledge management is important. But knowledge management should simply be one of many cooperating means to an end, not the end in itself. That is, unless and individual's job turns out to be corporate knowledge management director or chief information officer. I'm quite sure it will come to this, for in some ways we are predictably consistent.

We associate the cause of our direction with the many companies and educational institutions we had been consulting to or associated with in the past. These companies had pursued TQM, Deming, Baldrige or reengineering, not in support of what they were trying to accomplish, but as ends in themselves because they simply didn't know what they were really trying to accomplish. And, since they didn't know what they were really trying to accomplish, their misdirection was actually a relief, and pursued with a passion even when it just didn't get them anywhere in particular.

Developing a Context of Knowledge Management

Data > Information > Knowledge > Knowledge Management

But, before attempting to resolve the question of knowledge management, it is appropriate to develop a viewpoint regarding just what this stuff called knowledge is, which there seems to be such a desire to manage.

Consider this observation as a basis for thought relating to the following:

A collection of data is not information.
A collection of information is not knowledge.
A collection of knowledge is not knowledge management.

The idea is that data, information, knowledge, and knowledge management are more than simply collections. Rather, the whole represents more than the sum of its parts and has a synergy of its own.

Data

We begin with **data**, which is just a meaningless point in space and time, without reference to either space or time. It is like an event out of context, a letter out of context, a word out of context. The key concept here being "out of context." And, since it is out of context, it is without a meaningful relationship to anything else. When we encounter a piece of data, if it gets our attention at all, our first action is usually to attempt to find a way to attribute meaning to it. We do this by associating it with other things. If you see the number 2, you can immediately relate it to being greater than 1 and less than 3, whether this was implied by this particular instance or not. If you see a single word, such as "time," there is a tendency to immediately form associations with previous contexts within which you have found "time" to be meaningful. This might be, "being on time," "a stitch in time saves nine," "time never stops," etc. The implication here is that when there is no context, there is little or no meaning. So, we create context but, more often than not, that context is somewhat akin to conjecture. Out of this conjecture we fabricate meaning, but it may or may not be the right meaning. The data contains no meaning by itself.

Information

Information is quite simply an understanding of the relationships between pieces of data, or between pieces of data and other information. A collection of data for which there is no relationship between the pieces of data is not information. The pieces of data may represent information, yet whether or not it is information depends on the understanding of the one perceiving the data. Data becomes information by acquiring meaning, context, or associations. It may be done for the viewer or by the viewer. What you can say at this point is that the extent of your understanding of the collection of data is dependent on the associations you are able to discern. And, the associations you are able to discern are dependent on all the associations you have ever been able to realize in the past. While information entails an understanding of the relations between data, it generally does not provide a foundation for why the data is what it is, nor an indication as to how the data is likely to change over time. Information has a tendency to be relatively static in time and linear in nature. Information is a relationship between data, with great dependence on its context for meaning and with little implication for the future (1).

Dependency and Relationship
After you have information, you have to analyze the dependencies to get to **knowledge**. Dependencies means how the data or information effects or is effected by other data or information. You need to find out what is dependent on what, what needs to happen so what else can or will happen. When something happens, what else always does or can happen. These are kinds of dependencies. Dependency embodies both a consistency and completeness of relations that, to an extent, creates its own context. Dependency also serves as a legacy with both an implied repeatability and predictability.

This is probably one of the main purposes of a college education – the collection and understanding of dependencies and relationships within and between disciplines and historical legacy threads. These then can become the building blocks for new knowledge coming from new experiences.

Knowledge
When a dependency relation exists amidst the data and information, the dependency has the *potential* to represent knowledge for decision-making. It only becomes knowledge, however, when you are able to realize and understand the dependencies and their implications. A dependency which represents knowledge also provides, when the

dependency is understood, a high level of reliability or predictability as to how the dependency will evolve over time, for dependencies are seldom static. Dependencies, which represent knowledge, have a completeness to them that information simply does not contain.

Knowledge Management

Having knowledge enhances decision making. And decision making, even more so than knowledge, tends to create its own context. **Knowledge Management** arises when you understand the foundational systems and operating principles* in an existing context, as well as other contexts. Knowledge Management is the organizational process of combining data and information technologies with the creative and innovative capacity of the human resources.

This facilitates predicting the outcome before taking action (Ripley and Ripley, 1992). So, now the viewpoint includes:

Information relates to description, definition, or perspective (what, who, when, where).
Knowledge comprises tactics, practice, method, or approach (how).
Knowledge Management embodies strategy, principle, insight, moral, or legacy (why).

(*Foundational principles refers to the fundamental truths or laws as the basis of reasoning or action. Systems principle refers to a set of connecting data and information parts in an organized structure or process. Operating principles refers to an individual's or an organization's values, ethics and morals,)

Illustration of the Continuum:

Savings Account Example:

This example uses a bank savings account to show how data, information, knowledge, and knowledge management relate to the principal, interest rate, and interest.

Data: The numbers 100 or 7%, completely out of context, are just pieces of data. Interest, principal, and interest rate, out of context, are not much more than data as each has multiple meanings that are context dependent.

Information: If you establish a bank savings account as the basis for context, then interest, principal, and interest rate become meaningful in that context with specific interpretations.

Principal is the amount of money, $100, in the savings account. Interest rate, 7%, is the factor used by the bank to compute interest on the principal.

Knowledge: If you put $100 in your savings account, and the bank pays 7% interest yearly, then at the end of one year the bank will compute the interest of $7 and add it to your principal and you will have $107 in the bank. This dependency represents knowledge, which, when you apply it, allows you to understand how the dependency will evolve over time and the results it will produce. In understanding the dependency, you have knowledge. If you deposit more money in your account, you will earn more interest, while if you withdraw money from your account, you will earn less interest. This knowledge enhances your decision making at the multiple choice level. Knowing how you arrive at acquiring more money is knowledge management.

Knowledge Management: Knowledge management is rooted in systems principles. In this case the principle is that any action that results in encouraging more of the same action, produces growth. Taking all the data and information in isolation, not showing their dependencies, you could never account for or predict growth.   If you studied all the individual components of this dependency, which represents knowledge, you would never discover the emergent characteristic of growth. To effectively predict growth you need to use knowledge management.

Now, knowing this knowledge, why doesn't everyone simply become rich by putting money in a savings account and letting it grow? The answer has to do with the fact that the dependency pattern described above is only a small part of a more elaborate pattern of dependencies that operates over time. People don't get rich because they either don't put money in a savings account in the first place, or when they do, in time, they find they need things or want things more than being rich, so they withdraw money. This depletes the principal and subsequently the interest they earn on that principal.   Knowledge management helps you see the choices and the consequences.

The Continuum
Note that the sequence data > information > knowledge > knowledge management (Value Added Intellectual Capital) represents an emergent continuum. That is, although data is a discrete entity, the progression to information, to knowledge, and finally to knowledge management does not occur in discrete stages of development. You progress along a continuum as your understanding develops. Everything is relative, and you can have partial understanding of the relations that represent information, partial understanding of the dependency patterns that represent knowledge, and partial understanding of the principles that are the foundation of knowledge management. As the partial understanding becomes more complete, you move along the continuum toward the next phase.   You learn by connecting new information to these dependency

patterns that you already understand. In doing so, you are able to enhance your understanding and your decision making.

The Value of Knowledge Management

Systematic Way of Utilizing Knowledge

In an adult learning context, **data** represents facts or values of results, and relations between data have the capacity to represent **information**. Dependency patterns of sets of information have the capacity to represent **knowledge**. For the dependency patterns to be of any utility they must be managed, and when managed this represents knowledge to the one that understands. Yet, what is the real value of information and knowledge, and what does it mean to manage it?

Without associations we have little chance of understanding the data or the world around us. We understand things based on the information we are able to discern. If someone says that enterprises revenue started at $3,000,000 per quarter and has been rising 20% per quarter for the last four quarters, you may confidently say that enterprise revenues are now about $6,220,800 per quarter. You are confident because you know what "rising 20% per quarter" means and you can do the math. (Data and Information level)

But, if someone asks what revenues are apt to be next quarter, you would have to say, **"It depends!"** You would have to say this because although you have data and information, you have no knowledge. This is a trap that many instructors and learners fall into, because they don't understand that data doesn't predict trends of data. What predicts trends of data is the activity that is responsible for the data. To be able to estimate the revenues for next quarter, for example in an airport, you would need information about the competition, market size, extent of market saturation, current tenant revenue input, customer satisfaction levels associated with current product or service delivery, current passenger capacity, the extent of resource capacity utilization, and a whole host of other things. When you are able to amass sufficient data and information to form a complete dependency pattern that you understand, you have knowledge, and then you can be somewhat comfortable estimating the revenues for next quarter.

In this example what needs to be managed to create value is the data that defines past results, the data and information associated with the enterprise, it's market, it's customers, and it's competition, and the dependency patterns which relate all these items to enable a reliable level of predictability of the future.

> Step 1 of knowledge management is the capture, retention, and reuse of the data-information-knowledge base that impart an understanding of how all these pieces fit together all the dependency patterns.

> Step 2 involves utilizing foundation principles, systems principles and operating principles. What too many people do is make decisions or choices at only the data or information level.

Utilizing Knowledge Management: On-Demand Access
The value of Knowledge Management relates directly to the effectiveness with which the managed knowledge enables the adult learners to deal with today's situations and effectively envision and create their future. Without on-demand access to managed knowledge, every situation is addressed based on what the individual or group brings to the situation with them. With on-demand access to managed knowledge, every situation is addressed with the sum total of everything anyone in the organization or group has ever learned about a situation of a similar nature. This is what a comprehensive automated management and strategic planning instruction methodology brings to today's adult

learner, knowledge management and not just disconnected, unintegrated data or information.

Vendors are doing their best to hawk a vast spectrum of distance learning products labeled "knowledge management." Combine this with an absence of common naming concepts and features, and it becomes difficult even for interested technology executives to get their arms around the subject. But there's a monster of an underlying reason why knowledge management is tough to grasp. Like the Holy Grail, it's an idea worth battling for even if it doesn't really exist.

Desktop applications are easy to understand and use because they're only trying to replace an existing machine with a computer. Word processing, for example, was a typewriter replacement; spreadsheets were a calculator replacement. More sophisticated applications are harder to understand and use because they replace a constellation of manual business systems and machines. Electronic document-management systems, for example, have designs based on known, understood business processes that occur without computers.

Knowledge management is still more difficult to understand because the learning process it aims to computerize doesn't exist in the real world for most organizations and educational institutions. Unlike replacing a machine such as a typewriter or an office procedure such as document control, education and training institutions have been trying unsuccessfully into this 21st century to make knowledge management a reality. With the specialized exception of units whose entire business is knowledge management, there's no obvious, proven model to follow. The results are product ivory towers built on conceptual quicksand.

We can, however, describe what knowledge management is by stepping back from technologies, products and services and taking a high-level view of the learning issues before jumping into technology-based solutions.

The learning problem that knowledge management is designed to solve is that knowledge acquired through experience doesn't get reused because it isn't shared in a formal way.

Knowledge Management: A Business Way of Life
Whether it's how to avoid remaking mistakes, to assure the reuse of proven best practices, or simply to capture what instructors and other adults have learned about theories, models, or applications, knowledge management is the concept under which information is turned into actionable knowledge and made available effortlessly in a usable form to the people who can apply it.

Knowledge management then, is a way of doing learning. In reality, it's more a learning practice than a product or service.

While some on-line, internet organizations may have proprietary systems that work for a single vertical market, no one has **successfully created a reproducible system that others can follow with a reasonable chance of success**. And there are vertical knowledge-management applications in departmental areas such as the help desk. But the ultimate goal isn't creating a departmental island of success recycling. **It's giving the organization the capacity to be more effective every passing day with the gathering of institutional memory** the way human beings have the capacity to become more effective and mature every day with the accumulation of thoughts and memories.

The system objectives that support the knowledge-management goal are knowledge gathering, organizing, refining, and distributing. Each of those objectives has a host of enabling functions. Knowledge organizing, for example, happens through searching, filtering, cataloging, and linking, to name a few. Technologies (products or features of products) combined with learning practices make these objectives achievable.

Barriers To Success

Even if you can cover all the required functions with technologies, you're going to face intractable challenges you most likely have no authority to overcome.

Because of the downsizing cult's belief in the disposability of employees, many knowledge workers have lost a sense of loyalty to the educational - learning organizations they work for. But the knowledge-management concept needs cooperation to work - instructors have to trust that their donations don't undermine their job security or, more commonly, their job competitiveness.

For example, in enterprises where evaluation, promotion, or compensation is based on relative numbers, individuals sharing their knowledge reduce their chances of success, and those holding back have an initial relative advantage, which discourages cooperative behavior.

Organizations about to go through another downsizing are never likely to measure group contributions more highly than individual ones - the individual stars get to keep their jobs, the cooperators are lucky if they get a Miss Congeniality award with their pink slips. And the laid-off knowledge sharer is worth relatively less because his or her knowledge is now shared across a wider population. It's therefore important that the system be designed around financial incentives that support the knowledge-management way of doing business.

And, of course, there's the more routine challenge of committing to making the knowledge-management concept a reality. More often than not, people are hammering away as hard as they can to get their current workload processed. The rewards of knowledge management are all mid-to-long-term.

The number of adult learning specialists that have a lever, a fulcrum, and a platform on which to stand to move this set of problems aside are few. The only thing that makes it worth the effort is the reward: the chance to institutionalize important lessons and create the self-perpetuating cycle of increased competency.

Overcoming Blockages to Knowledge Management

Knowledge management is more a marketing slogan than a basis for buying a product. You should define your adult learning goals in trying to implement the knowledge-management concept and lay out a set of supporting objectives. You should examine the education - learning organization's incentive systems for kinds of behaviors and internal data storage and distribution models. You need to also look at what functions a distance learning product supports and how easily one could integrate it with other distance learning products that support complementary functions.

If an education-learning organization is not going to treat the knowledge-management initiative as a strategic and high-priority effort, you shouldn't waste time trying to deploy it. And even if the deployment is purely departmental, some strategic changes might need to be made by the management of the department to address issues such as financial compensation based on contribution of knowledge to the corporate or educational institution information store. This is because a knowledge-management implementation requires a shift in philosophy for most organizations-not only in how people work, but more importantly in how they behave and interact with each other. In the end, the key to whether you should embark on this journey is understanding whether your organization has the ability to make wholesale changes to become a business or distance learning specialty built around the knowledge-management concept.

Implementation of Knowledge Management
What is a Knowledge Management entity, department, unit?

Knowledge Management (on-line instructing and learning) is the combined business, technology and human enterprise entity that helps capture, organize, store and spread knowledge of individuals or groups across an organization, nationally or worldwide.

A well-developed knowledge management system will stimulate the creativity and thinking of each instructor by providing exactly the knowledge that an instructor and their distance learners need for optimal performance.

Ideal End Situation
Knowledge Management is getting the Right Information within the Right Context to the Right Person at the Right Time for the Right Learning Purpose.

Knowledge is the ideas, information and the relationships between various ideas and information. Functionally, knowledge management Infrastructure takes advantage of existing knowledge, stimulates the development of new knowledge and ideas, acquires knowledge directly and painlessly, automatically classifies and interrelates knowledge, makes knowledge globally accessible so that the right knowledge can be obtained and effectively utilized by any instruction provider or adult learner within the system who needs it.

This applies the same way to most businesses interactions with potential and actual customers. They can collect and record all information and enter into a data base for continuous improvement, knowledge of the customer and their business. This can have a great cumulative effect.

How it can work
A Knowledge Management system needs to be well planned and carefully designed.

Knowledge is collected from all existing sources including people, systems, data stores, file cabinets and desktops. All knowledge of value is stored in the organizational knowledge repository.

For virtual teams, this knowledge would be immediately conveyed to those people and systems that could use it. The right knowledge will go to the right person or system at the right time. Current knowledge can be entered and retrieved from the system at any time in the future. As knowledge becomes obsolete or expires, that knowledge can then be put into long-term storage (attic) or removed from the system. This stored information and knowledge needs to also be about what hasn't or doesn't work on projects, with customers, services, design, specific locations and process developments. A "playbook" can be easily compiled and managed for each customer, industry and other potential customers. This can be the development of the educational organization's own internal data base incorporated into the distance learning knowledge management tool.

Knowledge Units
Knowledge units are groups of people or interests that come together to share knowledge that affects their performance and the adult learners performance. Knowledge groups (business units) operate independent of traditional organizational structure to find common ground for their category of interest. They are virtual units that are boundary-less and are not hindered by organizational or physical barriers. Their common interest is the specific knowledge or focus.

Practitioners of Knowledge Management have found that a critical success factor in the implementation of knowledge management is the cultural environment that encourages the sharing of information. Knowledge sharing requires the balancing of the protective instincts of where one's perceived special value versus the value of sharing that can give the enterprise knowledge units a competitive edge. This means that people work together and trust each other.

Knowledge Assets
Knowledge assets are similar to capital assets. They are usually independent of those who created them and they can be used, moved, and leveraged by others to solve broad-based problems (limited scope problems) and to enhance performance. A knowledge artifact is a specific instance of a knowledge asset. These knowledge artifacts may be presented by a browser-based system. They may be embodied as text, diagrams, graphics, audio, video, or animation.

Knowledge groups have separate knowledge assets and knowledge access requirements. A knowledge group will have knowledge requirements specific to its area of interest. Because knowledge groups may have overlapping areas of interest as well as overlapping membership, there are often common knowledge requirements across groups. This can become a "test drive" of any future salable distance learning systems.

A Process at a Time
The complexity of this task is easy to be oversimplified. Just taking one process or reporting system and analyzing it and creating the program needed to implement knowledge management can a time consuming challenge for even the technically trained.

However, once in-place it can be a huge time saver, helping 'instruction makers' make more accurate, yet quicker required units of learning. So, bite (byte) by bit - a process at a time may be a way to go.

What is Knowledge Module Architecture?
A knowledge module architecture is a representation of the underlying set of interrelated parts that define and describe the solution domain required by the distance learning to attain its objectives and achieve its learning vision.

A module is a self-contained, reusable building block that can be used independently or assembled with other modules to satisfy learning enterprise requirements. A module handles a specific event, or related set of events, and provides a particular function or group of related functions through a well-defined and stable interface. Focus units (people) activate or access various knowledge modules.

How Computer Handles the Knowledge
The Knowledge Management modular architecture consists of knowledge portals, knowledge components, and the knowledge repository.

A Knowledge Portal is a starting point web site where members of a knowledge group begin to enter, find, and access knowledge using the various knowledge modules (icons). The knowledge portal may be designed to focus upon the type of work expected to be done by the knowledge user. Knowledge portal profile modes so far determined are: (1) knowledge subject matter access, (2) collaboration, (3) group description and, (4) a combination of the above. At times, the knowledge user may wish to focus on knowledge relevant to a project being worked on within the context of the knowledge group, or he or she may wish to take an enterprise knowledge view.

A knowledge module is a self-contained, reusable object that can be used independently or assembled with other modules to satisfy knowledge management requirements. There is the generic set of architecture issues relevant to all modules. Knowledge modules have to interface with the knowledge portal, with the knowledge repository, and with other knowledge components. A knowledge module may need to be customized to handle knowledge of events specific to a given knowledge group. In a like fashion, module behavior may need to be customized to satisfy the special needs of the specific knowledge group.

The Knowledge Repository consists of servers where knowledge indices and, often knowledge artifacts (documents, presentations, databases, charts, graphs, plans, audio files, and/or video files) are made accessible. Some searching may cross knowledge servers.

Organizational Virtual Knowledge Repositories are inter-connectable Knowledge Repositories, globally distributed, that look to be a single entity to portals and knowledge modules. One search searches all.

Maintaining Knowledge Quality
While knowledge modules are crucial to a knowledge management system, experts have estimated that 90 percent of the success of knowledge management is involved with gaining the buy-in of knowledge users and encouraging knowledge sharing. One important aspect of knowledge sharing is obtaining high-quality knowledge and in maintaining its excellence.

One essential aspect of knowledge quality is meaningful classification. Although it may be possible to perform some classification automatically, a considerable amount of manual effort will be required initially. "Knowledge (referrants) (librarians) " will be required to perform some of these activities. This is not to say that Knowledge reference librarians are essential for a functioning Knowledge Management System. What it means is that those organizations that require **high-quality** information need to consider developing Knowledge reference catalogers and librarian professionals.

Knowledge archivers (Review Board)
Archiving we are defining as the careful and responsible management of something entrusted to one's care. Knowledge does not belong to a knowledge group; it belongs to the enterprise. Therefore, selected knowledge group members should act as archivers of the knowledge to maintain and enhance the **quality** of the knowledge.

Knowledge archivers need to take responsibility for both appropriate knowledge content and appropriate knowledge presentation.

One knowledge archiver approach is to set up a Review-Editorial Board for this purpose. The Review - Editorial Board will be responsible for ensuring that both content and presentation of knowledge is appropriate. Presentation would consider aesthetics as well as the medium (for example, text, graphics, data, audio, video) by which knowledge is conveyed.

Knowledge Content Administration
In addition to Review-Editorial functions, members of the organization will also need to perform Knowledge Management administrative functions. Functions that need to be provided include reviewing and maintaining knowledge, archiving appropriate knowledge, organizing knowledge etc.

Knowledge Management Tool Administration
Of course, all the tools of the Infrastructure will have to be maintained. Maintenance will include common network management functions, server maintenance, as well as administration of all the Knowledge Management tools.

Conclusion
The value of Knowledge Management then relates directly to the effectiveness with which the managed knowledge enables the members

of the enterprise to deal with today's situations and effectively envision and create their future (3). Without on-demand access to managed knowledge, every situation is addressed based on what the individual or group happens to bring to the situation with them. With on-demand access to managed knowledge, every situation is addressed with the sum total of everything anyone in the organization has ever learned about a situation of a similar nature.

Summary: knowledge management gathers institutional memory, stimulates knowledge, takes advantage of new knowledge, creates reproducible system, improves seeing choices and consequences, and enhances distance learning enterprise's multiple dimensions.

PART III
(♪) *THE INSTRUCTOR - SKILLS* (♪)

The more knowledge and skills the instructor has in the areas of human behavior and learning, the more effective and versatile is their capability.

Chapter 14
< • // • # • >   The Pygmalion Effect   < • // • # • >

Betting on the flip of a coin doesn't change the odds, but letting the learner know that you have bet on them can considerably affect their performance.

One person's prediction of another person's behavior somehow comes to be realized. The expectation is communicated to the other person, sometimes in unintended ways, thus influencing his or her actual behavior.

Many studies have been done to illustrate the effect of the trainer on the learner. The research model has been basically the same with the same resulting outcomes. The potential learners are given a "new test of learning ability" prior to training. The trainers are then casually given the names of five or six learners who are designated as "HAPS" (High aptitude persons), possessing exceptional learning ability.

In each case, what the trainers didn't know was that the learners names had been picked in advance of the testing on a completely random basis. The difference between the chosen few and the other learners existed only in the minds of the trainers.

The same tests were taken by the learners at the end of the training revealed that the "HAPS" had actually soared far ahead of the other learners by several points. The trainers described the identified "HAPS" as happier than the other learners, more curious, more affectionate and having a better chance of being successful on the job and in later life.

Again, the only change had been one of attitudes. Because the trainers had been lead to expect more of certain learners, those learners came to expect more of themselves.

The explanation probably lies in the subtle interaction between the trainer and the learners. The instructor's tone of voice, facial expression, posture, and body movements may be the means by which the trainer unwittingly communicates their expectations to the learners. This communication may be what helps the learners change their perceptions of themselves.

Adult learners very often have become what has come to be expected on them. What other people's expectations and opinions are concerning them change their personalities and affect their behavior. The way we imagine ourselves to appear to another person is an essential element in our conception of ourselves. Different people bring out different traits in us. We are reluctant to be evasive with people who expect us to be straightforward, or cowardly with those who think of us as brave.

The knowledge that others believe in us and are counting on us acts as a self-fulfilling prophecy and helps us to become as good as they think we are. When the late Roger Bannister began training to beat the four-minute mile, hardly anybody believed it could be done. "At first I wasn't sure either," said Bannister.   "But I knew my trainer believed in me and I couldn't let him down."

In adult learning, where the end results of attitudes can be measured in dollars and cents on the job, experience has shown that it pays to overestimate, rather than to underestimate the learner's abilities. A good trainer makes the learners realize they have more ability than they think they have, so that they consistently do better work than they thought they could.

Conversely, negative expectations of a person's ability or behavior tend to come true in undesirable and even damaging ways. For example, in a self-managing work team on the job, members of the team are often "assigned" roles, such as - the leader, gate-keeper, the blocker, opinion-giver or the one who holds us back. All are self-fulfilling prophecies because the characteristics they predict are incorporated in the worker's picture of themselves. He or she is told, in effect, "This is what we expect of you" Eventually, the role becomes second nature to them.

Almost any assertion you make about a learner - including yourself - can become a self-fulfilling prophecy. All of us carry on a constant dialogue with ourselves and replay our mental tapes. We are constantly making predications about what we can and cannot do. And there are very few of us who could not do a lot more if we simply expected more of ourselves.

You Are a Pygmalion

The prediction or expectation of an event can actually cause it to happen. The expectation of personal empowerment becomes a self-fulfilling prophecy.

As indicated earlier in the book, the most famous lines that illustrates the Pygmalion effect is in George Bernard Shaw's play (later the movie "My Fair Lady") when Eliza Doolittle explains: "You see, really and truly, apart from the things anyone can pick up (the dressing and the proper way of speaking and so on), *the difference between a lady and a flower girl is not how she behaves, but how she's treated,* I shall always be a flower girl to Professor Higgins, because he always treats me as a flower girl, and always will; but I know I can be a lady to you, because you always treat me as a lady, and always will."

The idea that one person's expectation can influence the behavior of another has its origin in Greek and Roman mythology. Pygmalion was a prince who carved a statue of the ideal woman out of ivory. So beautiful and lifelike was his creation that he fell in love with the statue. Belief in his love caused Venus to come to the rescue, and the statue was brought to life.

As a trainer, if your personal empowerment expectations are high, their success is likely to be excellent. If your personal empowerment expectations are low, your success is likely to be poor. Your training empowerment will rise or fall to meet your expectations. You are a

Pygmalion to yourself and others whether you want to be or not. What you expect of yourself and how you treat yourself will largely determine your performance and training progress. More often than not, you do what you believe you are expected to do. The basis for this self-fulfilling prophecy is that the prediction or expectation of an event can actually cause it to happen. The expectation of personal empowerment and success becomes a self-fulfilling prophecy. When you predict an event, the expectation of the event changes your behavior in such a way as to make the event more likely to happen.

Self-Fulfilling Prophecies can have both positive and negative results, so be careful to work only on the positive. You've heard parents say, "Look out, you're going to fall. You're going to fall." The child falls. "See I told you so." The truth is most children actually have exceptionally good balance, but the power of the negative Pygmalion *scripts* the child for the future.

Your mind set becomes self-fulfilling. "I have personal empowerment in my training. I am a successful trainer and I am a Pygmalion to the successful learning of the participants." ***You don't have choice, you are a Pygmalion whether you want to be or not, so be a Positive Pygmalion to yourself and others.***

Positive Pygmalion Characteristics

1. Belief in themselves and confidence in what they are doing.

2. Belief in their ability to develop the talents of their learners - To care, train and motivate them.

3. Ability to communicate to learners that their expectations are realistic and achievable.

4. Preference for the rewards that come from the success and increased skills, knowledge, and problem solving demonstrated performance of their learners over the rewards they get from their company or boss.

Positive Pygmalion Factors

1. Easy to talk to, even under pressure.

2. Tries to see the merit in your ideas even if they conflict with his or hers.

3. Tries to assist learners to understand the organization's objectives.

4. Consistent, high expectations of the learners.

5. Encourages learners to reach out in new directions.

6. Takes the learner's mistakes in stride, so long as they can learn from them.

7. Tries mainly to correct mistakes and figure out how they can be prevented in the future.

8. Expects superior performance and gives credit when the learner does it.

Chapter 15
ßß&&&ßß   Instructor "B's"   ßß&&&ßß

1. **Be yourself**. These are adults you are dealing with and they are usually masters at spotting phony behavior.

2. **Be honest**. They will understand when you make mistakes because they have had the same feeling (probably many times).

3. **Be accepting**. An atmosphere of acceptance is necessary before the adult learner will contribute to the class. Help them to recognize their needs. **Remember**, your needs are not their needs.

4. **Be patient**. **Remember** that adult learners can and will learn but they also tire more rapidly than children. They can't go the same pace as they used to.

5. **Be brief.** Say what you are going to say. Sometimes trainers feel they have to expound and are notorious for this!

6. **Be generous with your praise**. Adults want and need sound and honest appraisal. Use appropriate reinforcement to achieve the learning objectives and to recognize the adult for risking participation and potential change. **Remember** you are a Pygmalion, whether you want to be or not.

7. **Be participative.** Adults learn best by doing and sharing after they have received the basic input and the goals to be accomplished. Break the whole learning into participative parts that builds back to the whole objective.

Chapter 16
0◊•◊0◊•◊0◊• **Adult Instructor** •◊0◊•◊0◊•◊0
Do's and Don'ts

Remember: "Start Where They Are At - Not Where You Want Them To Be." Dr. Ripley

<u>DO</u> the following:

1. Treat the learners as adults.
2. Find out each learner's educational/training goals.
3. Assist learners to make a realistic plan for accomplishing their educational/training goals.
4. Let learners find success in every learning task. Give sincere praise. A word or two of praise, a pat on the back, or an appreciative smile can work wonders.
5. Determine the learners' education handicaps -- reading level, mathematical skill--informally and individually during the first few sessions or classes.
6. Periodically check the learner's progress. Keep good records on work they have completed. Each learner should have a personal folder showing the learner's goals, assessment results, and accomplishments.
7. Make the learning experience meaningful to the learners' everyday lives. Adults want to learn things that can help them on the job, at home, and in social situations.

8. Alternate the kinds of learning activities. Utilize lecture, group discussion, experiential learning activities, role-playing, individualized instruction, Q & A sessions, buzz groups, films, videos and teach back methods.

9. Provide materials for enjoyment and further self-instruction. These might include video-tapes, films, audio-cassette tapes, magazines, and supplementary short self-directed workbooks .

10. Have a sense of humor. Let the learners know you are good-natured, cheerful, enthusiastic, and capable of laughing with them.

11. Listen to their problems, aspirations, fears, likes, and dislikes. If they know you care about them and sincerely want to help, they will make every effort to come to the learning and training sessions.

    The adult learner doesn't care how much you know until they know how much you care.

12. Have the adult learners share their experiences and knowledge with the class.

13. tolerant of the learners' beliefs, customs, and mannerisms. Many of these adults may reject the current middle class values. Accept the learners for what they are. We are all different. Diversity increases the creativity of the learning. This makes for a more interesting world.

14. Anticipate and plan ahead. Nothing is more boring than an unprepared trainer. A trainer must plan-evaluate-plan constantly in order to provide the most stimulating learning atmosphere possible.

15. Plan for the learners' physical and social comfort. Provide comfortable chairs and informal seating arrangements. Adults like tables on which to put things. Keep the training room at a proper temperature. Keep the training room well lighted. Have a refreshment center handy (preferably in the room) and let the

learners share the responsibility of bringing in snacks. Adults like to feel some ownership and responsibility for the learning.

DO NOT DO the following:

1. Don't treat adults like elementary or high school pupils.
2. Don't expect rapid learning. Sometimes adults who have been out of a formal school setting for many years take a little longer at learning tasks.
3. Don't let the learner become overly frustrated. When the adult learner gets too frustrated they don't come back. A Zen learning frustration level is OK, but you the trainer need to be very timely and behaviorally alert if you use this master role technique.
4. Don't ridicule or put down the adult. As a trainer you must work to assist the adult to feel good about themselves as a person.
5. Don't give the adult a test the first session. Wait until the adult has developed some self-confidence about attaining the desired outcome goals.
6. Don't conduct a highly structured training session. Trainers of adults must be very flexible and adaptable. You need to be very organized, prepared and well-structured but provide the learning experience in a relaxed manner. Remember the secret is being very knowledgeable in the training topic and enthusiastic about imparting this to others.
7. Don't make the adult feel he or she knows nothing or very little. Use the adult's knowledge and experiences.

Chapter 17
ç • ç • ç • ç Communication Skills   ç • ç • ç • ç
Purposeful and Controllable

Effective verbal communications and group dynamics are key to instructing and the adults learning. The following two chapters will aid the instructor in conveying these important skills to the adult learners.

COMMUNICATION SKILLS: Purposeful and Controllable

I.   Introduction
This material will allow some of you to understand why you are so effective, others of you to add to your repertoire, and for the remaining group to start to develop new techniques and skills.

You Are The Words You Use
You become the words you use all day long. People infer what kind of person you are by your words and your total body presentation. If your present words are not leading people to see you as you wish to be seen, then change your words and non-verbal messages. In other words, start managing your communications. This includes: understanding your objectives, structuring your communication, establishing good rapport, utilizing questions and silence, re-directing resistance and limiting ambivalence.

Managing your communications also means understanding the other person. ***To Be Understood Is One Of The Primary Things People Want In Life.***

The first point of purposeful verbal communications is: **You Are Responsible For The Other Person Understanding You.** People in other countries are much wiser about communications than we Americans and they save billions of dollars a year in clear-cut contract agreements, joint ventures, and personal negotiations. For instance, in Europe, with so many languages, people talking to someone from another country always make sure they are understood and never <u>assume</u> comprehension. The Europeans take responsibility for having their message understood. Here in America we put the burden on the listener to comprehend our words and level of language. This can be dramatically brought home when teaching Asian graduate students. You can think you are being a good professor and very kind when you ask them if they understand what you just said. They will politely say, "Yes, we understand honorable professor." But to your dismay, at exam time they will not have understood your pearly words of wisdom. The fault is yours. Ask people to repeat what they think they just heard you say. This will avoid many, many misunderstandings. Don't kill them with kindness, be kind to them.

II. Different Cultures and Changing Language

Importance of Understanding Our Changing Language and Different Cultural/Gender Backgrounds

New Words and New Meanings

Our American-English language is alive with new words and new meanings for old words. Scientists and engineers are prominent among the new-word makers for the purpose of short-cutting communications. Business and government leaders wallow in this season's "buzz words." Minority groups add words through "in" music and street language. Marketers and advertising agencies create and refashion words to sell their product. Finally we are also a melting pot of immigrants speaking their native language and half

American-English.   Fore instance, in the Los Angeles school system over 169 different languages are spoken by the students. On the other side, words drop out of use and suddenly a thirty year old word will gain a new meaning, and you unconsciously date yourself by the words you use. If you are going to communicate effectively you must be aware of our fluid language and attempt to understand the other person's comprehension level and cultural background. Every sub-cultural group is a new-word generator for the purpose of short-cutting communications.

Countries Cultures, Taboos and Customs

To be an effective communicator today, you must be aware of cultures and their communication taboos and customs. For instance with the Japanese, do not use words or language constructions that cause them to lose face, do not hurry a decision, know they will go for a group decision, and realize that their use of time is different than ours.

The French people, like the Japanese, have a great deal of subtleties in their language. This leads to many important misunderstandings. Many French executives, scientists and engineers, whom we have trained, have stated they are shy about attempting to speak American-English because they can't quite find the right shading of a word to express their precise meaning. If you study their culture of art and expressions of beauty, or even their cooking this can give you a better understanding why our language creates difficulty for them.

We Speak American - English

Of course you realize we do not speak British-English, let alone write it. Their taboos and difference in meanings for lorry, lift, (let alone "Will you knock me up") are merely the simple examples that get us into trouble. When the "Brits" speak to each other they are frank, precise and maintain the word as 'officially' defined.

And then with the Germans their language may often appear to us as inside-out. Example: "I been here no long time." They can often times sound angry with their boisterous method of delivery, even when they   are not.

U.S. Geographical Differences

These were examples of some of the countries where you need to see and understand the different cultures. However, right here in our own country are some equally strong geographical differences.

Many of you have lived in different parts of the United States. Think about some of the differences you have noticed. Have you seen differences in communications from people who live East and West of the Mississippi? Have you noticed any differences in the communications from people living in New York, New Jersey and Texas or California?

Then have you noticed in difference in the communication messages in the rural towns and large cities? What about a difference between the subculture groups that live in the urban and suburban parts of the large U.S. cities?

As you know and can quickly learn from others in this learning event, there are geographical, cultural and ethnic differences in our human communications in various parts of the United States.

Business Communication

However, the real purpose behind these questions of different parts of our country is to have you realize you also do business communicating differently in different parts of the country. Just like other countries, there is a format and a plan to follow and there are ritualistic ways of doing business communication. In one industry or part of the country first you do business communicate and then go socialize.   In another part of the country you must first socialize before any consideration is given about the business communication. And in the other part of the country you do business communication but never socialize. (In all parts of our world, Japan is the number one place where you need to know their rituals and business communication etiquette before ever sitting down to do business.)

The purposeful business communications techniques, skills and methods of making an impact while obtaining power and maintaining control are the same, only the underlying cultures and ways of conducting the business communication are different. Always inform yourself or have someone who will be responsible to keep you abreast of the local taboos and customs.

Gender, Ethnic/Racial Differences
A lot of misunderstandings between adults arise from everyday gender communications. Each individual is different with varying amounts of feminine and masculine communication characteristics. By recognizing, understanding and exploring these differences you can discover ways to improve gender relationships. Affection and respect for another person motivates a person to overcome these communication frustrations in the relationship.

Why do gender differences exist? This is not totally understood but biological differences, parental modeling and treatment, education, birth order, societal conditioning, sub-cultural expectations, history and mass media are all contributors.

However, there are childhood social patterns that assist in explaining these developing differences. As this is a dynamic culture with constant subtle changes, these childhood gender social patterns will follow the subtle changes in the larger adult culture.

Again, there are many, many books written on each of these subjects relating to communications with different groups of people or a person who is tied to one particular sub-group.

Be Believable

It's best to communicate in a comfortable, believable manner. Adults tune out people who primarily preach, moralize, lecture and instruct in their conversations with them. Adults resist changing when they are threatened or commanded. Adults also feel guilty after evaluations and name-calling. Also, blaming and criticizing messages reduce adult's self-respect and self-worth. These are some of the reasons to spend time thinking about what message you communicate to a particular person or group of people. What other ways could you attempt to say what you really mean, and what skills could you practice to better guide yourself into becoming a more effective communicator? This is what is being provided for you in this book.

No One Best Way – But, Skills To Be More Effective and In Control

Is there one best way to say things to another person? Not really, you have to communicate in your own way. There are some ways that seem to create more problems for the adult and some techniques have been found to be more effective in creating good relations with an adult. The hundreds of books on how to communicate with each other wouldn't have been written if there were only one or two ways that had been found to be the best. It is up to you to discover how you best communicate being authentic, trustworthy, caring, loving, sympathetic, and understanding. What is included in this purposeful communication and active listening manual are all those skills that we have researched and trained other adults to use effectively when communicating with each other. Also, included are some examples and ideas to stimulate you in becoming a more aware adult in guiding yourself through your methods of communicating.

Own What You Say
When you start your verbal communications with: blaming and shaming the other person.
"You stop that, don't you ever...."
"If you don't stop that I'll...."
"Why did you do that, you're mean...."
"You're acting like a kid, you just want attention...."
"Why can't you be good, you should know better."

Think how these blaming responses make you feel. It's the same for your child or other adults when they hear these verbal messages from you.

Instead, when you start with your describing, owning and the consequences of your verbal message.
Your complete message to the other person must include a description of the unacceptable behavior, the feelings you are experiencing and the resulting effect on you or more concrete consequences.
"When you said you were going to drop out of school, I got upset and felt hurt, because of what the consequences would be for your future."

Another Major Point
Talking about "them" to other people
What the adult hears you communicating to others about them is what they take to their heart and their mental computers. These often are far more powerful builders of self-esteem, self-confidence, self-respect and self-worth than anything you say to them directly.

Example: Adult A talking to Adult B with Johnny within listening distance.
"When he was working on the histogram and Pareto chart, I knew we were going to have trouble with him and that he would never be a

good learner. He does such dumb things and doesn't seem to try hard enough. Well, I should have expected it, he does so many dumb things in other places."

Don't ever "kid" yourself that the other person doesn't hear what you say about them. Whatever you say about "them", to other people will be taken by "them" at face value. Then if you later say something different to them about the same subject, it will carry little weight.

Instead try to catch the person doing something positive and focus on what they can do well or get excited about. Then when they hear you say positive and complimentary things about them to other people they will believe this is how you really feel and will respond the same way to what you verbally communicate to them directly.

III. General Overview With Some Specifics

Understanding Your Objectives

You want the other person to buy into what you are saying. You have to convince them to take ownership or responsibility. Purposeful verbal communication differs from casual conversation because it has <u>specific objectives</u> and <u>purposeful outcomes of ownership by both communicators.</u> You are looking to be productive as a result of your communications. You are seeking results. The resulting accountability can lead directly to improved productivity.

Structuring Your Communications

Aristotle wrote, "Everything has a beginning, a middle and an ending." This is the structure of purposeful communication. The structure includes the predetermination of objectives. In the **Beginning** both parties become at ease; comfortable enough to discuss the theme or objectives at hand. If you are the initiator, <u>you</u> must clearly state the purpose. Do this early and whenever necessary. Do not leave the other person 'in the dark.' The beginning may involve talking for a few moments about the difficulty of getting started. And remember: begin where your listener is at, not where you want them to be.

The **Middle** employs specific techniques explained in this chapter. Ninety percent of your time should be spent in appraisal of the existing topic or problem. The greatest problem new executives and managers have is that they don't spend enough time in thoroughly defining problems or concerns. Here's an illustrative example we first heard in Iowa. An elementary teacher asked her fifth-grade pupils to write the most succinct story they could about a famous person. The winning story was about Socrates. The pupil wrote, "Socrates was a wise man. Socrates advised the people. The people poisoned Socrates." If advice were the solution, we would all have solved our communications problems years ago.

The **Ending** is the time to review "ownership" of problems and agreed upon action steps. Make certain those who came in with the problem leave with it -- unless it was your problem in the first place. But then keep it and ask for their feedback and recommendations. You are there to assist others to appraise and analyze a problem, and guide them in solutions, but it is still their accountability. Don't collect other people's problems, you have enough of your own. The ending is normally short because there are only a few alternative solutions to any problem. Such a simple format assists you in moving to a productive conclusion.

While much of the effectiveness of your communication is dependent on your skill and discipline, **Time** itself has a structural influence. Adults can sit in one place just so long. Schedules of busy people are often crowded. Learning to allot the proper amount of time for a conversation can significantly increase your productivity.   While learning the art and methods of purposeful verbal communication, remember that the dynamic processes are spontaneous.   Yet these processes can never be divorced from the structural   and   time elements. The flow of verbal exchange is integrally welded to the timing of specific actions you employ along the way.

You will be determining the direction of the communication.   In working conversations the questions asked most often direct and limit the scope of the conversation. The verbal responding skills can also do this in a non-limiting way so as to flush out underlying core causes and influences.

You must also be aware of silent language: what the person is really saying, aside from the words they are using. Note any significant omissions that are relevant.   Observe the variations in facial expression, movements of the body, muscular tensions, changes in volume and quality of voice, rapidity of speech or silence. Correct interpretation is as important as the observed data itself.

A. Rapport and Ownership

Establishing rapport, as well as overcoming resistance and conscious use of authority, can help create movement in communication.

Consider some of the following as aids in enhancing rapport:

- Be friendly and courteous.
- The surroundings should be comfortable and reasonably private.
- Appear unhurried, even though many others may be waiting to see you.
- Be patient and gracious with awkwardness, nervousness or hesitancy on the part of the other person.
- Express neither moral or ethical judgment, nor approval or disapproval of their attitudes and ideas.

➤Accept the other person as a conversational equal.

➤Always make clear the limitations of the conversation so that the other person doesn't expect more than can be delivered.

➤And last, make clear what responsibility for planning and final actions rests with the other person.

B. Direct Questions

After rapport has been established and after the purpose of the questions has been explained, questions may be asked directly. The other person should not have to defend their self <u>against you.</u> When this is the case, it indicates a misuse of your authority and a lack of skill. The use of <u>leading</u> questions is a dubious technique. This method implies cleverness rather than a desire to understand another person. Also, avoid questioning that leads to "yes" and "no" responses. Ask questions that evoke explanation or description.

Example: "what plans have you considered to overcome
                these difficulties?"

Note: Engineers be careful not to browbeat with **WHY**, because it can evoke justification and rationalization. Save this word for a design-problem session not for a human relations encounter. This also tends to hold true for lawyers. Try not using it at home. Your spouse will appreciate this change.

C. Silence

Silence has its uses. It connotes a thoughtful, meditative "sorting out" of what has been said and felt. Silence allows you time to recognize nonverbal indicators and to assess where the conversation has gone. Silence may also be used to maintain poise or to direct the conversational course into a new channel.

Difficulty in managing silence is often due to the mismanagement of tensions and your own prejudices. If you feel that every void of silence must be filled, you should know that your eagerness to talk has more to do with your own comfort than with concern for the other person. **Actually**, in the course of silence, the other person draws on his or her own inner resources to ponder meanings and solutions to problems.

Silence can indicate anxiety or emotional blocking, or it can be a passive expression of anger or hostility.

The secure person is never afraid of silences. You don't feel compelled to rush in to fill a vacuum. Knowing when <u>not</u> to talk can be critically important. You need to understand why another person is unable or unwilling to continue, and what your response should be.

D. Resistance

Resistance can take the form of a person who acts uncooperatively or clings unyieldingly to a point of view. Resistance (or hostility) is seldom directed against you as a person. A negative reaction to authority can cause the resistance.

Hostility is usually an expression of futile rebellion. You merely afford a temporary target for pent-up feelings. When hostility is directed at you as a person, it may signal justifiable resentment against misuse of authority or a dislike of personal characteristics.

You must recognize resistance as symptomatic. You must not yield to irritation and discouragement over another's unexpected or irrational behavior. Neither should you insist on your own plan of action. Seek to help the other person search for the real causes of resistance. Both you and the other person need to face resistance directly to have a favorable outcome.

This is not the place to use intimidation. Many of you have used this fashionable way of rising up the American business ladder, but save it. You always have it in your bag of verbal tricks (negotiation and power techniques) for times when you really need it.

E. Ambivalence

Ambivalence is the existence of equal and opposing forces. The Niels Bohr's Law of Complementarily (Haas, 1983) states that two opposing forces can be in the same space at the same time, (love and hate; desire to work and not to work; desire for friends and avoidance of contacts). Ambivalence is constantly encountered. Knowing its significance can help you better understand others. Indecision is the behavioral aspect of ambivalence most often seen by the executive or manager, and is normally caused by an inability to visualize the probable or unintended consequences of alternatives.

Gaining a better understanding of **Ambivalence, Resistance, Silence, Direct Question** and **Rapport** will enable you to more quickly and accurately recognize needs and problems. To the extent that you can discipline the expression of your own fears and prejudices, you will become more adept at comprehending the wider meanings of other people's responses.

IV. The Seven Basic

PURPOSEFUL VERBAL RESPONDING SKILLS

Verbal Sending Skills

Verbal responding skills give you control and force. But before we go to those skills, we should first cover **Verbal Sending.**

When you speak to another person, you receive two feedbacks. First, you hear your own voice. Second, you observe the reaction of the other person. Too often, observing the other person comes second. We talk primarily to hear ourselves. You must make sure that the other person really heard and understood what you said. Interestingly enough, on the receiving side, people hear with their eyes first and react immediately to non-verbal body language.

Here are some additional ideas to assist you in verbal sending messages:
•Know the purpose of your message before you try to verbalize.
 As your mothers and fathers told you, "Put your mind in gear before you put your mouth in motion."

**•"Own" your words by using personal pronouns such as I and
 my.**
 Take clear responsibility for your ideas and feelings. You "disown" your message when you use terms like "most adults", "you", "our company", etc. The receiver (the other adult or adults) can't tell whether these are your real feelings or meanings.

•Make your messages complete and specific.
 Include all information the other person needs to comprehend your message.

•Be redundant if it helps.
Repeating your message can increase the person's understanding - but guard against being overbearing.

•Ask how your words are being received.
You must be aware of how the other person interprets and processes your message.

•Make your words appropriate to the other person's frame of reference.
The same information may be explained differently to a person in your sub-cultural local group than to a person from another part of the city or country.

•Describe behavior without evaluating or interpreting.
When reacting to the behavior of a person, describe behavior ("You keep interrupting me"), rather than evaluate it (You don't like to listen").

While clear speaking and careful listening are at the heart of training your communications, specific basic verbal responding skills can and have been identified. Seven of the most basic are **Acceptance, Reflection, Clarification, Abstraction, Interpretation, Summary** and **Selective Reinforcement.** Included next are definitions, explanations and verbal responses used by highly successful business executives and managers and trainers who effectively use purposeful responding skills.

Verbal Responding Skill #1 – ACCEPTANCE

Acceptance is both an attitude and a skill. As an attitude it conveys a respect for the worth and integrity of the other person. Evaluative judgments are avoided, and an attempt is made to accept the other person unconditionally. As a skill, it is simply a verbalization of acceptance. It is a way of expressing "I am here and I am with you.

Acceptance is a simple skill of responding mainly with short phrases, such as, "umm-hmm" and "yes, go on." It is employed particularly when much narrative material is presented. Very often the person merely needs to 'ventilate' before real content is forthcoming.

Acceptance maintains the flow of communication by indicating, in effect: go on; it's safe; you needn't be hesitant about expressing your opinion or how you feel.

Acceptance can reinforce discussion through the use of expressions like, "I see,", "uh-huh." These expressions also afford a transitional bridging between ideas, giving a smooth movement to the discussion.

The simple **Acceptance** skill, besides the verbal response, has at least three observable elements.

> **Facial Expression and Nodding.** You must convey genuine expression of interest. Anyone who doesn't will be unmasked by the sensitive discussion participant.

> **Tone Of Voice and Inflection.** Your tone of voice and inflection also convey messages of acceptance.

Distance and Posture. If you sit comfortably close, the other person will infer a friendly attitude. "Towardness instead of "away-from-ness" by posture conveys the qualities of openness and sincerity.

Many people are hypersensitive to these kinds of cues and they may interpret the slightest negative gesture by you as rejection or disinterest. Yawning, crossing and re-crossing of legs, grasping the arms of the chair tightly are negative cues easily discerned and often interpreted as disinterest. This oversensitive interpretation of body language appears to have come from three sources: (1) Books on "body language," (2) Instant experts (the seminar sellers); and (3) the television fad presenters.

Practice this skill by trying to keep a person talking by only saying "umm hmm" or nodding your head. See how long you can go before you have to enter the conversation. Don't worry about what they are saying. Your sole goal is to keep them talking. We once told a group of executives that we had kept a person talking for 20 minutes just by smiling and saying "umm hmm". Sure enough, one of them called us the next week and said, "I tried it and you were right. I kept one of my vice-presidents talking for an hour and twenty minutes." Please, no more new records. Just try these skills for yourself to prove that they work.

Verbal Responding Skill #2 – REFLECTION

This powerful skill will help you in guiding others to reach conclusions and to initiate action steps. During the process you will have not added new content to the conversation or slipped in any of Socrates' advice. In fact, executives and managers have reported, "They left thanking me for being so helpful, and saying it was the first time someone had really understood them." A major advantage of this skill is that it forces you to listen. It also stops you from making one of the most common and fatal mistakes in communication: mentally preparing your own statement while they are still talking. What you are really saying to them when you do this is: "would you please hurry and shut up so I can talk."

This Refection is a deceptively easy skill. You merely reflect back or paraphrase in fresh new words what you have heard. However, to own this skill and use it purposefully at will it takes a few weeks of practice and an occasional **Reflection Skill Day** where you use the skill consciously for half a day.

Reflection (or paraphrasing) may be broken down into **Content** and **Affect** (of feelings).

Reflection of Content

The **Reflection of Content** is the paraphrasing of what the other person says. When restating you attempt to feed back to the other person the essence of what they have just said you are mirroring. Don't just parrot words. Attempt to crystallize the other person's comments and make them more concise.

Examples of reflection of content:

Example #01

Colleague: "I don't know about him. One moment he's nice as
                can be, and the next minute he is a real jerk."

You: "He's pretty inconsistent"
                    or
              "You're saying he is pretty inconsistent."

Don't turn your response into a question by raising your voice at the
end of the statement. You are making a reflection response, not
asking a question.

Example #02

Associate: "Everyday there is something new to do. There must
                be ten different activities going on at one time around
                here."

You: "So there are lots of things for you to choose from."
                    or
              "Something new is always added to the activities you
              already have going."
                    or
              "With so many activities going on it's hard to add on
              something new to do."

A well-stated reflection will let the other person make his or her own
clarification. Don't respond, "So are you trying to tell me you are
overloaded and can't take on this new project?" or "Are you trying to tell
me we're doing too many things at one time?" These go beyond the other
person's statement. If this is what he or she is trying to tell you, they will
get there soon enough. Never worry about making a misinterpretation in
your verbal response. If you are wrong, the other person will correct you

(give you a clarification), which will move the process along very effectively. Don't try to be perfect in your verbal responses. That only leads to stress, tension and anxiety. You already have enough of those.

Here is another example
:

Example #03

Personnel Manager: "He's really crummy. His degree is from a non-accredited school, he's had very little training and he has a very poor
relationship with his wife."

You: "Putting all the pieces together leads you to have concerns   about him as an employee."
or
"He's questionable both as to the skills in his specialty and as an individual."

Reflection of Affect

This is the attempt to express in fresh words the essential <u>attitudes</u> of the other person. You mirror attitudes back so they can realize what affective signal they are giving off. This also shows the other person that he or she is being understood. This will reinforce the free expression of feelings.

The word "affect" is used to demote the underlying feeling, belief, idea, or opinion about what is being said, not just the content.

The following are examples of **Reflection of Affect:**

Example #01

Associate: "I could hardly believe it. That was probably one of the most wonderful things that ever happened to me."

You: "You were really happy."
                              or
                 "You feel excited and happy but still in somewhat disbelief."

Example #02

Computer Graphics Artist: "I couldn't think of anything to say when she said that she liked my new idea."

You: "It made you feel good but a little embarrassed."
                                     or
                            "In your excitement it was hard to find the right words to respond with."

A common reflection error is the overworked introductory phrase, such as "you feel - - -." This procedure will tend to arouse the other person's resentment. Other words that most express the attitudes are:

"You were mad (sorry, confuse, etc.) when that happened."
"You believe..."
"It seems to you..."
"As I get it, you felt that..."
"In other words..."
"I gather that..."
"I hear you saying..."

Verbal Responding Skill #3 – CLARIFICATION

Clarification is the attempt to ask for more information or to request a restatement. It is used when you feel a need to clear up meanings. In other words, you are saying to the other person, "This is what I am hearing. Is this what you want me to hear?" **Clarification** is also used with semantic problems and bilingual conflicts. If during the communication you feel you can simplify or more clearly state an idea put forth by the other person, go ahead and use clarification. Remember that the **Clarification** must not lose the original idea or train of thought.

Here are some examples of statements requesting more information:

"Is this what you are trying to tell me?"

"Could you tell me more about that?"

"Could you expand more on that?"

"I don't quite get what you mean; is it... ?"

"I don't know if I quite understand, is this what you're trying to say? "

Example of Clarification
Example #01

New Employee: "Nobody will put me on the scene because I got busted with a lid."

You: "Are you telling me that no will hire you because you were arrested for possession of drugs?"

(Aside: These sub-culture words like "lid" are continuously changing but other new words will have the same camouflaged meaning.0

Example #02

Accountant: "This past quarter's results are in line with industry
               results but lower than our forecasts; yet close to
               prior years' results established goals if the last
               quarter is like the second quarter of two years
               ago."

You: "Is what you're trying to tell me is that the company
               lost money this last quarter?"
                      or
               "I don't quite get what you mean; is it that the
               numbers appear to be indicating the only way the
               company can meet this year goals is if the conditions
               are just like two years ago?"

Clarification and the next skill, **Abstraction** ensure better understanding with individuals from another country or from the vast number of sub-cultures of our country..

Verbal Responding Skill #4 – ABSTRACTION

An **Abstraction** is a special kind of clarification. This is a request for the personal or internalized meaning of a word or phrase. For example, the other person might say, "Working is a real bummer." You can respond by **Abstracting** -- "Bummer. . . ", or "Bummer?".

You are asking the other person to elaborate with other words or ideas. This leads to more concreteness of explanation and specific examples by the sender.   **Abstracting** can expand either the content or affect by focusing on the significant.   You can almost "steer" the course of the communication at a specific point.

Examples of Abstraction
Example #01

    Engineer: "I really shouldn't spend so much time away from my children."

    You: "Shouldn't !"

Example #02

    Salesperson: "We are close to having stupendous results in Japan this year."

    You: "Close to...?"
                or
          "Stupendous !"

The other person will normally respond with a more concrete explanation.

With this skill you need never worry about the latest language fad, minority street language, bilingual phrase or foreign word.

Use the **Abstraction** skill to get others to use more concrete terms. The more abstract the word, such as good, bad, right, wrong or should -- the more the need for **Abstractions**.

Practice listening for key words or phrases. If you have children, try it with them. You may find that you can communicate. "Awesome?" "Cool?" "Bad?"

Verbal Responding Skill #5 – INTERPRETATION

Interpretation goes beyond their verbal remarks to the underlying causes. Such causes may or may not be understood by the other person making the verbal remarks. With your verbal interpretation response the other person is presented with a hypothesis about relationships between attitudes and behaviors and their consequences.

Examples of Interpretation
Example #01

Young Manager: "I just couldn't get along with my boss on the last job."

You: (Knowing the young manager still lives at home and has stated previously he has problems with his parents.)

"You have trouble getting along with people in authority."

Example #02

Restaurant Manager: "I . . . I don't know if I . . . If I want to get that multi-unit job . . . .It's so hard. I'd just rather stay here and take care of my customers."

You: "You're afraid to get out of your comfort zone for fear you may not succeed in a more responsible position."

or

> "So, fear of failure is keeping you from succeeding in a more responsible position."

Interpretation then, is going beyond mere content. It is making a guess. You may be surprised that you will be right with your verbal interpretation response about 95% of the time. After all, you have had years of social learning and observation of behavior.

Although your **Interpretation** may be "right on," the other person may deny it. The person may not be able to admit the truth, or the person may be shocked that you interpreted it so correctly. Very often that person will come back to you a week or a month later and say, "Remember that conversation we had a couple of weeks ago? Well, you were right on."

Overuse of **Interpretation** can lead to hostility. If the other person comes back with "That's not so," just go on with the communication at hand. If the denied idea is the key issue or recurring theme, it will come up later in the purposeful communication.

Verbal Responding Skill #6 – SUMMARIZATION

Summarization is used to recapitulate, condense and crystallize the essence of what has been said. This is an excellent verbal responding skill to use with those who have "verbal diarrhea." A summary may be an expression of emotion or descriptive content or both.

A **Summarization** puts together a number of the other person's paragraphs, or a particular phase of a session, or may cover the entire conversation.

Summarization can be done either by you or the other person, or can be done as a collaborative act.

The following are examples of statements inviting **Summarization**:
"Let's see if we have the whole picture then. . . "
"Tell me how you think the picture looks now."
"How would you pull everything we have been saying together."
"Could you summarize for me what you think we have
    accomplished today."
"As I see it, three main points have been covered...."

Summarizations are frequently used in the following situations: (This is not an inclusive list.)

1. When you wish to structure the beginning of a conversation session by recalling the high points of a previous session.
2. When the other person's verbal presentation has been confusing, lengthy or unorganized.
3. When the other person seems to have expressed everything of importance on a particular topic. (This helps a conversation either move on to a new topic, or repeat the present topic at a different level)
4. When the next action steps require mutual assessment and agreement.
5. When you wish to re-emphasize what has been discussed in order to give an assignment for the next meeting.
6. When you feel someone is about to gain a new insight if only a few points could be stressed.

Verbal Responding Skill #7 –
SELECTIVE REINFORCEMENT

Selective Reinforcement lets you create the outcome you desire. This skill requires purposeful attention and careful control. You have to live with what you produce.

<u>**You must**</u> reinforce only one attitude, verbal output or behavior at a time. **Selective Reinforcement** must be consistent and demonstrated immediately following the desired attitude, verbal output or behavior. This scientific verbal and nonverbal responding method merely follows the time-honored laws of learning and reinforcement.

An increase in the desired output by the other person will tend to occur within minutes. Rarely, if ever, will the recipient, the other person, be aware of what you are doing.

During an interval of high national unemployment, we were hired by the Labor Department's Unemployment Compensation Division to develop a method for getting the unemployed back to work more quickly. We were able to effectively apply **Selective Reinforcement** in a practical way. (First, we had to get the Unemployment Compensation people to change their thinking about these people as being welfare recipients. After all, they had to have held a job for months to be eligible for Unemployment Compensation. These unemployed people had already successfully held a job.) As a result of our project they were renamed as Claimants.

We trained claims assistants in five major cities to use the **Selective Reinforcement.** This skill included the use of "Umm Hmm" or "Good" or nodding their head whenever claimants made a positive statement about **Work** or **About Themselves.** The result was that those who received the **Selective Reinforcement** during their interview sessions returned to work on an average of six weeks earlier than the group who just received the usual traditional assistance.

Now, let us shift **Selective Reinforcement** to the behavioral side of communications. Let us say that you want someone to be more communicative. This person also has the arms closed tightly. You could use a smile or a head nod every time you saw a finger move. Then don't smile or nod again until you see further finger or arm movement. This takes patience, but in a little while you probably will see the arms open and even gesturing.

You may say, as others have, "But if I do that, I can't really be listening and we're not building a relationship." Our response has been, "If they are already so closed up, nothing could happen anyway." So go ahead, change their posture, if that is what is needed to improve communications.

Selective Reinforcement can also be used to limit irrelevant material or unacceptable behavior. Cross your arms, move back or just sit still (this is the best) when the other person is talking about irrelevant material or is behaving unacceptably. Then, when they make any change to the desired outcome, move forward and smile. A person can be quickly trained to stay on the topic or behave appropriately. In other words, you can punish or reward, steering the other person toward more effective behavior and saving considerable time in the long run.

This can work just as effectively on you. Every year my graduate students would select a reinforcer (such as lifting their pencils) when I moved to the left. Sure enough, I would find myself over at the window lecturing to the birds.

This is a powerful technique, use it purposefully, appropriately and selectively.

V. Purposeful Communication Impacts

Another question is: "How can I purposefully make a **Communication Impact** on a customer or employee?" By communication impact we mean having influence over the outcome.

This module describes some determinants that we have found to operate in communication sessions.

❖ Talk Ratio:
The proportion of one person's talk to all the talking is an impact determinant. Let that person make an impact. You encourage their talking initially. Then when all problem datum has been presented, increase your talking to increase your impact. We have often wished this wasn't true, especially with "talk-ratio hogs" in group meetings. The talk-ratio impact material may not be the most significant, but it often steals the opportunity from other people who could make a significant contribution.

❖ Selectivity:
Responding to only a portion of what the other person is saying increases the impact you make. When the other person introduces several ideas or feelings and you reflect only one, then you are making a choice point for them and increasing your impact.

Example:

Associate: "I need help to get some things straightened out in my
                 thinking, and then my job. . . Well, anyway, it seems
                 to me that I can profit from some expert advice.

You: "Your job, , ," (like abstraction)
                             or
                 "You don't sound too confident about what are
                 saying. Is that the message you're trying to
                 communicate about the project?

❖ Time:

Time and time-related changes you make in the discussion will
increase the impact on the other person. Using discussion materials
more or less remote in time from the other person's responses will
increase your impact.

Example:

Associate: "I don't think I can get caught up this month—just
                  can't seem to make it."

You: "Why just last week you said that at last you thought
                  you had it licked.

Another example:

Associate: "He is a horrible person to work for and never sees
                  all the extra work I do."

You: "So it won't matter how hard you work, next week or
                  next month, he won't appreciate or recognize your
                  effort."

❖ Inconsistencies:

The more inconsistencies pointed out in the other person's story, the greater the impact you can make. However, abuse or overuse of this impact increases hostility, defensiveness and resentment.

❖ Contrasts:

The more contrasts in your views compared to the other person's, the greater your impact.

Example:

Employee: "I just can't work with her. She's always criticizing, always griping. It just isn't worth it."

You: **(Minimal)** - "You find it difficult to get along with her.

You: **(Stronger)** - "None of the others seem to have any trouble with her."

You: **(Much Stronger)** - "Strange that two persons just last week commented on how easy and nice she was to work with.

❖ Direct Address:

The more you use the other person's name or the second person singular (you) during the verbal communication, the greater the impact. Overuse will seem awkward and can lead to irritation.

❖ Perspective:

Abruptly changing the frame-of-reference of the topic under discussion increases the impact. For instance, if the other person is discussing feelings in the present communication session and you suggest the possible generality of such feelings outside the present discussion, impact is increased. Another way to use perspective to make an impact is when the other person is talking of an extraneous event.   By calling attention back to the present conversation, you make your impact.

Switching from abstract to concrete terms or from concrete to abstract will also increase the intensity of the impact

❖ Alternatives - Choices:

Narrowing the range of decisions heightens your impact.   Another form of this impact technique is when the other person allows only one alternative.   Here you increase the impact by enlarging the scope or number of alternatives.

Examples:

You: "Well, there are several choices open to you. You can quit the training right now, or you can switch to a different course, or you can even try to continue in your same class but get some help in the operations. What do you think would be best?"

You: **(Stronger)** "There really isn't much choice. You've got to get some help and lick that problem in the operations so that you can go ahead with meeting your training goals.

❖ Evidence:

The greater the use and amassing of evidence the greater the impact.

Example:

You: "Well, let's look at your record; three times absent without notifying us, late any number of times, difficulties with Jones. Now do you really think you've got a promotion coming? You just haven't earned it."

❖ Authority:

Impact intensity is increased by using rules that govern all parties or are beyond your manipulation. This can be called going to a higher authority.

Example:

You: "It's the operations department's policy that when
one is as far behind in their assignments as you
are and when they are not in serious distress that
we must suspend further service until some
projects have been completed."

❖ Urgency:

Here impact is increased by imparting a mandatory quality to choice. (As with Authority, Urgency as a technique presses toward decision or action.)

Example:

You: "Unless you can get more rest and take it easier on
the job, this tension is going to combine with your
physical condition and could produce a heart attack."

❖ Personal Reference:

The greater the extent that you refer to yourself or use first-person pronouns, the greater the impact. However, non selective use (such as 'old war stories') leads to the other person being "turned-off" and "tuned-out."

Example:

You: "I wonder if you would tell me something about your
last design problem as you remember it?"

❖ Tone:

Another person's likes, dislikes, desires, interests, biases, prejudices and annoyances communicated are reflected back to them by the tone of your response rather than by its content. In general, the more you express your feelings and emotions, the greater will be the intensity of your impact.

❖ Evaluation:

Impact intensifies when you express values or judgments. Managers and Associates bring their values and judgments into the communication session more than is usually recognized through such forms as approval, disapproval, criticism, praise, exhortation, etc.

At first glance there may seem to be a conflict between purposeful verbal responding skills and impact intensity techniques. However, you must remember the different goals for purposeful communication. In the beginning, establishing rapport and creating open communication is the goal. Active listening skills help to put others at ease so they can frankly discuss the situation. Purposeful verbal responding skills assist in bringing out causes and possible courses of action. But when it is time for you to make an **impact** and sway others, the impact intensity techniques come in handy. By knowing these you will also be able to recognize when they are being used on you, purposefully or not.

The authors are not implying that any one purposeful communication impact characterize good communications. Rather, the purposes of the purposeful communication session determine the appropriateness of techniques and levels of use. In addition, each individual has his or her own style. For example, a purposeful verbal communication session to tell an associate what a good job he or she has done would have a pattern of techniques and tone far different than a purposeful verbal communication session about a serious infraction of operating policy.

TWO ROLE MODEL EXAMPLES

Most board chairperson's, CEO's and presidents have highly developed listening, reflection and abstraction skills. Two of the best examples the authors have known and observed are Bob Galvin, past chairman of the board of Motorola and Bob Wian, past chairman of the board and developer of Bob's Big Boy Restaurants.

Bob Galvin, would sit with his chair slanted back and foot up against a table; would actively listen, smile and nod appropriately; and would let all speak their minds. Then he would come in with a well-modulated voice to give a summary-reflection of what he had heard and observed. He would ask for clarification and feedback as to whether he was understanding correctly. He did not hurry others and allowed them to get their message out in their own way. Because he modeled active listening all present actively listened when he spoke. However, one should not assume that his use of verbal communication skills and techniques means that he didn't have strong convictions or positions. However, by encouraging open discussion, he was assuring himself a broad view of the situation. He could re-examine his own ideas before coming to a conclusion.

Bob Wian, would operate in a similar manner. He would lean forward on the desk or table in front of him, occasionally writing on a pad of paper. When all verbal communication had stopped, he would sit back, take his pad of paper and say, "Maybe I'm the only one who doesn't understand" or "Perhaps someone could clarify for me or help me to better understand how this will improve what we are already doing." After one more set of inputs, he would then present his position and rationale. The others would follow his modeling and actively listen. Seldom did he receive much resistance to his ideas or much lack of understanding. He also provided a positive reinforcer to others by thanking them for their verbal-communication and for giving him their time.

Chapter 18
((ß))((ß))((ß)) Group Dynamic Skills ((ß))((ß))((ß))
Understanding, Communicating and Controlling

LEARNING GROUP LANGUAGE

During the past thirty years, the authors learning, drawing on small group work literature, research and applications, has developed to the point of having its own language and meanings. Some significant words are **TRUST, OPENNESS, COHESIVENESS, TASK, MAINTENANCE, LEARNING MEMBERSHIP ROLES** and **EARNING GROUP NORMS.**

> ➤ **TRUST AND OPENNESS**   relate to the self-disclosure and feedback system.

> ➤ **COHESIVENESS** is the attractiveness of the learning group for its members and need for members to maintain the learning's group orderly existence.

> ➤ **TASK AND MAINTENANCE** refers to how a learning group moves in their communications between the task at hand and the relationships of the members. A group tends to move back and forth between task and maintenance in relation to their discomfort level.

> ➤ **LEARNING MEMBERSHIP ROLES** are 'played' by group members if all human resources in the group are to be utilized and if the group is to successfully perform its self-determined task.

➤ **LEARNING GROUP MEMBERSHIP** is a feeling of belonging and having influence.

When you are new to a learning group, you often have to pay some type of "entrance fee." This fee can be related to such things as seniority in the learning group, or being given permission by the leader to make a contribution. The fee can also be related to recognizing how decisions are made, how information is brought forth, how problems are solved and how conflicts are resolved. One of the primary tasks of "old timers" is to assist the new learning group member and not make the initiation be too hard or too long.

➤ **LEARNING GROUP NORMS** are the learning group's spoken and unspoken 'set rules' for its task and maintenance activities.

Each learning group develops its own norms very quickly. In the week-long seminar (Workshop for Effective Management), conducted for executives, managers, engineers, scientists, accountants technicians and supervisors, the participants were randomly assigned to learning groups when they arrive on Sunday. They performed all their learning experiences together in the total learning group or their assigned smaller learning group. On Thursday they were given the learning group task where they were observed in person and on television by another learning group. The observed learning group was then given feedback by the watching learning group's members. Typical comments were: "I don't know how they ever get anything accomplished;" " Thank goodness I'm in my group;" "Now I know why they've never won anything;" "I'm sure glad I'm in our learning group." We then ask if any of them would like to move to the other learning group. Not once in over 50 such seminars had a participant wanted to move to the other learning group. They came as strangers on Sunday, but by Thursday each learning group had developed strong norms for task and maintenance activities. We then talked about how norms of operating were effective for their learning group functioning but would be ineffective for another learning group, and how difficult it would be for new members to enter their well-functioning learning groups. From this activity they also learned about Gestalt, where the whole is greater than the sum of the parts and synergy, where learning group energy is more than would be possible from individuals.

If learning groups can be formed so tightly, so quickly and be such powerful motivators, what do you look for in learning groups or learning events? First, you must realize that predictable normal human behavior is always functioning in learning events. Behavior relates to our role in the learning group at that time, as well as to our personal "hidden agendas."

LEARNING GROUP TASK FUNCTIONS AND MAINTENANCE ROLES

Understanding the learning group functions and learning group member roles is necessary for effective group learning activities. In all learning group interactions, there are two major ingredients, **TASK (content)** and **MAINTENANCE (process).**

Task refers to the selecting, defining and solving of common problems. The task functions of effective learning group members are identified in relation to the functions of facilitation and coordination of learning group's problem-solving activities.

Maintenance refers to what is working. Maintenance refers to such variables as participation, influence, conflict, leadership struggles, competition, cooperation, accountability, and so on.

LEARNING GROUP TASK FUNCTIONS AND LEARNING GROUP MEMBER ROLES

Functions 1 -- 6

Learning group task function are behaviors directed toward helping the learning group get the job done. **Learning group member task roles** are related to the task the learning group has undertaken. These roles coordinate learning group effort in solutions. The following types of behavior and roles are necessary to fulfillment of the learning group's task.

1. *Function:* **INITIATING:** Proposing tasks or goals; defining a learning group problem; suggesting a procedure or ideas for solving a problem.

   Member Role: **INITIATOR:** Suggests or proposes new ideas. These may take the form of suggestions of a new learning group goal or a new definition of the problem.

2. *Function:* **SEEKING INFORMATION OR OPINIONS:** Requesting facts; seeking relevant information; asking for expressions of feelings; requesting a statement or estimate; soliciting expressions of value; seeking suggestions and ideas.

Member Role: **INFORMATION SEEKER:** Asks for clarification of suggestions in terms of their factual adequacy for authoritative information and facts pertinent to the problem.

Member Role: **OPINION SEEKER:** Asks primarily for a clarification of the values pertinent to the learning group undertaking or of values involved in a suggestion.

3. *Function:* **GIVING INFORMATION OR OPINIONS:** Offering facts, providing relevant information; stating a belief about a matter before the group; giving suggestions and ideas.

Member Role: **INFORMATION GIVER:** Offers facts or generalizations which are "authoritative" or relates personal experience to the group problem.

Member Role: **OPINION GIVER:** States beliefs or opinion pertinent to a suggestion being discussed. The emphasis is on the proposal of what should become the group's view of pertinent values.

4. *Function:* **CLARIFYING AND ELABORATING:** Interesting ideas or suggestions; clearing up confusions; defining terms; indicating alternatives.

Member Role: **CLARIFIER:** Shows or clarifies the relationships among various ideas and suggestions, tries to pull ideas and suggestions together, or tries to coordinate the activities of learning subgroups.

Member Role: **ELABORATOR:** Spells out suggestions, offers a rationale for suggestions, and tries to foresee how suggestions would work out if adopted by the learning group.

5.   *Function:*   **SUMMARIZING:**   Pulling together related ideas; concisely restating suggestions; showing relationships among suggestions.

Member Role: **SUMMARIZER:**   Reviews discussion; summarizes the relationships of suggestions; pulls ideas and suggestions together in a compact way; offers a conclusion for the group to accept or reject.

6.   *Function:*   **CONSENSUS TESTING:**   Asking if the learning group is nearing a decision; "sending up a trial balloon" to test a possible conclusion.

Member Role: **CONSENSUS TESTER:**   Raises questions to test whether the group is ready to come to a decision.

LEARNING GROUP MAINTENANCE FUNCTIONS AND MEMBER ROLES
Functions 1 -- 5

Learning group maintenance functions refer to types of behavior that keep the learning group in good working order, promote good climate for task work, and foster relationships which permit maximum use of member resources. Learning group maintenance member roles build learning group-centered attitudes. The members of a learning group who assist in the perpetuation of group-centered behavior also use these roles.

1.   *Function:*   **HARMONIZING:** Reconciling disagreements; reducing tension; getting people to explore differences.

        Member Role: **HARMONIZER:** Mediates differences; relieves tension through jesting or "pouring oil on the troubled waters;" reconciles various points of view.

2.   *Function:*   **GATE-KEEPING:** Keeping communication channels open; facilitating participation; suggesting procedures that permit the sharing of ideas and feelings.

        Member Role: **GATE-KEEPER:** Attempts to keep communication channels open by encouraging participation of others; proposes regulation of communication so that everyone has a chance to contribute.

3.   *Function:*   **ENCOURAGING:** Being friendly, warm and responsive indicating verbal and non-verbal acceptance of contributions.

        Member Role: **ENCOURAGER:** Praises and accepts the contribution of others; indicates warmth and solidarity by attitudes toward others; offers recommendation and accepts other points of view, ideas and suggestions.

4. *Function:*   **COMPROMISING:**   Offering compromise which yields status; admitting error; modifying in the interest of group cohesion or growth.

    Member Role: **COMPROMISER:**   May offer compromises by yielding status and admitting error to maintain learning group harmony.

5. *Function:*   **STANDARD SETTING:** Testing whether learning group is satisfied with its procedures; suggesting procedures; pointing out explicit or implicit norms for testing.

    Member Role: **STANDARD SETTER:**   Expresses standards for the learning group to attempt, applies standards in evaluating learning group maintenance.

In a group that is achieving its learning goals and getting work done, members perform both **TASK** and **MAINTENANCE** functions.   A learning group that limits itself only to task functions will be highly productive for short periods of time, but its long-term effectiveness will be diminished.   A learning group that exercises only maintenance functions will be at first happy and "country clubbish," but will not work fast enough.   We went through a time in American education and business of "touch and feely sensitivity groupies" that pushed us to the edge of non-competitiveness. An ever excelling, superior learning group needs a balance of **TASK** and **MAINTENANCE** functions.

Unfortunately there are other learning group member roles that add nothing to either the task or maintenance functions. We refer to them as **SELF-ORIENTED LEARNING GROUP MEMBER BEHAVIORS**. (We will cover these later.) These are attempts to satisfy individual needs that are irrelevant to the learning group and may be negatively oriented. A high incidence of "individual-centered" as opposed to "learning group-centered" participation always calls for self-diagnosis by the learning group. The diagnosis may reveal conditions that may include an inappropriately chosen and inadequately defined learning group task; low-level learning group maturity, low level of skill-training; and prevalence of "authoritarian" or "laisse faire" points of view toward learning group functioning. This last item is often true in education, business and government of presidents and top executives who rose to their top positions through intimidation. These are the greatest **BLOCKERS** of innovative learning. They tend to limit the learner's "brain power."

Other task and maintenance blockers include the devil's advocate, who is more devil than advocate, and the help-seeker who is only calling for sympathy. You as the instructor or learning group member must confront these blockers directly and explain how they are detrimental.

In addition to task and maintenance functions, other important variables occur in all learning events. Some of the important ones are summarized below, along with some observational guidelines.

Various Variables Necessary for Success

When certain role players are missing from a learning group and if no present learning group member is willing to assume that task or maintenance role, a learning group will be less than effective.

Task Oriented Learning Group Member
If there is no task oriented member, then the team may lack task focus, use time and resources poorly. The few members who complete their tasks will resent those who don't.

Team Goals Member
Without a team goal focused member, the team will lack clarity about perspective and purpose. This member helps and keeps the new team from floundering and losing interest because goals were never formulated. Without help from a team goals member, only the leader or a few members will get recognition for team accomplishments and the other team members will become resentful.

Process Oriented Member
Without the process oriented member, the team climate will be formal and the team will limit itself to task-oriented interactions. There will be excessive talking and little
listening. Success will be measured by task completion, with little positive recognition for contributions or accomplishments. There will be no maintenance of interpersonal relations of the group process.

Challenger Member
Without the challenger team member there is the tendency to lean toward group-think. The team plays it safe in the effort to just complete its work and gain recognition. Unless challenged, the members tend to lose interest and retreat. Little continuous improvement is accomplished.

ADULT LEARNER TEAM BUILDING

Adult Learners Self-Managing Teams typically pass through four levels in becoming an effective, self-directing, self-sustaining, empowered learning team. The following chart illustrates one progress model path to becoming an empowered self-managing adult learning team. (Adapted from the popular stage model of **Forming, Storming, Norming** and **Performing**)

Level I

Diverse collection of individuals
Members not linked by goals and roles
Members not certain about what to expect
Not totally willing to commit to the process as they don't grasp it's full scope
Individuals at "What am I?" stage
Question each other and withhold full participation
Desire clear definitions, boundaries and work expectations
Requires a lot of time in learning.
Need positive team models and skilled facilitators

Purpose	Learning purpose and Mission Unclear. Confusion, Ambivalence, Avoidance
Commitment	Need to assist team members to see themselves as independent and interdependent-by design and necessity Members don't know yet what they bought.
Involvement	Have histories of individual recognition and reward for past individual initiative. Few have experience to work in collaboration and subordinating self to the team.
Trust	Wait and see. Little basis to build on.

Process
Orientation   Unfamiliar - Confused

Communication   Tentative - Leader to members
                     Questions and explanations

Level II

Teams often feel letdown do to new learning challenges.
Are being asked to do new aspects of learning.
Become involved with team meetings, project planning, and problem solving besides maintaining responsibilities for their learning.
Cohesiveness of the team tested.
Leaders and members struggle with relinquishing control.
There is team stress, conflict and rejection.
"I told you so" critics arise.
Information and learning now even more important.
Need to review the team's mission statement
Need to compare or measure team's performance to goals.
Need to discuss how to operate more effectively as a team.

Purpose   Begins to understand mission and
                    purpose but need guidance and reassurance.

Commitment   Tends to be subgroups.

Involvement   Members feel more comfortable as to what a
                     adult learner team is and how they are to work
                     together in the team.
                    However, one or two members still dominate the group.

Trust   Members categorized into those they
                    trust, those they don't trust and the
                    unknowns.

Process Orientation	With learning, standard processes beginning to operate but still unfamiliar and difficult to use. Need to become more skilled at leading and participating in meetings. Need to learn to trust the process.
Communication	More aggressiveness and conflicts arise. Individual members assert themselves. Still little empathy or support with limited active listening.

Level III

Team becomes more goals focused.
The learning vision and mission must be kept in focus.
Team leaders begin to become coaches. and reinforce more team empowerment and self-direction.
Learning now needs to expand to interdisciplinary groups.
Contact with outside sources is encouraged.
Team is now a consultative unit for within and outside the learning event.

Purpose	Need to be reminded of learning event/course vision and mission and the team's mission. The focus is now on performance and achieving team goals.
Commitment	Cross-training taking place. Team members can now rely on each other during peak production or other demands. Members now committed to getting the job done.
Involvement	Begin to rely on each other's talents. Need for different skills and talents identified. Potential problem of allegiance being

sworn to the team over the course requirements.
Members begin to show comfort as
to their role in the team.

Trust   Working together begins to create trust.

Process   Processes become more natural.
Orientation   Cohesiveness observable.

Communication   Still heavy emphasis on task
                        orientation.
                        Members begin to develop
                        networks and support groups
                        outside the team.

Level IV

Adult Learners Team becomes proactive, anticipates demands.
Are more focused on continuous improvement
Now fully capable of organizing and improving own learning methods
and processes.
Now want to be in charge of their own learning destinies, including
accepting new team members and budgeting of time.
Is now a self-sustaining learning group.

Purpose   Are now flexible and adaptable to change
                        to new demands.
                        Clear learning vision and mission are reviewed,
                        revised and maintained.

Commitment   Committed to the learning , the team
                        and themselves.

Involvement   All members participate from making
                        presentations to facilitating.
                        Product and process innovations
                        are developed.

Trust	Now extended openly. Now fairly stable.
Process Orientation	Now viewed as a regular part of their learning. Continuous improvement and quality become the internalized values.
Communication	Frequent team meetings. Now complex and multi-faceted. Solution thinking and Quality oriented. Active Listening and Purposeful Communications.

SELF-ORIENTED TEAM MEMBERS

The processes described so far have dealt with the learning group's attempt to work out problems of task and maintenance. There also are forces that disturb work and represent a kind of emotional undercurrent in the stream of learning group life. These underlying personal issues produce behaviors that interfere with learning group functioning. They cannot be ignored or wished away; they must be recognized and their causes understood. As the learning group develops, conditions must be created that permit these self-oriented energies to be channeled into the learning group task and maintenance effort.

Causes of these **SELF-ORIENTED** activities include:

1. The problem of **IDENTITY**. Who am I in this group? Where do I fit in? What kind of behavior is acceptable here?

2. The problem of **PERSONAL GOALS** and **NEEDS**. What do I want from this group? Can the group goals be made consistent with my goals? What can I offer to the group?

3. The problem of **POWER, CONTROL**, and **INFLUENCE**. Who will control what we do? How much power and influence do I have?

4. The problem of **INTIMACY.** How close will we get to each other? How personal? How much can we trust each other, and how can we achieve a greater level of trust?

Behaviors produced in response to these SELF-ORIENTED problems include:

1. **DEPENDENCY-COUNTERDEPENDENCY**: Leaning on or resisting anyone in the learning group who represents authority.

2. **FIGHTING and CONTROLLING:** Asserting personal dominance, attempting to get one's way regardless of others.

3. **WITHDRAWING:** Trying to remove the sources of uncomfortable feelings by psychologically leaving the learning group.

4. **PAIRING-UP:** Seeking out one or two supporters and forming a sub-learning group in which the members protect and support each other independent of the learning group's task and maintenance.

5. **BULLYING:** Deflating, putting down the status of others; actively disapproving of group values; joking aggressively, attacking the problem that the group is working on, showing envy toward another's contribution.

6. **BLOCKING:** Being negative and stubbornly resistant; disagreeing and opposing beyond reason; bringing up issues after the group has rejected them.

7. **RECOGNITION-SEEKING:** Calling attention to one's self; boasting; talking about person achievements; grabbing and holding onto the group's attention.

8. **SELF-CONFESSING:** Using the group as an audience to express "feeling," "insight," ideology, etc.

9. Acting as a **PLAYBOY** or **PLAYGIRL:** Publicly displaying lack of involvement in group task or maintenance. This may take the shape of cynicism, nonchalance, horseplay, or "out of the room" behavior.

10. **SPECIAL INTEREST PLEADING:** Arguing for the underdog, minority groups, "grass roots community," labor, small business person, etc.

Many decisions are made in learning groups without considering their effects on the total learning group. Some try to impose their decisions, while others want all members to share in making decisions. Some decisions are made consciously with reference to the tasks at hand; others are made without much awareness. Usually these decisions relate to learning group procedures or standards of operation.

Some unproductive methods by which learning groups make decisions:

1. **SELF-AUTHORIZER:** Does a group member or the leader make a decision and carry it out without first checking with other group members? What effect does this have?

2. **HANDCLASPER:** Does one member's support of another's suggestions or decisions result in the two members deciding the topic or activity for the group? How does this affect other group members?

3. **MAJORITY SUPPORTERS:** Is there evidence of a majority pushing a decision through over other members' objections? Do they call for a vote?

4. **THE PLOPPER:** Does a member make a contribution which receives no response or recognition? What effect does this have on that person?

COMMUNICATION SUGGESTIONS

HOW TO TALK WITH LEARNING GROUP MEMBERS

1. Assume that the listener is always right. If they misunderstand you, assume it's your fault, and go back and try again.

2. Use language that is appropriate to the situation and the audience and your purpose. Don't talk over your listener's head - but don't talk "down" to them either.

3. When you listen, try to understand what the speaker means by his or her words, not what the words mean to you - or what you think they should mean.

4. Words are not things. Don't confuse the word symbol with the reality it tries to represent.

5. Language is a marvelous tool - but not a perfect tool. Never expect the speaker to, or never think you can say everything about a subject or always be precise and exact.

6. Beware of the word "is"; concepts can never be exactly equated. When you say "John is a cheat," what your are really saying is "on this and this occasion John seemed to act in such a way that did not seem to be honest." Beware especially of the judgment words like dishonest, bad, unfair.

7. Beware of the word "all" - when you use it and when you hear it. It is impossible to make statements about groups of people that are always true about all people. When a person says, "All Hottentots are money-hungry," what he or she probably means is, "On a few occasions I have dealt with a few Hottentots who seemed to act in a way that was greedy."

8. Check in your speaking and your listening the "black-and-white fallacy." Most of life tends to be "gray." Statements like,

"You're either a success or a failure, you're either honest or dishonest; you're either for or against us" don't live with reality and lead us into mistakes.

9. Check the facts - not the words. Observe, verify, check with experience all your ideas and concepts.

10. Don't demand that all language be precise communication. Accept the stock phrases of polite conversation as being merely ways of making for smooth social relationships. When a person says, "it's a nice day, " don't quibble about the literal meaning.

11. Pay attention to the results of your own words; not carefully how your listener is responding or failing to respond, and modify your language accordingly.

12. Learn to listen actively; pay attention to people. Listen to understand, and actively concentrate on getting the underlying thought he or she is trying to communicate.

13. Develop the habit of putting yourself in your listener's place - try to see how he or she sees you and he or she hears you.

14. Don't criticize a person's appearance or their manner of speaking. The rudest person in the world is the one who calls attention to someone else's rudeness.

15. Don't be hasty to dismiss a subject as "boring" or "dull." Often it is only the listener who is dull.

16. Don't yield too easily to distractions; the speaker deserves your complete attention.
    As you listen to a speaker who seems to be proceeding too slowly, don't let your mind wander, but use the time to think ahead of them, weigh their evidence, review what you have heard, listen "between the lines."

HOW TO <u>DIFFER</u> WITH LEARNING GROUP MEMBERS

1. In dealing with other people, the first step is to see the world through their eyes - to enter into what they are trying to do, however strange their idea's seem.

2. While exactness is desirable, always insisting that a person "define their terms" is foolish on two grounds: definitions are words about words and often confuse rather than clarify; the statement ignores that fact that both speaker and listener have responsibility to understand.

3. When people disagree, they usually do so in one of five ways.
   a. Mood of dismissal: "I refuse to listen."
   b. Expressing suspicion and distrust: "What are you hiding?"
   c. Inclination to laughter: "Don't be too hard on Bill. He's had a hard day."
   d. Air of incredulity: "How did you ever get that idea?"
   e. The inquiring-investigative attitude: "That's interesting. Why do you think so?"

4. Generalizations in themselves aren't bad; sometimes they're very useful. In a discussion of generalizations, refer them back to specific instances and particulars: "You say that recruits fail only because they don't study. Have you known any recruits who have studied and still failed?"

5. In any discussion it is often helpful to try to restate what the previous speaker has just said. This accomplishes two things: it helps you see the world through their eyes, and it helps them look at their own ideas objectively.

6. In any discussion learn the distinction between statements about things observed, statements which refer to what is assumed, and statements which refer to what is felt about a situation.

   a. "Two-thirds of the class failed." This is a statement that can be verified; if there is disagreement, it is relatively easy to check on its truth. This is observed.
   b. "The high failure rate was due to the recruits' lack of basic preparation." This is a hypothesis. One only assumes its validity. Other hypotheses, equally as valid, might be asserted.
   c. "That team facilitator is doing a lousy job." This is essentially a statement of feeling or emotion and must be handled as such.

7. When a real difference arises, try to find a middle ground: A compromise is a decent, honorable, demonstration of practical intelligence.

8. When a person makes a strong statement that you disagree with, "All labor leaders are thieves." Try one of these approaches:

   a. "That's one way of looking at it. Is there any other?"
   b. "Your feelings about that are clear. Does it exhaust what can be said about it.?"
   c. "Is that true all the time?"

9. When people criticize your ideas, don't take the attack personally. Try the soft, gently answer: "Maybe you're right But I wonder if.."

10. When you encounter anger, don't try to thwart or repress it. Merely ask the angry person to take another look at the thing or person that made them angry.

11. Don't challenge minor slips or errors. Challenge the big mistakes that need challenging. And challenge in such a way that the speaker isn't put on the defensive, but is led quietly to examine their own beliefs.

12. Every opinion is worth listening to, no matter what advances it. But examine all opinions on controversial issues with great care. And criticize the idea, not the speaker.

13. Refrain from disagreeing with a speaker until you've heard them out completely. Be sure to get the total picture; don't act on the basis of partial information.

14. Misunderstanding arises when someone assumes that the person who disagrees with them has no good reason for doing so.

LEARNING GROUP MEMBER FEEDBACK

Keys For Giving Effective Feedback

1. The feedback needs to focus on the behavior of the person.

2. The current behavior needs to be measured in objective terms.

3. Knowledge of the desired results should be known and understood.

4. The feedback is intended to help the person perform better.

5. The feedback is focused on those aspects of performance over which the person has control.

6. The feedback is given immediately following performance or as soon as is feasible.

7. The system of feedback is well known and is a permanent part of the job.

8. The feedback is based on the standards which have agreed on by giver and recipient.

9. The feedback is descriptive of performance.

10. The feedback is specific

11. The feedback is given by the lowest level possible in the chain of command.

12. The feedback is based on positives rather than negatives.

13. The feedback is based on alternatives rather than solutions

The feedback is given with due respect to the readiness of the person to receive it and learn from it.

HANDLING SPECIAL SITUATIONS

The Over-Talkative Group Member

- There is often one group member who is constantly talking. His or her ideas might be good; but unless the excessive talkativeness can be controlled, the other group members may become frustrated and lose interest because they don't have an opportunity to express themselves. This group member may be an excellent contributor but is undermining the total group process.

- One idea could be to give them assignments which will make it more difficult to talk and work at the same time, such as being the participant observer of the session.

- Also, this group member may find it difficult to talk much if writing down the ideas as the scribe/recorder during a brainstorming session.

- You as the leader or facilitator can address questions to specific group members rather than asking them so that anyone can feel free to answer.

- Another approach is responding, "You've given us some good ideas. Let's hear what some of the other members have to say."

- Sometimes giving the member the special assignment of getting more involvement on the part of the other team members can be very fruitful.

The Non-Verbal or Quiet Learning Group Member

- The use of the Sequential Brainstorming technique and the Analysis techniques which seek group members' opinions by going in rotation, is an excellent way of bringing out the non-verbal or quiet team member.

- Using that group member's first name in directing a question to them is sometimes necessary.

The Negative Learning Group Member

- In many groups there are members who disagree with nearly every suggestion made. When this happens, the other group members soon become discouraged and, typically, will threaten to drop out unless this problem is brought under control.

- The real danger is that negativism is contagious. The best way to counter negativism is with enthusiasm and a positive outlook. This may be frustrating for you as the leader or facilitator, but you must remember that enthusiasm is even more contagious than negativism.

- Ask the negative group member, "What would you do?" This forces them into a position of put up or shut up. When he or she does make a suggestion it may evoke the same treatment that they have been giving to others. One or more of these experiences may result in improvement.

- Use a Verbal Responding Skill of Reflection or paraphrasing the negative input back to the group member. The shock of hearing how badly his or her statement sounds can often assist in causing a change.

- Give the negative group member additional assignments to carry out. This type of person is often an energy source that feels that his or her capabilities are being underutilized. If this the case, the leader or facilitator has nothing to lose and everything to gain by making this person a hard working contributing member of the team through increasing his or her responsibilities and workload.

- Giving the negative group member the task of being the substitute leader or facilitator for a session often gives them insight into their behavior.

- When all else fails, you as the leader or facilitator must have a private counseling/coaching session with the negative group member.

The Recognition Seeking Learning Group Member

- This group member likes to let the team know who he or she is by boasting and by telling of his or her personal achievements. The braggart can be an annoying disruptive force in the learning group.

- Give recognition to the whole learning group and not the individual. Give recognition to a learning group member who has been a good participant without the need for recognition. Give little to no recognition to the recognition seeker.

- Again this learning group member's need for recognition can be used to the advantage of both the individual and the whole learning group.

The Playboy or Playgirl

- These disruptive learning members flaunt their disinterest in the learning with nonchalance, horseplay, cynical remarks, and "cute" jokes.

- As the instructor or facilitator you can direct attention away from the playboy or playgirl by failing to reward them with attention.

- Again this negative behavior learning member may require a private coaching session to determine the cause of the disruptive behavior.

Chapter 19
◊X◊X◊X◊ Adult Instructor's Self-Appraisal ◊X◊X◊X◊

HOW DO I RATE?

ATMOSPHERE FOR LEARNING
- Do I know the names of my learners?
- Do my learners experience a feeling of being welcome?
- Is there a genuine feeling of cooperation between trainer and learner?
- Is the classroom or learning space attractive, well lighted, and comfortable?
- Do I create an atmosphere that "We are going to learn something worthwhile in this course"?

IMAGE AS THE INSTRUCTOR
- Am I interested in each individual learner's needs and responses.
- Do I speak clearly and distinctly?
- Is my classroom or learning space appearance pleasing?
- Do I smile and radiate enthusiasm?
- Do I earn the respect of my learners?
- Do I make learning an exciting experience?
- Am I on time for my classes?
- Do I really enjoy facilitating the learning of adults?

INSTRUCTING PROCEDURES
- Do I prepare a detailed lesson plan for each learning experience?
- Do I provide special lesson materials to meet individual learning differences?
- Am I versatile in the use of teaching devices?
- Do I make full use of training aids (audio-visual, interactive learning materials)?
- Is imagination exercised in developing lesson materials?
- Is there an element of surprise in every lesson?
- Is the material *learner focused* with shared, participative activities?
- Have I structured and sequenced the material according to the levels of learning?

PSYCHOLOGY OF APPROACH
- Do I treat my learners as adults?
- What efforts do I make to motivate the learners' learning?
- Am I effectively using knowledge of motivation and management of behavior?
- Is three-way communication encouraged?
- Do I develop an attitude of supportiveness in the learning process?
- Do the learners share in identifying and developing goals?
- Do I utilize every opportunity to praise and commend learners?
- Am I a good Pygmalion and Model for facilitating adults to learn?

PART IV
□•□•□•□• *EVALUATING* •□•□•□•□

Chapter 20
∫◊∫◊∫ The Instructing and the Instructor ∫◊∫◊∫
Benchmarking

Evaluation of the instructing and the instructor are important for the continuous improvement for the next group of learners. Without feedback the trainer does not know how effective or ineffective the training has been as a whole and whether some particular unit needs revamping or is fine the way it is.

LEARNING EVALUATION FORM

Instructor_____

Date_____

Course_____

Your assistance is needed in providing feedback as to the quality of the trainer and the training you received. The purpose is to provide honest and candid information so that improvements can be made or material kept the same in future presentations.

Make a check after each item. Please refer to the **Rating Standards** on the following pages for clarification and definitions of each area. Thank you for taking the time to complete this evaluation form.

INSTRUCTION - TRAINING

		Unsatisfactory		Average	Outstanding	
		1	2	3	4	5
01.	Knowledge of Subject	----	----	----	----	----
02.	Preparation and Planning	----	----	----	----	----
03.	Lesson Introduction	----	----	----	----	----
04.	Lesson Development	----	----	----	----	----
05.	Lesson Summary	----	----	----	----	----
06.	Questioning Technique	----	----	----	----	----
07.	Learner Participation	----	----	----	----	----
08.	Selection and use of Training Aids	----	----	----	----	----
09.	Introduction to Exercises	----	----	----	----	----
10.	Conducting of Exercises	----	----	----	----	----
11.	Achievement of Objectives	----	----	----	----	----

INSTRUCTOR

12.	Interest and Enthusiasm	----	----	----	----	----
13.	Appearance and Bearing	----	----	----	----	----
14.	Speech	----	----	----	----	----
15.	Platform Manner	----	----	----	----	----
16.	Control	----	----	----	----	----
17.	Management	----	----	----	----	----

GUIDE TO RATING STANDARDS FOR THE
INSTRUCTOR/INSTRUCTING EVALUATION FORM

DIRECTIONS

Ratings: Use the rating standards defined below to assign a numerical grade to each of the listed items. If any item is not applicable to the particular training, use the letters NA - not applicable. Obviously, it is unlikely that any individual will match perfectly the description of any level. The placement of an individual at a particular level for any item is an approximation; that is, the description of the assigned level comes the closest to describing the training or the trainer.

Comments.   Any comments or explanatory remarks may be written on the back of the rating form.

RATING STANDARDS - BENCHMARKS

INSTRUCTION - TRAINING

1.   Knowledge of Subject
UNSATISFACTORY – 1   Fundamental knowledge lacking; appears devoid of allied information; frequent errors of fact; many ambiguities and misleading statements; frequently bluffs to cover up inadequacies; avoids answering direct questions on subject.

BELOW AVERAGE – 2   Information bordering on the inadequate; information disjointed, superficial; occasional errors in fact; occasional ambiguities and misleading statements; sometimes tries to bluff.

AVERAGE – 3   Knowledge limited to specific area of training responsibility but clearly adequate for present training duties; average command of information in instructional field; organized.

ABOVE AVERAGE – 4   Accurate and well-organized knowledge of field; a strong background in subject being trained; comfortable knowledge of allied fields; uses variety of illustrative materials.

OUTSTANDING – 5   Demonstrates mastery of subject; genuine scholarship; rich store of information pertinent to situation; exceptionally well-chosen illustrations; wide knowledge of related fields; well organized.

2.   Preparation and Planning

UNSATISFACTORY - 1   Little or no planning in evidence; no provision made for individual differences, objectives undefined, unattainable, or unrealistic; organization haphazard; fails to provide for integration with other lessons.

BELOW AVERAGE - 2   Planning incomplete and superficial; provision made for meeting needs of faster or slower learners with little regard for others; objectives not clearly defined; organization and continuity somewhat lacking; extremely limited provision for integration

AVERAGE - 3   Obviously planned, and with some imagination; shows consideration for individual and class differences; objectives clearly defined; organization adequate; simple to complex order emphasized; recognizes the need for integration; method and techniques appropriate.

ABOVE AVERAGE - 4   Very well prepared; material well organized; evidence of thoughtful planning; objectives clearly and well defined; plans for meeting individual and class differences; selects an appropriate variety of techniques and materials; provides for integration.

OUTSTANDING - 5   Completely and thoroughly prepared; imaginative planning; intelligent comprehensive organization of material; evidence of complete and thoughtful planning for meeting individual and class differences; objectives valid, attainable, and clearly set forth; techniques sleeted require learner participation; provision for integration.

3.   Lesson Introduction

Each initial lesson in a sequence of lessons requires a clear explanation of purpose, scope, and importance. Succeeding lessons in a continuous block of instruction require only that the trainer show how the lesson ties in with the complete sequence.

UNSATISFACTORY - 1   Introduction completely devoid of imagination and ingenuity; fails to secure learner attention; purpose and objectives not clearly stated; importance of material not mentioned; fails to relate instruction to preceding or succeeding lessons.

BELOW AVERAGE - 2   Secures class attention, but with considerable effort; superficially defines purpose and objectives; outlines scope of lesson; stresses importance of material; inadequately relates instruction to preceding or succeeding lessons.

AVERAGE - 3   Secures class attention; adequately defines purpose and objectives; outlines scope of lesson; stresses importance of material. For the second and succeeding hours of a continuous block of instruction, secures attention and ties in the work of the hour to that of preceding hour(s).

ABOVE AVERAGE - 4   Captures attention effectively and effortlessly; clearly explains purposes and objectives; stresses importance of material to individual; fully defines the scope of the lesson; and/or refers the learner to related materials.

OUTSTANDING - 5   Uses imagination and ingenuity in securing immediate and undivided attention of class; defines purpose and objectives of lesson clearly and fully; sells importance and meaningfulness of material to the individual; provides an interesting overview of the scope of the lesson; and/or clearly relates present instruction to materials previously learned.

4.   Lesson Development

UNSATISFACTORY - 1   Presentation   fails   because   of   poor organization, lack of unity, or inappropriate method or techniques; techniques bungled; individual differences ignored; fails to understand learner difficulties; instruction is unquestionably dull, prosaic, and plodding; learner reaction neither solicited nor encouraged; "floored" by the unexpected; examples need illustrations lacking.

BELOW AVERAGE - 2   A barely acceptable presentation because of faulty organization, abrupt transitions, marginal application of techniques; instruction borders on the dull, prosaic, and plodding; no use made of learner leads; trainer relatively inflexible; reads notes frequently; treatment of learners impartial but unsympathetic; frequently fails to understand learner learning difficulties; illustrations or examples infrequently used or inappropriate.

AVERAGE - 3   A reasonably good presentation, well organized; techniques appropriate but limited in variety; attends to obvious learner difficulties; subject matter sometimes emphasized to the exclusion of individual learner needs; uses note inconspicuously; usually makes transitions smoothly; some use made of learner leads; handles most unexpected situations well; uses appropriate illustrations and examples.

ABOVE AVERAGE - 4   A very good lesson, well organized, interesting and informative, understandable and clear; good transitions; appropriate variety in techniques and materials; effectively uses learner contributions and leads; handles the unexpected quite well; adapts work to individual needs with better than average success; uses examples and illustrations effectively.

OUTSTANDING - 5   A fine lesson, exceptionally well organized, interesting, coherent, unified; variety of techniques and materials used skillfully; smooth transitions from one phase of lesson to another; clever and unique approach; flexible; resourceful in meeting unanticipated situations; ingeniously exploits learner contributions; thoroughly understands learning difficulties of learners; uses many vivid and apt illustrations and examples.

5.   Lesson Summary

Each concluding lesson in a block of instruction requires a complete and comprehensive summary, in which the main teaching points are emphasized and further applications are delimited, and a strong closing statement. Preceding lessons within the block require only periodic internal summaries.

UNSATISFACTORY - 1   No summary provided - or simply makes a token effort to summarize.

BELOW AVERAGE - 2   Internal summaries lacking; merely restates scope of lesson or hurriedly recaps training points.

AVERAGE - 3   Recaps main learning points; clears up learner confusion.

ABOVE AVERAGE - 4   Evidence of careful attention to summary; recaps effectively; re-emphasizes main training points; clarifies difficult areas; uses a closing statement.

OUTSTANDING - 5   Uses imagination and originality in concluding the lesson; recapitulation is complete and comprehensive; primary training points are emphasized and difficult areas clarified; new relationships are defined; strong closing statement.

6.   Questioning Technique

UNSATISFACTORY - 1   No evidence of planning; questions unsuited to class situation because of irrelevance, vagueness, or vocabulary level; learner questions discouraged; questions fragmentary or inconsequential; handles responses poorly; often misunderstands learner questions or the reason for the confusion that prompted the question.

BELOW AVERAGE - 2   Inadequate planning in evidence; questions call for little learner thought; questions not well distributed; frequently violates mechanics of asking questions; questions poorly framed; responses not fully exploited; learners afforded very limited opportunity to ask questions; sometimes fails to understand learner questions.

AVERAGE - 3   Some   evidence   of   planning;   questions reasonably well formulated and understood by learner; uses some thought-provoking questions; mechanics of questioning satisfactory; learner questions and responses handled adequately.

ABOVE AVERAGE - 4   Evidence of planning; uses suitable questions which produce interested and generally effective learner responses; frames thought-providing questions; uses correct procedures; distributes questions and provides excellent answers.

OUTSTANDING - 5   Evidence of careful planning for the use of questions; unusually skilled in asking questions which elicit responses related to the objective; questions widely distributed among class; handles learner questions and responses exceptionally well; employs learner responses to move the lesson forward; encourages learner questions and provides clear and complete answers.

7.   Learner Participation

UNSATISFACTORY - 1   Trainer unable to obtain participation or trainer unwilling to encourage participation; learners obviously sullen or rebellious; learners hesitate or afraid to take part because of poor trainer-learner rapport.   Trainer obviously unable to generate interest; learners bored, restless, or inattentive.

BELOW AVERAGE - 2   Environment created by trainer fails to elicit general interest and participation; many learners reluctant to take part; participation obtained by compulsion; trainer depends upon a few aggressive learners for reaction; some imbalance in learner-trainer active participation.   Learner interest and attention marginal; lapses in attention frequent and sustained.

AVERAGE - 3   Real interest in participating aroused in most learners; timid and weaker learners not responding; adequate balance of learner-trainer active participation, consistent with method used.   Trainer attends more to capable, self-confident learners.   Learners interested and attentive with only occasional and temporary lapses.

ABOVE AVERAGE - 4   Most learners willing to participate; learners with the trainer all the way; only a few learners must be cajoled into taking part; excellent balance of learner-trainer active participation.   Learners interested, show that they are with the trainer; lapses in attention rare.

OUTSTANDING - 5   Participation spontaneous; atmosphere created by trainer encourages learner participation; all learners eager to take part; learners assume responsibility for their own learning; proper balance of learner-trainer active participation maintained, consistent with method used.   Learners evidence high interest in the presentation, "hanging on every word" and eagerly participate in every exercise; attention sustained throughout the session.

8.   Selection and use of training aids

UNSATISFACTORY - 1   Training aids inadequate or lacking; aids fail to illustrate the point; trainer and class unprepared for use of aids; aids used as crutches; aids do not augment verbal instruction; aids handled in a clumsy fashion; explanation sketchy and insufficient.

BELOW AVERAGE - 2   Poor judgment in selection of types of aid; incomplete preparation for use; lesson constructed around aids prepared for other instruction; aids used solely as "eyewash"; transition between aids lacks smoothness; mechanics of using aids occasionally mishandled.

AVERAGE - 3   Training aids adequate - illustrate the point; evidence of preparation and acquaintance with aids; aids introduced at proper time and used with satisfactory skill.

ABOVE AVERAGE - 4   Shows imagination and originality in the selection and development of aids; well prepared for the use of aids; aids smoothly displayed; aids integrated into lesson; excellent accompanying explanation; mechanics of use of aids well handled.

OUTSTANDING - 5   Shows exceptional imagination and ingenuity in the selection and development of training aids; evidence of careful and complete preparation for the use of the aids; aids displayed smoothly and skillfully; aids completely integrated into the lesson; accompanying explanation crystal-clear and complete; mechanics of use of aids exceptionally well handled.

9.   Introduction to Exercises

The initial lesson of an extended practical exercise requires a clear definition of purpose, scope, and importance. Succeeding lessons require only a definition of the relationship of a specific exercise to the complete sequence.

UNSATISFACTORY - 1   Introduction devoid of imagination; fails to secure learner interest and attention; purpose and objectives not clearly stated; standards of acceptable performance not defined; importance of the exercise not mentioned; fails to relate the experience or practice to preceding of succeeding sessions; directions learners incomplete or unclear.

BELOW AVERAGE - 2   Secures class attention, but with considerable effort; purpose and objectives superficially defined; importance of experience or practice session not mentioned; inadequately relates experience or practice to preceding or succeeding sessions; directions to learners bordering on the inadequate.

AVERAGE - 3   Secures class attention; adequately defines purpose and objectives; emphasizes importance of the experience or practice; presents specific and clear directions; answers questions about procedures and succeeding hours of experiences or practice in a long practical exercise secures attention and ties in the work of the hour to that of preceding hour(s).

ABOVE AVERAGE - 4   Captures attention effectively and effortlessly; clearly explains purposes and objectives; stresses importance of the material; clearly defines what the student is to do; sets standards of performance that are realistic; demonstrates where necessary; answers questions clearly and lucidity.

OUTSTANDING - 5   Uses imagination and ingenuity in securing immediate and undivided attention of the class; defines purposes and objectives clearly and fully; sells importance of the experience or practice session sets realistic standards; demonstrates procedures when necessary; follows up by setting standards for individual learners (where applicable); ties lesson in neatly with preceding and following experience and practice sessions.

10.   Conducting of Exercises

UNSATISFACTORY - 1   An unprofitable experience; poorly organized, unrealistic; inappropriate techniques used; session drudgery for learners; learner difficulties ignored; fails to check on learners' progress and performance; discourages learners; provides no direction or guidance.

BELOW AVERAGE - 2   A barely acceptable exercise; organization barely adequate; main techniques appropriate; some lack of imagination evident; practice borders on drudgery; monotony evident; insufficient direction provided for some learners; checks on learner progress are spotty; little encouragement given; not all learners are informed of their progress.

AVERAGE - 3   A worthwhile exercise or practice session; well organized and realistic; techniques appropriate but limited in variety; attends to obvious learner difficulties; repeats instructions when needed; keeps learners busy; checks effectively on individual progress; encourages learners; informs learns of the quality of their performance at intervals.

ABOVE AVERAGE - 4   A very good exercise or practice session, well organized and realistic; used a variety of techniques to overcome monotony of exercise or practice; cleverly adjusted work and standards to individual needs; understands and attends to specific learner difficulties; keeps learners constantly informed of their progress; uses encouragement and praise judiciously. In initial exercise or practice session, provides close supervision of step-by-step performance. May give instruction to individuals and small groups apart from the remainder of the class. Where applicable; singles out specific element of skill for isolated practice; combines specific elements of skill into exercise for overall practice; uses problems.

OUTSTANDING - 5   An excellent exercise, exceptionally well organized, interesting, and realistic; variety of techniques used; clever and unique approaches; cleverly adjust work to individual needs; ideal exercise and practice conditions set up for each group and learner; exceptionally effective motivational techniques used; learners kept purposefully occupied; progress of learners continually checked; competition with past records emphasized.

11.   Achievement of Objectives
UNSATISFACTORY - 1   No apparent check made of learner learning; check made are totally ineffective; lesson objectives clearly not achieved.

BELOW AVERAGE - 2   Inadequate check made of learner learning; remedial techniques ineffective or inappropriate; achievement of objectives questionable.

AVERAGE - 3   Uses some means for determining extent to which learners have learned; utilizes adequate remedial techniques; indications point to satisfactory achievement of most learners.

ABOVE AVERAGE - 4   Uses excellent means for determining the extent to which objectives have been achieved; checks periodically on learner understanding and achievement; uses good remedial techniques; all learning checks and other observations indicate that lesson objectives have been thoroughly achieved by the class, with a few possible exceptions.

OUTSTANDING - 5   Uses clear-cut and definite means of determining level of learner achievement; checks periodically and thoroughly on learner understanding achievement; difficulties revealed by checks receive immediate attention; remedial training exceptionally effective; all indications point to superior achievement of lesson objectives by the class.

INSTRUCTOR – TRAINER

12.   Interest and Enthusiasm
UNSATISFACTORY - 1   Unenthusiastic; always seems to say the wrong thing; uncouth or impolite; flustered, hurried; strained and impatient; negligent; critical and fault finding; harsh; definitely unfriendly or too familiar, no real interest shown in the subject.

BELOW AVERAGE - 2   Somewhat oversensitive; easily upset; often hurts learner feelings; somewhat unconventional in terms of polite practices; aloof; talks down to learners; impatient; cold; hesitant, timid, apologetic, wavering; somewhat, little enthusiasm shown

AVERAGE - 3   Somewhat upset by the unexpected, usually patient; civil; conforms to conventional practices; somewhat serious, reserved, or exacting; generally says the wise thing; constant, moderately, sometimes shows enthusiasm.

ABOVE AVERAGE - 4   Cheerful; well balanced; courteous; poised, but with some effort; tries to be objective; tactful in most situations; friendly, with an understanding, adult point of view; decisive; determined; steady, enthusiastic.

OUTSTANDING - 5   Enthusiastic about the subject, the learners and demonstrates it at all times; always courteous and poised; objectively decisive; enthusiastic; conveys interest in subject; considerate of students; friendly, but avoids over familiarity; dynamic and assertive; displays sense of humor; able to see learner's point of view; confident.

13.   **Appearance and Bearing**

UNSATISFACTORY - 1   Untidy in attire and personal care; posture and bearing poor.

BELOW AVERAGE - 2   Somewhat careless in attire; details of personal care show neglect; posture and bearing somewhat deficient.

AVERAGE - 3   Moderately neat and well groomed; details of personal care generally satisfactory; adequate posture and bearing.

ABOVE AVERAGE - 4   An excellent model and standard in appearance; clothing person neat, clean and well groomed; good posture and carriage, excellent bearing.

OUTSTANDING - 5   A near-perfect model and standard in appearance; evidence of special attention to fit and press of clothing; scrupulously neat, clean and well groomed; fine bearing and posture.

14.   **Speech**

UNSATISFACTORY - 1   Very deficient in grammar or vocabulary; uneven, excessively choppy speech; too rapid; too slow and drawling; noticeably defective, frequent mispronunciations.

BELOW AVERAGE - 2   Slurred; not articulate; may grope for words; choppy - many vocalized pauses; limited vocabulary; repeats pet words and phrases; uses slang; uses words beyond the comprehension of the class; careless in use of English.

AVERAGE - 3   Speaks without difficulty; fee from undesirable speech habits; makes few errors in English usage; uses reasonably good choice of words.

ABOVE AVERAGE - 4   Speaks with ease and precision; conversational, with informal correctness; good choice of words; uses appropriate inflection and emphasis.

OUTSTANDING - 5   Articulates and enunciates clearly, correctly, naturally and vividly; superior command of English; fluent expression; colorful vocabulary.

15.   Instructing Manner

UNSATISFACTORY - 1   Body movements stilted, meaningless, or affected; stares at floor, ceiling or one spot in the room; continually shifts eyes without fixing on any individual; depends completely on notes; possesses extremely distracting mannerisms; movements awkward, repetitious, or meaningless.

BELOW AVERAGE - 2   Body movement or gestures infrequently used; stays rooted to one spot; movements bordering on the stilted or affected; indecisive - often loses eye contact; frequent distracting mannerisms; often stiff, unnatural, or excessive.

AVERAGE - 3   Body movements typically natural and meaningful; usually decisive; usually maintains eye contact; occasional distracting mannerisms in evidence; Movements are decisive, and purposeful (in contrast with random, excessive movements which serve only as an outlet for nervous energy).

ABOVE AVERAGE - 4   Body movements appropriate, natural, purposeful; eye contact consistently maintained; mannerisms rarely distracting, movements purposeful and natural; few unplanned and random movements.

OUTSTANDING - 5   Body movements always natural, meaningful, decisive, emphatic, eye contact smooth and continuous, direct - encompasses entire class; personal; completely free from distracting mannerisms of movements and actions; no evidences of nervousness; movements in the room or on the platform, always planned, decisive, and purposeful.

16.   Control

UNSATISFACTORY - 1   Disrespect and disorder in evidence; trainer not aware of centers of difficulty; lacks ability to individualize problem areas; uses ridicule, sarcasm, threatens.

BELOW AVERAGE - 2   Some control problems in evidence; trainer recognizes centers of difficulty but deals with them ineffectively; uses threats, reprimands, ridicule, or sarcasm to maintain order.

AVERAGE - 3   Control adequate; some minor difficulties may be in evidence; control secured through setting limits, giving expectations, infrequent reprimands, cajolement, or coaxing, uses praise and reinforcement

ABOVE AVERAGE - 4   Group well controlled; control secured primarily through trainer's personality, effectively uses praise and selective reinforcement to obtain desired course results; learners desire for trainers approval; handles problems well, sets limits.

OUTSTANDING - 5   Class interested, attentive; control strong; control primarily secured through interest in class activities, trainer patients, excellent use of praise, corrections, selective reinforcement of desired behaviors and learning outcomes; trainer tactfulness, effectiveness in dealing with problems, and having learners accountable for their own learning.

17.   Management

UNSATISFACTORY - 1   Haphazard management practices; routines poorly managed; materials of instruction unavailable when needed; continuous confusion; little or no regard shown for environmental conditions (heat, light, ventilation, etc.); seating arrangement inappropriate for type of training or lesson.

BELOW AVERAGE - 2   No consistent management practices; some confusion; materials of instruction on hand but in disorder; only token attention given to environmental conditions: classroom and seating arrangements marginal.

AVERAGE - 3   Training room orderly; routines satisfactorily managed; materials of instruction available but not ideally arranged; some attention paid to environmental conditions; room and seating arrangement adequate.

ABOVE AVERAGE - 4   Training room routines well managed; adequate attention given to environmental conditions; instructional materials available and ready to use; room arrangements suited to training; seating adequate.

OUTSTANDING - 5   Training room techniques managed rapidly, quietly, and efficiently; careful attention to environmental conditions; instructional materials readily accessible and ready to use; room arranged most advantageously for planned training; seating arrangements ideally set up. **(End)**

Chapter 21
(((((o))))) Learning Effectiveness Assessment (((((o)))))

Need for Evaluation:

Instruction and development staffs have become more and more accountable for the effectiveness of their programs. Evaluation can be used to determine whether the instruction achieves its objectives. Evaluation can also assess the value of the learning, identify improvement areas, and identify unnecessary learning that can be eliminated. (Kirkpatrick, Kramer & Salinger, 1994).

Many instructing professionals agree that evaluation is important to successful learning, but few conduct complete and thorough evaluations. Evaluation can seem anti-climatic to the excitement and creativity of creating a new course. Typically evaluation is an afterthought or not done at all. Evaluation builds in rigor. It's an integral part of the whole quality effort. If you don't measure, how do you know whether what you've done is worthwhile?

With more emphasis on return on investment (ROI), organizations and educational institutions are asking what is the value of instruction. Too often, instruction departments have little or no idea how their instruction relates to the objectives of the organization. This could be due partially to instructors' lack of measurement and evaluation skills, which result in measurements that are not valid, reliable or even useful to the management of the organization.

The training department that measures increase in number of participants is in trouble. A training department that is concerned only with counting the number of participants in seats probably isn't measuring whether the trainees learned anything or whether the skills they learned are helping them to perform their jobs more effectively.

One of the most widely used models for evaluating training programs is one that was proposed in 1959 by Donald L. Kirkpatrick when he was at the University of Wisconsin. The model maintains that there are four levels to measure the quality or effectiveness of a training course. Moving down the column, the matrix presents these levels, in order, from simple and inexpensive to complex and costly. Each level has its advantages and disadvantages. It is important to plan the evaluation process as the instructing is being planned. It is important to consider all levels at the outset, even though only one or two levels may be used ultimately.

The following is a description of Kirkpatrick's 4 levels of evaluating training:

Donald Kirkpatrick's 4 Levels of Evaluating Training

Levels		Description	Comments
Level 1	Reaction	Trainee reaction to the course. Does the trainee like the course? Usually in the form of evaluation forms, sometimes called "smile sheets".	Most primitive and widely-used method of evaluation. It is easy, quick, and inexpensive to administer. Negative indicators could mean difficultly learning in the course.
Level 2	Learning	Did trainees learn what was based on the course objectives?	Learning can be measured by pre- and post tests, either through written test or through performance tests.
Level 3	Transfer Behavior	Trainee behavior changes on the job - are the learners applying what they learned?	Difficult to do. Follow up questionnaire or observations after training class has occurred. Telephone interviews can also be conducted.
Level 4	Results Outcome Measurable Outcome Purpose of the Training	Ties training to the company's bottom line. Offenders - Job Retention	Generally applies to training that seeks to overcome a business problem caused by lack of knowledge or skill. Examples include reductions in costs, turnover, absenteeism and grievances. May be difficult to tie directly to training.

(Kirkpatrick, 1959), (Kirkpatrick, 1975)

Information from each prior level serves as a base for the next level's evaluation. Thus, each successive level represents a more precise measure of the effectiveness of the training program, but at the same time requires a more rigorous and time-consuming analysis.

Level 1 Evaluation - Reactions
You evaluate the reaction of people to a training course. What participants felt about a learning.

Survey participants and ask them questions about the quality of the learning and their satisfactions with it.

Just as the word implies, evaluation at this level measures how participants in a training program react to it. It attempts to answer questions regarding the participants' perceptions - Did they like it? Was the material relevant to their work? Every program should at least be evaluated at this level to provide for the improvement of a training program. In addition, the participants' reactions have important consequences for learning (level two). Although a positive reaction does not guarantee learning, a negative reaction almost certainly reduces its possibility.

This is the most commonly-used method of evaluation, probably because it is the easiest type of evaluation to administer and evaluate. This level produces what some people dub the "smile sheet", which measures how well the students like the learning.

Level 2 Evaluation - Learning
You evaluate the learning of people by seeing what facts, techniques and principles are learned.

Criteria: Relate Course Objectives - Performance Objectives against desired Measurable Outcomes over a 3, 6 month and one year period of time.

You assess participants as to what knowledge they learned from the training. For example: You give a test at the start of the course and another test at the end of the training. The difference shows the learning that took place.

Assessing at this level moves the evaluation beyond learner satisfaction and attempts to assess the extent students have advanced in skills, knowledge, or attitude. Measurement at this level is more difficult and laborious than level one. Methods range from formal to informal testing to team assessment and self-assessment. If possible, participants take the test or assessment before the learning event (pretest) and after the learning event (post test) to determine the amount of learning that has occurred.

Level 2 (Learning) is not as well-used in business settings as an evaluation technique; school settings are more likely to use Level 2 evaluation techniques. The message that managers are delivering is that the training department needs to show concrete evidence that learning is achieving its goals of changing behavior on the job (Level 3) and is also contributing to the company's bottom line (Level 4). Reasons for this include the influence of the quality movement and its emphasis on measurement, cost cutting measures which forces training departments to use money more wisely. Instructors are realizing that their goal is to effect results, not just to put people in seats. Another reason attributed to the increased interest in evaluation is the rise of technology, which has eased much of the burden of data-gathering for evaluating learning. (Geber, 1995).

Level 3 Evaluation - Transfer: Behavior, Skills, and Attitude Change
Measure Actions and Behavior Change - compare with Plan created in the course building phase.

Need measure of their behavior and skills at time of entering the instruction and after completion of the learning event.

You evaluate behavior by seeing whether the course actually modified people's behavior and skills. You are evaluating not just the knowledge learned during or from the learning event, but how it impacts on their job and other areas of their life. For example, you might look at someone three months after the instruction to see if they do their job better. (Need a criteria - measurable - What objectively is: "Do their job better.")

This level measures the transfer that has occurred in learners' behavior due to the training program. Evaluating at this level attempts to answer the question - Are the newly acquired skills, knowledge, or attitude being used in the everyday environment of the learner? For many instructors believe this level represents the truest assessment of a program's effectiveness. However, measuring at this level is difficult as it is often impossible to predict when the change in behavior will occur, and thus requires important decisions in terms of when to evaluate, how often to evaluate, and how to evaluate.

Level 4 Evaluation- Results: Outcomes - Measurable Changer - Adult Learners

Instructors, Facilitators, Organization and Community

You evaluate the effectiveness of course on the results of an organization. This evaluates not whether the course helps the individual, but whether it helps the business aims of the organization.

For example: work out whether the organization meets its business aims better or is more profitable because of the learning.

Frequently thought of as the bottom line, this level measures the success of the program in terms that managers and executives can understand -increased production, improved quality, decreased costs, reduced frequency of accidents, increased sales, and even higher profits or return on investment. From a business and organizational perspective, this is the overall reason for a training program, yet level four results are not typically addressed. Determining results in financial terms is difficult to measure, and is hard to link directly with training.

Measurable Outcomes - Against a predetermined Criteria: evaluations may be actually easier to accomplish than Level 3, since Level 4 evaluations are tied to measurable information. Some instructors believe that a positive Level 3 evaluation implies success at Level 4. Some executives are willing to assume that if employees are exhibiting the desired behavior on the job (Level 3) that it will have positive influence on the company's bottom line.

Unfortunately, for most instructors, doing Level 3 and Level 4 evaluations are the "trainer's equivalent of flossing your teeth" Instructors will probably not do Level 3 and Level 4 evaluations unless they are told to do so. However, executives who are getting sophisticated measurements from the rest of the organization also expect the same from the training department.

Even though more difficult, Level 3 and Level 4 evaluations do provide other advantages besides contributing to company goals. These evaluations can be a "value added" service that the training department can provide. They can also be instrumental in overhauling current curriculum; if a course is not meeting organization objectives, then either change the course or stop offering the course all together. Eliminating unnecessary training could positively affect the company's bottom line. Another benefit of deeper evaluations is that it can uncover the barriers that prevent the learning from being applied to the job.

Design and Implementation

To collect accurate information with evaluation instruments, you need a basic knowledge of statistics and research methods. You need to know how to use various instruments and be able to select the most appropriate instrument for each evaluation. Multiple instruments should be used in any evaluation. Each instrument has inherent strengths and weaknesses. Multiple instruments can compensate for the weakness in another instrument or complement the strengths in another. Multiple instruments also provide more credibility and may produce different results that could be missed with a single evaluation instrument.

Conducting evaluations, particularly Level 3 and Level 4 evaluations, can seem overwhelming, and if it is done as an afterthought it can be very difficult to do. However, it is much easier to design evaluation into the training as the course is being developed. Evaluation must be plotted while the course is still a fresh idea.

(Here the Instructing and Instructor (Benchmarks) comes in - see previous chapter)

Evaluation Matrix Worksheet

Levels	What might be measured?	What are the data sources?	How should data be collected?	What are potential problems?
Level 1 (Reaction)				
Level 2 (Learning)				
Level 3 (Behavior on job)				
Level 4 (Results)				

The following evaluation matrix worksheet could be used to assist in the design of the evaluation:

Interviews (Level 1, Level 2, Level 3)A face-to-face interview involves an individual responding orally to oral questions asked by an interviewer. Interviews can be either structured or unstructured. Structured interviews consists of a list of predetermined questions. Unstructured interviews begin with standard questions but bases subsequent questions on the interviewee's responses to the previous questions. Interviews provide a means to collect in-depth information from participants who are reluctant to fill out a questionnaires. Interviews can be time-consuming and expensive and must be given by a skilled interviewer. Some participants may be less willing to reveal information in an interview. However, interviews (vs. surveys) are most likely to get people to "tell stories" and give specific illustrations.

Interviews can also be done in small groups of 5-12 people. This type of group interview is often called a "focus group" and can be used to collect in-depth qualitative information. Before the focus group meets, methods for recording, reviewing and synthesizing information need to be established.

Tests (Level 2, Level 3)

Tests can be administered as a standardized method for measuring knowledge (paper and pencil test) and skills (performance test). To be able to measure training effectiveness, pre- and post tests are given to determine change after training.

To increase the effectiveness of the test, the following are suggested:

Draft sample questions during program development; make sure all objectives are included and all questions not related to objectives are deleted. Relevant tests yield more valid results. Review test before administering.

Plan test details: schedule, timing instructions, scoring.

Avoid trick questions or questions with more than one answer. Write questions as clearly as possible.

Use a random arrangement of answers to keep test-takers from guessing the pattern of correct answers.

Vary the difficulty of the questions.

Observations (Level 2, Level 3)

The work behavior of trainees is observed before, during, and after training. A trained observer watches and records the behavior. Sometimes the behavior is videotaped or audiotaped to be able to study later. This method provides evaluation of both verbal and nonverbal behavior. The major disadvantages of observations include modified behavior of the participants as a result of the observers presence, poorly trained observers who collect unreliable data, and observations that are expensive and time-consuming. The impact of the observer can be minimized by carefully choosing observers, giving observers standard forms to fill out, and trying to minimize the presence of the observer.

Performance should be measurable with observable results, based on the objectives for the training program. There should be a systematic appraisal of performance on the job both before and after training to determine changes, if any. The observers could include instructors, supervisors, co-workers or professional observers. As with any post-training evaluation, it must be determined if the performance is a result of training or some other factors. Barriers to using knowledge could include lack of management support, low priority, or lack of proper tools or equipment. Control groups, who do not receive training, can be used to measure other factors. (Kirkpatrick, Kramer & Salinger, 1994).

Performance Records (Level 4)

Performance records can be used to evaluate a training program's effect on the company's bottom line. Data such as costs incurred, amounts produced, revenue generated, or time required to complete tasks, would be measured both before and after training to be able to quantify the effects of training. Any measurable savings to the company could be compared with the actual cost of delivering training.

For example, 360 Feedback, focus on the change in performance of the participants after the learning event: immediate, 3 months, 6 months, one year. Have a control group. Use a pre and post for change in attitude or behavior. Reduction in turnover, illness, absenteeism, EEOC, Affirmative Action inquiries, etc. Improved production and performance outcomes against a predetermined criteria. **Must be criteria based.**

Appendices

Appendix.
(∫) *Behavior Clarifying Approaches* (∫)

Today there are hundreds of books, journal articles and opinion papers and electronic resources espoused "New" information to "up-date" you on theories, approaches and techniques about the subjects in this book. However, to build a house of knowledge you need to start at the base, the foundation upon which the many stories of the house are built. These Appendices are three basic focal points that are major connecting points in creating the solid, lasting foundations. Provided here is a glimpse of what the true scholar of understanding and instructing the adult learner needs to acquire a strong set of building blocks for their body of knowledge.

Appendix A01
// • # • > Motivation and Needs Hierarchies // • # • >

To explain, predict, and control adult behavior the instructor needs to understand motivation. Behavior is a function of the adult interacting with a specific environment. Existing approaches can be conveniently described within this framework. To provide some answers several clarifying approaches are presented for you to integrate into your unending quest for a better understanding and motivation of the adult learner. By examining these approaches you can draw upon them selectively concerning how to better understand and motivate the adult.

Dr. Abraham Maslow

Dr. Abraham Maslow stated that experienced needs are the primary influences on an individual's behavior. When a particular need emerges, it determines the individual's behavior in terms of motivations, priorities, and action taken. Thus motivated behaviors is the result of the tension - either pleasant or unpleasant, - experienced when a need presents itself. The goal of the behavior is the reduction of this tension or discomfort and the behavior itself will be appropriate for facilitating the satisfaction of the need. Only *unsatisfied needs* are prime sources of motivation.

Understanding behaviors and their goals involves gaining insight into presently unsatisfied needs. Dr. Maslow developed a method for gaining insight by providing *categories of needs in a hierarchical structure*. He placed all human needs, in terms of the behaviors they foster, from primitive or immature, to civilized or mature, into an eight leveled need system. He believed that there is a natural process whereby individuals fulfill their needs in ascending order from the most immature to the most mature. This progression throughout the need hierarchy is seen as the climbing of a ladder where the individual must have experienced secure footing on the first rung in order to experience the need to step up to the next higher rung. The awareness of the need to climb further up the ladder is a function of having fulfilled the need of managing the preceding rung. Only satisfactory fulfillment of this need will allow the individual to deal with the new need or rung. Inability to fulfill a lower-order need or difficulty in fulfilling a lower-order need may result in an individual's locking in on immature behavior patterns. This may produce a tendency to return to immature behaviors under stress. When the satisfaction of higher needs are temporarily blocked, the adult may also revert to behaviors which fulfilled lower-order needs This not to say that any need is ever completely satisfied; rather, He indicated that there must be at least partial fulfillment before an adult can become aware of the tensions manifested by a higher-order need and have the freedom and desire to pursue its fulfillment.

Dr. Maslow was concerned primarily with the progressive development of each individual to their fullest potential. He saw the human as having purpose, values, options, and the right and capacity for self-determination. Through their own freewill, they can maximize their potential for growth and happiness.

Dr. Maslow started with the assumption that adults are "wanting humans" and are forever striving for goals of various kinds. He proposed that adults *want* because they need these goals. Furthermore, while the finite expression of these needs may vary from individual to individual and from culture to culture, there are certain fundamental stages of need and growth common to all adults, or at least the potential is present in everyone. Whether an adult reaches the upper plateaus of these potential stages of growth depends upon the degree to which lower-level needs are adequately fulfilled. Dr. Maslow categorized these needs into a conceptual hierarchy - called: **the hierarchy of needs**.

Dr. Maslow's **hierarchy of needs** states that (1) needs are arranged in a hierarchy of importance. and (2) only unfulfilled needs serve to motivate the adult. Also, that until one level of need is fairly well satisfied, the next higher need does not even emerge. Moreover, once a particular set of needs is fairly well satisfied, it no longer motivates. One is not driven to find food if they have a full stomach, or to find safety if one is already safe - although if safety is taken away or threatened, it once again becomes the driving force or motivation. The adult is not motivated to achieve goals that they have already reached. Thus to Dr. Maslow, the adult is driven by different needs: some people for physiological concerns, food, shelter, or clothing, others for security, others for belongingness, self-esteem, and so on. The direction, to Dr. Maslow, is toward *"Self-actualization."* It is important to keep in mind that an adult's motivation is not static, fixed, or "set in concrete." Whatever need is operative at a given time becomes the focus of an adult's striving to achieve satisfaction. Despite the tendency to fall back to a lower-level if a lower-level need is insufficiently met, this lasts only until the need is again satisfied. The adult's motivation is once again directed at the appropriate higher level of need.

Dr. Maslow states explicitly that an adult can be identified as being primarily at a specific level - their current level of prime motivation - at any point in life. Emotionally healthy and mature adults are found striving to satisfy upper-level needs. (Portions from personal communiqués between the authors and the late Dr. Maslow.)

RIPLEYS' HIERARCHY OF HUMAN NEEDS
Updating and Beyond Maslow

	Level	Human Needs
Pair 4	8	Self-Actualization --> Being values
	7	Beauty
Pair 3	6	Understanding
	5	Information
Pair 2	4	Self-Esteem
	3	Belongingness
Pair 1	2	Security
	1	Survival

Many current writers on Maslow show a real lack of depth of understanding of the original hierarchy and only indicate five or six levels in the hierarchy thus the reader is cheated out of a complete picture and understanding of the adult needs. Placing the needs into four pairs can assist in understanding what has happened in our society and where the needs are for the adult learner.

Pair 1 Survival and Security
These levels are primarily taken care of by basic physiological requirements of food, shelter, clothing, and other necessities. However, adults adapt this basic level upward to include such needs as avoidance of physical discomfort, pleasant working environment, or more money for providing creature comforts.

The adult also has to feel secure and safe. When the adult has at least partially fulfilled the basic survival needs, he or she will experience the tensions relating to needs of security, orderliness, protective rules, and general risk avoidance. These needs are often satisfied by an adequate salary, insurance policies, and a good burglar alarm system. The security need is also fulfilled by employment without fear of being fired or replaced.

Pair 2 Belongingness and Self-Esteem

When these survival and security needs have been met, the individual will become less preoccupied with self and will endeavor to form interpersonal relationships. The relative success of this need for Belongingness will result in the adult feeling accepted and appreciated by others. This need used to be nurtured in the early primary grades of the school, on up through high school and on into the workplace. However, today with restrictions on teachers and the school system, the child does not get this feeling of *belongingness* fulfilled and there is a big void that has yet to be filled in later in the workplace. Today there are self-managing teams in the workplace to assist in fulfilling this unfulfilled need. Outside of the workplace, clubs, religious institutions, or even gangs fulfill these needs.

The *Self-Esteem* also used to be fulfilled in the school setting by the teachers and the school system. The clubs, the achievements, the awards, the recognitions, and the school pride were important as developers of Self-Esteem. Today, the adult strives to fulfill these under-developed self-esteem needs in all aspects of their life. It is important for the trainer to understand this societal unfulfilled need development.

If Belongingness and Self-Esteem are increasingly not taken care of by the normal development of the human during the earlier growing up years, then the result is that the adult learning and work environments have to more and more fulfill these needs.

Note: A side result is that little true information or understanding is sought voluntarily without external consequences until this Pair 2 is fulfilled.

Pair 3 Information and Understanding

The schools in our society, do to current laws and personal contact restrictions, have jumped over the belongingness and self-esteem to just pumping information at and into the pupils. The pupil is getting information overload, feeling unfulfilled with seemingly irrelevant information. This leads to a desire to move out of the unfulfilling formal educational environment as quickly as possible.

On the other hand a large percentage of adults in learning situations have moved past just having the need for information. They want to understand what the information means and how to apply what is learned. The adult wants to be involved in their learning and participate in sharing this process with other adults.

Pair 4 Beauty and Self-Actualization

The adult then moves to a need for beauty in their environment. They want beauty in spaces in their home, at their workstation and in their external visited environments. They see beauty in things previously taken for granted and will expend energy to improve the aesthetics of their surroundings.

When the adult is getting their needs, at least partially fulfilled, at all the lower levels, and feel secure in their relationships with others, he or she will probably seek to gain special status within the group. The adults need tension will be associated with ambition and a desire to excel. These needs will motivate the adult to seek out opportunities to display their competence in an effort to gain social and professional rewards. At this Self-Actualization level, the adult is concerned with personal growth and may fulfill this need by challenging themselves to become more creative, demanding greater achievement for himself or herself. In general, they direct themselves to measure up to their own criteria of personal success. Self-Actualizing behaviors must include risk-taking, seeking autonomy, and developing freedom to act.

In fact, most adults of our society are found striving and partially satisfied and unsatisfied in their basic needs at the same time. Everyone has a self-actualizing potential and most reach it in some area of their lives.

What is the relevance of all this?
Well, this contains a wealth of insights into human motivation and can be useful in broadening the trainer's understanding of human nature, and the motivations of those who comprise their learning courses. For example, Dr. Maslow further defined self-actualization to include what he termed **"B-values"** or **Being-values**:. When adults approach levels of self-actualization, they seek after B-values. A large portion of the adults move on into the Being-values. If they fail to realize these values, they can regress into what Maslow termed "meta- pathologies." Say, for example, that a worker is invested in truth but sees the boss telling a half-truth or "white lie." The boss' activity then throws the individual worker into the

dilemma of either confronting the boss or living with the resulting bad feelings which, if repeated time after time, produces chronic bad feeling. With energy going into this area, the worker's productivity will decrease.

In the modern industry and business setting, most employees have their physiological and basic/safety needs - and to a large extent their belonging needs - satisfied by the job. The important part is what the employee does not have satisfied - their psychological needs of self-esteem and self-actualization. The key to real motivation lies in providing the adult the opportunity to satisfy the upper-level needs. And remember that "a satisfied need no longer motivates." However it can become a dissatisfier should it be temporarily unmet.

As these needs are being met, the adult need fulfillment moves more into the **Being-values**. These are the needs of mature adults that need to be filled or act as motivators for unfulfilled needs. (personal communiqué with the late Dr. Abraham Maslow)

Dr. Maslow said that adults have certain needs that go far beyond the physiological needs of hunger and shelter, or psychological needs like safety and security, or even love and esteem and a sense of belonging. These others -- which he called "growth needs" -- grow out of the adult's hunger for things like truth and goodness, which he called **being-values**. These growth needs produce a kind of hunger of the spirit for which the **being-values** provide a kind of food.

Think back to some activity that you found very satisfying -- or, from a negative viewpoint, one that you found very unsatisfying. It can be from your experiences in jobs, learning, work or play. Then begin drafting a description of it in terms of the being-values listed below.

Truth Did the activity allow you to know and to experience some sort of truth? Did it give you a chance to offer this truth to other people?

Goodness Did it get you beyond yourself, doing some good for other people in some way?

Beauty Did it allow you to create or experience what you felt to be real beauty: If so, how? Was the activity itself beautiful? Or was the product beautiful? Or the setting? Or the other people who were involved?

Unity Did the activity allow you to create some new whole, some new unity? Did it give you a chance to take things or situations that were broken up or disorganized and to put them together? Was there a sense of cooperation in the activity?

Completion Did it allow you to feel that you have really accomplished something, really completed it? How did you know when you were done with a complete act?

Order Was there a kind of orderliness about the activity? Did the orderliness seem natural or artificial? How did the orderliness avoid becoming monotonous? Did you yourself get the feeling that you were somehow helping bring order out of chaos?

Meaningfulness Did it seem to have some larger or more general meaning beyond itself? Is so, what was it? Would you have done it anyhow, without pay or pressure, just because of its basic meaningfulness? If it was meaningful beyond itself, how did it avoid becoming solemn and heavy?

Simplicity   Did the activity have a satisfying simplicity about it? If so, how exactly?   And how did the simplicity keep from becoming monotonous? Or on the contrary, did the activity seem to appeal to some sort of need for richness and variety? If so, how did it avoid becoming cluttered and busy? Were there general patterns or rhythms at work in the variety?

Aliveness   Did the activity seem to be involved with life? With fullness rather than with emptiness or hollowness? Did it involve a zest and lustiness? Or was it perhaps more quiet and contemplative?

The more you can differentiate where different people are at on the needs hierarchy and being-values the better you can reach them personally. The more closely you meet *their* needs the better their response to the education or training.

Appendix A02
// • # • > Achievement, Affiliation, Status // • # • > and Power Needs

Dr. David McClelland's need approach proposes that behavior is guided by desire to satisfy unfulfilled needs. However, this approach does not propose a hierarchy that defines one's level of progression. Instead, this approach proposes that each adult has common needs within three broad categories;

- •**Need for Achievement (nAch)**
- •**Need for Affiliation (nAff)**
- •**Need for Status (nSta)/Need for Power (Personalized or Socialized)**

Need for Affiliation (nAch)

Need for Achievement is the need for measurable personal accomplishment. Adults who have high achievement motives seek out challenging or competitive situations that have both realistic and achievable goals.

1. **Out-performance of someone else**. The adult is engaged in an activity in which winning or doing better than others is a primary

concern. Typical examples are needing to win a golf game or contest so that he or she can look better than others.

2. **Meeting or surpassing a self-imposed standard of excellence.** Often the standard of excellence does not involve competition with others, but is a self-imposed standard of high-quality performance. Typical examples include wanting to do an excellent job, wanting to find a better method, working carefully on the plan, etc. However, a distinction must be made between intensity and quality. Working hard or working fast is not evidence of concern over a standard of excellence. Only when the task demands intense effort, a concern for accuracy, or quality is a self-imposed standard of excellence indicated.

3. **Unique accomplishment**. The adult is involved in accomplishing other than an ordinary task or is using unique methods which will mark him or her as a personal success. An example is an extraordinary business innovation.

4. **Involvement in advancing one's business**, where the adult is involved in attaining a long-term business goal. The mere mention of a business goal is not the basis for assuming need for achievement; there must be evidence of involvement in a long-term businesses goal, some statement of wanting or feelings about goals that lie 3 to 5 years away.

5. **Plans for overcoming personal and environmental obstacles**. The high achiever carefully plans for the future by trying to anticipate any blocks to achievement of his or her goals. Evidence of this type of planning can be found in adult's talking about how they have overcome or are planning to overcome any barriers to goal achievement.

Need for Affiliation (nAff)

To decide whether or not an adult shows evidence of affiliation motivation, you must first look to see if that person is concerned about attaining an "affiliation goal"; i.e., does the individual have as his or her goal being with someone else and/or enjoying mutual friendship? Five concerns indicate the need for affiliation:

1. **Concern about being liked, acceptance, and friendship.** The individual talks about wanting to establish, restore, or maintain a close, warm, and friendly relationship with others.

2. **Characterization of a setting as a social situation**. The adult expresses a desire to participate or a concern with participating in friendly activities, such as parties, club activities, and reunions.

3. **Concern about the disruption of a positive inter-personal relationship.** The adult expresses an emotional concern about separation from another person, indicating a desire to restore a close relationship which had previously existed.

4. **Concern for people in the work situation**. The adult talks about people and working with people as the primary concern in his or her business life.

5. **Concern for people in other than work settings.** The adult talks about the importance of being with other people as a primary reason for his or her activity.

Need for Affiliation exists only when there is some evidence of concern about establishing, maintaining, or restoring a positive emotional relationship with another person. This relationship is most adequately described by the word "friendship."

Need for Status (nSta)

In deciding whether or not an adult shows evidence of the status motive, you must first look to see if the individual is concerned about attaining an "influence goal." Three categories indicate a status concern:

1. **Manipulative actions**. These reactions in themselves express an individual's concern for status. For instance, one might give bad advice to another person so they look good by comparison. Second, the actions might be giving manipulative assistance advice or support which may have been solicited by the other person but which goes beyond the mere answering of a request. These actions might be trying to control another person though regulating his or her behavior. These actions include influencing or persuading another person.

2. **Arousal of strong positive or negative emotions in others**. The adult's status is shown by the emotional reaction of others, e.g., fear, pressure, delights, awe, despondency, anger, or offense, because of something he or she has done. The distinction must be made that mere interest or listening intently is not strong feelings and must be intentional,

such as "he was absolutely fascinated." Further, the actions arousing the strong feelings must be under the control of the status-oriented person.

3. **Concern for reputation or position.** The adult is concerned with pure public evaluation; i.e., how someone else or "the world" will think of his or her status. The person is concerned about his or her reputation and others' judgment of his or her powerful position, but he or she does not necessarily talk about any particular actions which he or she takes relative to this concern. You are interested in whether or not the individual is interested in basking in the glory of high status or if he or she is disappointed by their inferior social position.

Need for Power (nPow)

Personalized Power and Socialized Power

Dr. McClelland, after many years and extensive research divided this status need into two parts representing two different people, the one with a Need for Personalized Power and the other with a Need for Socialized Power.

The most effective educators, trainers and upper management leaders of the twenty-first century will tend to follow the emerging socialized power model. This socialized power trainer/leader (manager) is interactive while the traditional personalized power trainer/leader (manager) tends to be command and control. Socialized power leaders encourage participation, they share power and information willingly and enhance the self-worth of others. They tend to adopt a style that includes vision, sensitivity, and involvement. Research of successful leaders/managers and their less successful colleagues, contrary to what one might think, has found a good manager is not one who needs personal success or who is primarily people-oriented, but rather is one who likes power. A desire to have impact, to be strong and influential is essential to good training and management. A strong power motivation is more characteristic of good trainers and managers than either a need for personal achievement or a need to be liked by others. Both achievement needs and affiliative needs appear to act counter to constructive power orientation and in the extreme are characteristics of unsuccessful trainers and managers. The highly self-centered nature of a strong need for achievement leads people to behave in very special ways that do not necessarily lead to good management. Because the trainer and manager with a strong need to be liked is precisely the one who wants to stay on good terms with everybody and therefore he or she is the one most likely to make exceptions in terms of particular needs. This kind of person creates poor morale because he or she does not understand that other people will tend to regard exceptions to the rules as unfair to themselves. Good training and management requires the appreciation of and desire for having impact, being strong and influential. However this desire for impact, strength and influence may take either of two forms: It may be oriented primarily toward (1) the achievement of personal gain and aggrandizement or by (2) a need to influence others' behavior for the common good. In the first instance, McClelland calls this power motivation Personalized; the need for power is essentially self-serving. The second power motivation he calls Socialized.; power is valued as an instrument to be used for the common good, on behalf of the whole organization, and for almost altruistic purposes. The quality empowering trainer and manager fits this second form and is (concerned with being a builder of systems, realistic goals, and people) collaborative, non-defensive, willing to seek help, respectful of other's rights, concerned with fairness, oriented toward justice, committed to the value of working per se, egalitarian, organization minded, a joiner, self-controlled in their use of power, concerned with fairness, a source of strength for others and replaceable by other managers. In other words a quality empowering trainer and manager leaves a system intact and self-sustaining. The movement toward continuous quality improvement and employee empowerment is a best fit for the socialized power trainer and leader.

Appendix A03
// • # • > Rewarded Behavior: Reinforcement // • # • >

Dr. B. F. Skinner (1953) and other behaviorists, i.e. people who concern themselves with observations of actual behavior, rather than with attitudes that are inferred from behavior, state that behavior is constantly being reinforced, positively or negatively, and that it is the shaping of behavior that causes the adult to do what they do. Behavior that is positively reinforced, i.e. the adult received the valued reward, will persist; extinction of the behavior occurs when the behavior is no longer adequately reinforced.

Pavlov and his dog, nicely illustrate the earliest recognized form of conditioning, which is now called classical conditioning. Pavlov observed that, over time, his dog had become conditioned to associate being fed with the bell that Pavlov rang to announce that it was feeling time, as shown in the following sequence.

Time	S -------->	R
1.	Food	Salivate
2.	Food-Bell	Salivate
3.	Bell	Salivate

The sequence relationship shows how the dog had become conditioned to salivate to a different stimulus.

While the above "experiment" may appear obvious, the simple principles of classical conditioning (Level 1 - Signal Learning) are not nearly so obvious in the learning or work settings. Classical conditioning suggests, for example, why there is crime, why there are rapes and murders, why politicians support their constituencies or take bribes, and so on. All adults have become conditioned over time to associate previously unconditioned stimuli, which then regulate the behavioral responses. In short, classical conditioning provides an explanation for changes in stimuli which produce identical behavioral responses.

Skinner then reasoned that if this S ---> R sequence could explain behavior, then it could also be used in a programmable sense to help individuals "operate" on their own environments. That is, if behavior is conditioned, then adults as elements of the environment of others can condition others, as well as themselves, to provide a desired response through alternations in the stimulus condition. In effect, Skinner identified an alternative form of conditioning, which is now called operant conditioning. (Level 2 - Reward the Response Learning) The distinguishing characteristic between operant and classical conditioning is that in operant conditioning the concern is with changing the response rather than changing the stimulus. Imagine the following sequence:

Time S ---------->   R < ------   Reward (positive or negative)

	S	R	Reward
1.	Bad Day	Drinks	Numb, Blocks out Bad Day
2.	Bad Day	Drinks	Paired with Aversive Stimuli (Pain)
3.	Bad Day	Doesn't Drink	No Pain

Having a bad day no longer results in problematic drinking. However, if the individual had no desire to change his or her behavior, i.e. believing the drinking does not represent a problem, then there would be no point to following this particular sequence.

This approach, like the others, attempts to answer the question, "Why do adults do what they do?"   The reinforcement approach answers the question by observing the S --> R connections and recognizing that a variety of stimuli may cause any particular behavior and that a particular stimulus may cause a variety of behavioral responses.   Also, that anything else that happened to be in the environment, i.e. a person, a picture, etc. at the time of the behavioral connection can also create stimulus or response effect just because it happened to be there.   This is called stimulus and response generalization. And a gradient of generalization would give a weight to every object that was in environment in relation to how close or far away from the conditioning act the object or person was at that moment.   Behavior then can be greatly influenced then by the type and scheduling of reinforcement that is employed.

Dr. Skinner and other reinforcement behaviorists have been attacked on the grounds that reinforcement seemingly ignores the "human" element -- that adults are thinking, breathing human beings with feeling, desires, motives and aspirations.   In response, Dr. Skinner denies that he is attempting to reduce human dignity or choice, but rather that the human should be aware that every action they take is itself conditioning some other aspect of the world around them.   Consequently, Skinner says, the human should not blindly condition the world in ways that are undesirable to them; they should attempt to selectively use positive and negative reinforcers, punishment, aversive stimuli, and other conceptual tools to create the kind of world they want to live in.

Reinforcement is a tremendous tool for predicting and controlling behavior in training settings.

The *reinforcement approach* is referred to as a process approach because it deals with the process through which motivation comes about, rather than with inner needs which may activate motivation. While the other behavior clarifying approaches, such as equity and expectancy, attempt to look inside the human mind to see how an individual's beliefs, expectations, desires and values lead to motivate behavior, Dr. Skinner's focus is almost entirely external. He maintained that behavior is determined by its consequences, what happens as a result of a person's actions. In other words, behavior which is rewarded or which has positive consequences will be repeated while behavior which receives either no rewards or negative consequences will cease. This simple idea can have profound consequences for trainers. For example, a trainee who is praised for their efforts on a project will continue to work hard on the project. On the other hand, if he or she is ignored or even reprimanded for their efforts then he or she will cease to produce in that area. Reinforcement has a very important implication in training; if trainers want to maximize goal attainment, it must carefully mange consequences so that the right behaviors are rewarded.

> **Note:** Behaviors learned as a result of this external motivating and manipulation will only continue to exist as long as some reinforcement is given. In a new environment this new learned behavior may or may not occur.

There are two important lessons that instructors must learn if they are going to get the best results from learners: (1) You get more of the behavior you reward. You don't get what you hope for, ask for, wish for or beg for. You get what you reward. People do the things that they believe will benefit them most. (2) In trying to do the right things, it is easy to fall into the trap of rewarding the wrong activities and ignoring or punishing the right ones. The result is that you hope for A, unwittingly reward B and then wonder why you get B. It does not matter what the instructor intends -- it's the reward and the punishment, from the learner's perspective that motivates.

INDEX

References, Resources and Bibliography

Authors Selected Bibliography

Ripley, R.E. and Ripley, M.J. (June, 2009) *Take Control of Your Life: With Your Lifestyle Wheel for Wellness,* ISBN 1448610338, Carefree Press.
Ripley, R.E. and Ripley, M.J. (August, 2009), *Road to Your Personal Success*, ISBN 1448626145, Carefree Press.
Ripley, R.E. and Ripley, M.J. (September, 2009) *Building Your Success Through Customer Relations*, ISBN 1449520049, Carefree Press.
Ripley, R.E. and Ripley, M.J. (2nd Ed., July, 2009) *Steering Your Ship on the Career Sea of Life*, ISBN1448625351, Carefree Press.
(All above and current book available at www.Amazon.com)

Ripley, R.E. (1969) *Report of Tucson Training Effectiveness Research Project Using the Ripley Interview Process System (RIPS),* Unemployment Insurance and Economic Services Division, U.S. Department of Labor, Washington D. C.
Ripley, R.E. and Ripley, M.J. (1970, 1974) *Career Families.* World of Work, Inc., Tempe, Arizona.
Ripley, R.E. and Ripley, M.J. (1970, 1974, 1976) *World of Work Inventory.* Scottsdale Arizona: World of Work, Inc.
Ripley, R.E. and Ripley, M.J. (1988) *Manage It All: Yourself, Your Company, Others,* Carefree Press.
Ripley, R.E. and Ripley, M.J. (1995) *Your Child's Ages and Stages*, Northwest Publishing.
Ripley, R.E. and Ripley, M.J. (1997) *Your Child's Ages & Stages: 0 to 6 Year Old*, Carefree Press.
Ripley, M.J. and Ripley, R.E. (1998) *Your Child's Ages & Stages: 7 to 12 Year Old*, Carefree Press.
Ripley, R.E. and Ripley, M.J. (1997) *It Takes a Parent...To Raise a Child,* Carefree Press.
Ripley, R.E. (1999) *Y2K: Planning for Crisis and Continuity*, April-May, Airport World.
Ripley, R.E., Ripley, M.J., Patch, K. (Two year grant of evaluation, effect and redesign – (2000-2001) *Offender Workforce Development Specialist Training*

Effect Evaluation, U.S. Justice Department, National Institute of Corrections, Washington, D.C.

Ripley, R.E., Ripley, M.J. (2001) - *BestFit Leadership*, BestPersonnelFit, LLC, Scottsdale, Arizona.

Ripley, R.E., Ripley, M.J. (2001) - *BestFit Performer*, BestPersonnelFit, LLC, Scottsdale, Arizona.

Selected Professional Juried Journal Articles

Ripley, R.E. and Ripley, M.J. (1992) *Empowerment, the Cornerstone of Quality: Empowering Management in Innovative Organizations in the 1990s*, Vol. 30, No. 4, Bradford, England: Management Decision Journal.

Ripley, R.E. and Ripley, M.J. (1992) *The Innovative Organization and Behavioral Technology for the 1990s,* Vol 57, No. 4, SAM Advanced Management Journal.

Ripley, R.E. and Ripley, M.J. (1993) *Empowerment: What to do with Troubling Employees*, Vol. 8, No. 3, West Yorkshire, England: Journal of Managerial Psychology.

Ripley, R.E. and Ripley, M.J. (1993) *How Ambitious are You?* January-February, Stateswest.

Ripley, R.E. and Ripley, M.J. (1994) *CREAM: Criteria-Related Employability Assessment Method: A systematic Model for Employee Selection*, Vol. 32, No.9,   Bradford, England: Management Decision Journal.

Adams, J. L. (1986) The Care & Feeding of Ideas: A Guide to Encouraging Creativity, Reading, Mass: Addison-Wesley.

Akerlind, G.S. and Trevitt, A. C. (1999). Enhancing self directed learning through educational technology: When students resist the change. Innovations in Education and Training International, 36(2), 96-105.

Aleger, G.M. and Janak, E.A. (1989) Kirpatrick's Levels of Training Criteria: Thirty Years Later, 42, 331-341, Personnel Psychology.

Alliger, G.M. & Janak, E.A. (1989) Kirkpatrick's Levels of Training Criteria: Thirty Years Later, Vol.42, 331-342, Personnel Psychology.

Allport, G. (1955) Becoming, New Haven: Yale University Press.

Allport, G. (1961) Pattern and Growth in Personality, New York: Holt, Rinehart and Winston.

Almenda, M. B. (1988) Speaking Personally with Gale B. Childs, 68-74, American Journal of Distance Education.

Alpander, G. G. (1991) Developing Managers' Ability to Empower Employees, 13-24, Issue 3. England: Journal of Management Development.

Alstete, J.W. (1995). Benchmarking in Higher Education: Adapting Best Practices to Improve Quality. (ASHE-ERIC Higher Education Report No. 5). Washington, DC.

Andrews, T. E. (1981) Adult learners: a research study. Washington, DC: Association of Teacher Educators.

Anthony, W. P. (1978) Participative Management, Reading, Mass: Addison-Wesley Publishing Co.

Anthony, W. P. (1981) Managing Incompetence, New York: AMACON.

Apps, J. W. (1994) Leadership for the emerging age: transforming practice in adult and continuing education. San Francisco: Jossey-Bass.

Apps, J. W. (1991) Mastering the Teaching of Adults. Malabar, FL: Krieger.

Apps, J. W. (1992) Adult Education: The Way to Lifelong Learning. Bloomington, Indiana: Phi Delta Kappa.

Araskog, R. V. (1989) The ITT Wars. New York: Henry Holt,

Argyris, C. (1964) Integrating the Individual and the Organization. New York: John Wiley and Sons.

Argyris, C. (1976) Increasing Leadership Effectiveness. New York: Wiley Interscience.

Argyris, C. (1990) Overcoming Organizational Defenses: Facilitating organizational learning. Needham Heights, MA: Allyn & Bacon.

Atkinson, C. (1941) Radio Extension Courses Broadcast for Credit. Boston: Meador:

Avis, J. (1995) The Validation of Learner Experience: A Conservative Practice?, October, 27, no. 2, 173-186. Studies in the Education of Adults.

Axford, R. W. (1969) Adult Education: The Open Door, Scranton, Pennsylvania: International Textbook Co.

Baillie, A. S. (1986) The Deming Approach: Being Better Than The Best, Autumn,15-23, SAM, Advanced Management Journal.

Baker, J. A. (1993) Paradigm Pioneers. Discovering the Future Series. Videotape. Burnsville, Minnesota: ChartHouse Learning Corp.

Baldwin, B.A. (1985) It's All in Your Head. Wilmington, North Carolina: Direction Dynamics.

Bandler, R. and J. Grinder. (1979) Frogs into Princes. Moab, Utah: Real People Press.

Bandura, A. (1969) Principles of Behavior Modification, New York: Holt, Rinehart and Winston.

Bandura, A. (1977) Self-Efficacy: Toward a Theory of Behavioral Change, Vol. 82, No. 2, 191-215, Psychological Review.

Bandura, A. and Walters, R. H. (1963) Social Learning and Personality Development. New York: Holt, Rinehart and Winston.

Bane, A. F. (1994) Technology and adult learning: a selected bibliography. Englewood Cliffs, New Jersey: Educational Technology Publishing.

Baridon, A. P., and Eyler, D. R. (1994) Working Together: The new rules and realities for managing men and women at work. McGraw-Hill.

Barnette, Ron (1995). Reflections on Electronic Frontiers in Education. Association of Small Computer Users in Education, Conference, North Myrtle Beach, South Carolina.

Baron, R. (1990) Countering the effects of destructive criticism: The relative efficacy of four interventions. Vol. 75, 3, Journal of Applied Psychology.

Beatty, P.T. (1996). Connecting with older adults: educational responses and approaches. Malabar, FL: Kreiger Publishing.

Beck, I. L., & McKeown, M. G. (1989) Expository text for young readers: The issue of coherence. In L. B. Resnick (Ed.), Knowing, learning, and instruction: Essays in honor of Robert Glaser (pp. 47-66). Hillsdale, New Jersey: Erlbaum.

Beckett, D. (2002) Life, work and learning: practice in postmodernity. New York: Routledge.

Belasco, J. A. (1991) Empowerment as Business Strategy, Executive Excellence, pps 15-17, June..

Belenky, M. F., Clinch, B. M., Goldberger, N. R. and Tarule, J. M. (1986) Women's Ways of Knowing: The Development of Self, Voice, and Mind. New York: Basic Books.

Belenky, Mary Field, Blythe McVicker Clinchy, Nancy Rule Goldberger, and Jill Mattuck Tarule. 1986. Women's Ways of Knowing: The Development of Self, Voice and Mind. New York: Basic Books.

Bennis, W. B. (1966) Changing Organizations, New York: McGraw-Hill.

Bennis, W. B. (1969) Organization Development: Its Nature, Origins, and Prospects, Reading, Massachusetts: Addison-Wesley.

Benson, T. E. (1991) Empowerment: There's That Word Again, 44-52, May, Industry Week.

Berge, L. Zane & Collins, P. Mauri (1995) Computer Mediated Communication. Cresskill, New Jersey: Hampton Press.

Best Practices in Adult Education: An individual Benchmarking Study. (1998). American Productivity & Quality Center, Texas, Houston.

Bigge, M. L.(1964) Learning Theories For Teachers. New York: Harper & Row.

Birkenholz, R. L. (1999) Effective adult learning. Danville, Illinois: Interstate Publishing.

Birnbrauer, H. (1987) Evaluation Techniques that Work, July, 53-55,Training and Development Journal.

Bischoff, L. J. (1969) Adult Psychology. New York: Harper and Row.

Blake, R. R. and Mouton, J. S. (1981) Productivity: The Human Side. New York: AMACOM.

Blanchard, K. (1990) How to Get Your Group to Perform Like a Team, July, 18-19, Executive Excellence.

Blanchard-Fields, F. and Hess, T. M. (1996) Perspectives on Cognitive Change in Adulthood and Aging. New York: McGraw-Hill.

Bligh, D. (1972) What's the Use of Lectures. Harmondsworth, England: Penguin.

Block, P. (1990) How to Be the New Kind of Manager, July, 51-56, Working Woman.

Bloom, B. S., Ed. (1956) Taxonomy of Educational Objectives, Handbook I: Cognitive Domain. New York: David McKay Co.

Bloom, B. S., Krathewohl, D. R. and Masia, B. B. (1956) Taxonomy of Educational Objectives, Handbook II: Affective Domain. New York: David McKay Co.

Bodi, Sonia. 1988. Critical thinking and bibliographic instruction: the Relationship. Journal of Academic Librarianship 14, no. 3: 150-153.

Borg, R. Walter; Gall, P. Joyce & Gall, D. Meredith (1993) Applying Educational Research: A Practical Guide. White Plains, New York: Longman.

Boud, D. and Griffin V. (eds.) (1987) Appreciating Adults Learning: From the Learners Perspective. London: Kogan Page.

Bransford, J.D., Sherwood, N. V. and Rieser, J. (1986) Teaching Thinking and Problem Solving, 1078-1089, vol. 41, American Psychologist.

Briton, D. (1996) The modern practice of adult education: a postmodern critique. Albany: State University of New York.

Brody, L. R., and Hall, J. (1993) "Gender and emotion," in M. Lewis and J. Haviland, eds., Handbook of Emotions. New York: Guilford Press.

Brookfield, S.D. (1991) Understanding and Facilitating Adult Learning: A Comprehensive Analysis of Principles and Effective Practices. San Francisco: Jossey-Bass.

Brundage, D.and MacKeracher, D. (1980) Adult Learning Principles and Their Application to Program Planning. Toronto:The Minister of Education.

Bruner, J. S. (1966) Toward a Theory of Instruction. Cambridge, Massachusetts: Harvard University Press: The Belknap Press.

Bruner, J. S. (1973) Beyond the Information Given. New York: W. W. Norton.

Brymer, R. A. (1991) Employee Empowerment: A Guest-Driven Leadership Strategy, 58-68, May, Cornell Hotel & Restaurant Administration Quarterly.

Burdett, J. W. (1991) What is Empowerment Anyway? 23-30, Issue 6, Journal of European Industrial Training.

Caffarella, R. S. (2002, 2nd ed.) Planning programs for adult learners: a practical guide for educators, trainers, and staff developers. San Francisco: Jossey-Bass.

Cahoon, B. ed. (1998) Adult Learning and the Internet. New Directions for Adult and Continuing Education, no. 78. San Francisco: Jossey-Bass.

Candy, P. C. (1991) Self-Direction for Lifelong Learning: A Comprehensive Guide to Theory and Practice. San Francisco: Jossey-Bass.

Cantor, J. A. (1992) Delivering Instruction to Adult Learners. Canada, Toronto: Wall and Emerson.

Cantor, Jeffrey A. 1992. Delivering Instruction to Adult Learners. Toronto: Wall & Emerson. (pp. 35-43.)

Carnevale, A.P., Gainer, L. J. and Meltzer, A. S. (1988) Workplace Basics: The Skills Employers Want, ASTD and U.S. Dept. of Labor Report 0-225-795--QL.2, Washington D.C., U.S. Government Printing Office.

Cavanaugh, J. C. and Blanchard-Fields, F. (2002, 4th ed.) Adult Development and Aging, Belmont, CA: Wadsworth Group, Thomson Learning.

Cervero, R. M. (1994) Planning Responsibly for Adult Education: A Guide to Negotiating Power and Interests. San Francisco: Jossey-Bass.

Chandler, L, A. (1994) Descriptive case studies of training, research, and development in computer and related instructional technologies for teachers. Chicago: Andrew University.

Chickering, A.W. & Reisser, L. (1993, 2nd ed.) Education and Identity. San Francisco: Jossey-Bass.

Clark, R. E. (1983) Reconsidering research on learning from media. 53(4), 445-459, Review of Educational Research.

Clark, R. E. (1994) Media will never influence learning. 42(2), 21-29, Educational Technology Research and Development.

Collis, B. (2001). Flexible learning in a digital world: experiences and e expectations. London: Kogan Page.

Commission for a Nation of Lifelong Learners. (1997). A Nation Learning: Vision for the 21st Century. Albany, New York: Regents College.

Conger, J. A. (1989) Leadership: The Art of Empowering Others, 17-24, February, Academy of Management Executive.

Conger, J. A. and Kanungo, R. N. (1988) The Empowerment Process: Integrating Theory and Practice, 471-482, July, Academy of Management Review.

Connolly, B.; Fleming, T.; McCormack, D.; and Ryan, A., eds.(1966) Radical Learning for Liberation. Maynooth, Ireland: Centre for Adult and Community Education, Saint Patrick' s College.

Cranton, P. (1996) Professional development as transformative learning: new perspectives for teachers of adults. San Francisco: Jossey-Bass.

Cranton, P. (1989) Planning Instruction for Adult Learners. Middleton, Ohio: Wall and Emerson.

Cranton, P. (1992) Working with Adult Learners. Canada, Toronto: Wall and Emerson.

Cranton, P. (1994) Understanding and promoting transformative learning: A guide for Educators of Adults. San Francisco: Jossey-Bass.

Cross, E.Y. (2000) Managing diversity: The courage to lead. Westport, CT: Quorum

Cross, K. P. (1978) The missing link: connecting adult learners to learning resources. New York: College Entrance Examination Board.

Cross, K. P. (1981) Adults as learners: increasing participation and facilitating learning. San Francisco: Jossey-Bass.

Cross, W. (1978) You are never too old to learn. Boston: McGraw-Hill.

Dacey, J. S. and Travers, J. T. (2004, 5th ed.) Human Development Across the Lifespan. New York: McGraw-Hill.

Daines, J., Daines, C. and Graham, B. (1993) Adult Learning, Adult Teaching. Nottingham, England: University of Nottingham.

Daloz, Laurent A. (1999) Mentor: guiding the journey of adult learners. San Francisco: Jossey-Bass.

Davidove, E. A. (1993) Evaluating the Return on Investment of Training, January, 1-8, Performance & Instruction.

Davis, M., and Denning, K. (1998) Learning in Virtual Space: Potential and Pitfalls in Electronic Communication. Paper presented at the 28th Annual SCUTREA Conference, July, Exeter, England.

Davis, Stan (1996) Slicing the Learning Pie, 32-38, Educom Review.

Day, R. (1995) The Information Revolution Transforming Teaching and Learning. Columbia, Magazine of Columbia University.

Deal, T. E., and Kennedy, A. A. (1982) Corporate Cultures.Reading, Massachusetts: Addison-Wesley.

Dean, G. J. (1994) Designing instruction for adult learners. Malabar, FL: Krieger Publishing Co.

Deming, W. E. (1982) Quality, Productivity and Competitive Position. Center for Advanced Engineering Studies. Cambridge, Massachusetts: Massachusetts Institute of Technology.

Deming, W. E.(1982) Out of the Crisis. Center for Advanced Engineering Studies, Cambridge, Massachusetts: Massachusetts Institute of Technology.

Dewey, J. (1933) How We Think: A Restatement of the Relation of Reflective Thinking to the Educative Process. Boston: D.C. Heath.

Diamond, R. M. (1998, 2nd ed.). Designing and assessing courses and curricula: a practical guide. San Francisco: Jossey-Bass.

Dirkx, J. (1998) Transformative Learning Theory in the Practice of Adult Education: An Overview, PAACE, 7, 1-14, Journal of Lifelong Learning.

Dirkx, J. M. (1997) A guide for planning and implementing instruction for adults: a theme-based approach. San Francisco: Jossey-Bass.

Dollard, J., and Miller, N. E. (1950) Personality and Psychotherapy. New York: McGraw-Hill, Inc.

Dominice, P. (2000) Learning from our lives: using educational biographies with adults. San Francisco: Jossey-Bass.

Draves, W. A. (1980) The free university: a model for a lifelong learning. New York: Association Press.

Draves, W. A. (1984) How to teach adults. Manhattan, Kansas: Learning Resources Network..

Driscoll, M. (1998) Web-based training: using technology to design adult learning experiences. San Francisco: Jossey-Bass.

Drucker, P. F. (1967) The Effective Executive. New York: Harper and Row.

Drucker, P. F. (1994) The Age of Social Transformation. The Atlantic Monthly.

Drucker, P. The age of social transformation. *The Atlantic Monthly,* Nov. 1994.

Early, V. (1991) Empowering Organizations, February, 13-14,Executive Excellence.

Erikson, E. Childhood and Society, (1950, 1963). New York: W. W. Norton & Co., Inc..

Evaluation: A Way to Stay on Track. (1992). December, 1-4, Meeting Management News.

Experience and Education. John Dewey (1997 reprint) Touchstone Books.

Feasley, E. C. (1983) Serving Learners at a Distance: A Guide to Program Practices. Washington, DC: Association for the Study of Higher Education.

Felder, R.M. and Silverman, L. K. (1988) Learning Styles and Teaching Styles in Engineering Education, 78 (7), 674-681, Engineering Education.

Festinger, L. (1957) A Theory of Cognitive Dissonance. California, Stanford: Stanford University Press.

Fetterman, D. M. (1996) Videoconferencing on-line: Enhancing communication over the Internet, 25(4), 23-27. Educational Researcher.

Findings From the Excellent Companies. (1980) New York: McKinsey & Company, Inc.

Fisher, A. B. (1991) Morale Crisis, 70-80, November, Fortune.

Flagg, B. N. (1990) Formative evaluation for educational technologies. Hillsdale, NJ: Erlbaum.

Flint, T. (1999) Serving Adult Learners in Higher Education: Findings from the CAEL/APQC Benchmarking Study. Council for Adult and Experiential Learning.

Freire, P. (1970) Pedagogy of the oppressed. New York: Seabury Press.

Freud, S. (1901) Zur Psychopathologie des Alltagslebens. Berlin: G.W. (Translated the Psychopathology of Everyday Life, 1904).

Frick, T. W. (1991) Restructuring Education Through Technology (Faster back service No. 326). Bloomington, Indiana: Phi Delta Kappa Educational Foundation.

Gadbow, N. F. (1998) Adult learners with special needs: strategies and resources for postsecondary education and workplace training. Melbourne, FL: Krieger.

Gagne, R. M. (1965) The Conditions of Learning. New York: Holt, Rinehart and Winston.

Galbraith, M. W. (1997) Administering successful programs for adults: promoting excellence in adult, community, and continuing education. Malabar, FL: Kreiger Publishing.

Gardner, H.(1993) Frames of Mind: The Theory of Multiple Intelligences. New York: Basic Books.

Garrison, D. R. & Shale, D. G.(1987) Mapping the Boundaries of Distance Education: The Concept of Control, 7-13, American Journal of Distance Education.

Garrison, D. R. (1987) The Role of Technology in Distance Education, 41-43, New Directions for Continuing Education.

Geber, B. (1994) Re-Engineering The Training Department, May, 1994, 27-34, Training.

Geber, B. (1995) Does Training Make a Difference? Prove It!, March, 27-34, Training.

Gerrity, T.W. (1976) College-Sponsored Correspondence Instruction in the United States:

Gilligan, C. (1982) In a Different Voice. Cambridge: Massachusetts: Harvard University Press.

Ginsburg, L. (1998) Integrating technology into adult learning. In C. E. Hopey (Ed.), Technology, basic skills, and adult education: Getting ready and moving forward (pp. 37- 46). Columbus, OH: ERIC Clearinghouse on Adult, Career, & Vocational Education.

Gitlow, H. and Gitlow, S. (1987) The Deming Guide to Quality and Competitive Position, Englewood Cliffs, New Jersey: Prentice Hall.

Glaser, R. (1976) Components of a psychology of instruction: Toward a science of design. Review of Educational Research.

Goldberger, N. R.; Tarule, J. M.; Clinchy, B. M.; and Belenky, M. F., eds. (1996) Knowledge, Difference, and Power: Essays Inspired by "Women' s Ways of Knowing." New York: Basic Books.

Goleman, (1995) Emotional Intelligence. New York: Bantam Books.

Goleman, D. When moods affect safety: Communications in a cockpit mean a lot a few miles up. New York Times, June 26, 1994.

Goleman, D. Working with Emotional Intelligence. New York: Bantam Books, 1998.

Goody, A. E. & Kozoll, C. E. (1995) Program development in continuing education. Malabar, FL: Krieger.

Gordon, I. J. (1968) Criteria for Theories of Instruction. Washington, D.C.: Association for Supervision and Curriculum Development, N.E.A.

Goski, K. L. and Belfry, M. (1991) Achieveing Competitive Advantage Through Employee Empowerment, 213-220, Summer. Employment Relations Today.

Graebner, C. (1998) "Enquiring into Group Learning On-Line." Paper presented at the 28th Annual SCUTREA Conference, July, England: Exeter.

Gregorc, A. F. (1982) An Adult's Guide to Style. Columbia, Connecticut: Gregorc Associates.

Griffin, Colin (1990) Curriculum Theory in Adult and Lifelong Education. New York: Nichols Publishing Company.

Haas, J. W., Jr. (1983) Complementarity and Christian Thought - An Assessment: The

Hamlin, R. (1991) A Practical Guide to Empowering Your Employees, Supervisory Management, pp 8, April.

Hart, L. A. (1975) Human Brain and Human Learning, Longman, White Plains, NY.

Hartman, V. F. (1995) Teaching and learning style preferences: Transitions through technology, Summer, 9, no. 2 Summer: 18-20, VCCA Journal.

Havinghurst, R. (1970, 2nd ed.) Developmental Tasks and Education. New York: David McKay.

Hayes, E.. (2000) Women as learners: the significance of gender in adult learning. San Francisco: Jossey-Bass.

Heimlich, J. E. (1994) Developing teaching style in adult education. San Francisco: Jossey-Bass.

Herrmann, N. (1990) The Creative Brain. Lake Lure, North Carolina, Brain Books.

Herzberg, F. (1966) Work and the Nature of Man. New York: World.

Herzberg, F. (1973) One More Time: How do you Motivate Employees?, 53-62, Harvard Business Review.

Hesburgh, T. M.. (1973) Patterns for lifelong learning. San Francisco: Jossey-Bass.

Higgins, R. N. (1991) Computer-Mediated Cooperative Learning: Synchronous and Asynchronous Communication Between Students Learning Nursing Diagnosis. Unpublished Doctoral Dissertation. Toronto: University of Toronto.

Hilgard, E. R. and Bower, G. H. (1966) Theories of Learning. New York: Appleton-Century-Crofts.

Hill, S. (1987) Trends in Adult Education 1969-1984. Washington, DC: Center for Education Statistics, Office of Educational Research and Improvement, U.S. Department of Education, (ERIC Document Reproduction Service No. ED 282 054).

Hoffman, B. (1995) Distance Education: The Elusive Definition. Vol 1, #1, The Distance Educator.

Holmberg, B. (1986) Status and Trends of Distance Education. London: Croom Helm.

Hopson, P., and Welbourne, L .(1998) Adult Development and Transformative Learning. 17, no. 2 .March-April, 72-86, International Journal of Lifelong Education.

Horney, K. (1939) New Ways in Psychoanalysis. New York: W. W. Norton.

Horney, K. (1967) Feminine Psychology. W. W. Norton.

Houle, C. O. (1984) Patterns of learning: New perspectives on life-span education. San Francisco: Jossey-Bass.

Houle, C.O. (1961) The Inquiring Mind. Madison, Wisconsin: University of Wisconsin Press.

How People Learn: Brain, Mind, Experience, and School: Expanded Edition. John D. Bransford, M. Suzanne Donovan, and James W. Pellegrino, editors. (National Academy Press, 2000)

Hoyer, W. J. and Roodin, P.A.(2003, 5th ed.) Adult Development and Aging. New York: McGraw-Hill.

Hume, A. D. (1995) Reward Management. Cambridge, Massachusetts: Blackwell.

Imel, S. (1982) Guidelines for Working with Adult Learners, ERIC Fact Sheet No. 25. Columbus: ERIC Clearinghouse on Adult, Career, and Vocational Education, The National Center for Research in Vocational Education, The Ohio State University, (ERIC Document Reproduction Service No. ED 237 811).

Imel, S. (1999) Using Groups in Adult Learning: Theory and Practice. 19, no. 1, 54-61, Journal of Continuing Education in the Health Professions.

Irving, R. (1995) A Study of Computer-Modem Students: A Call for Action. American Educational Research Association.

James, W. (1892) Psychology: The Briefer Course. (1961, edited by Gordon Allport), (originally published by Henry Holt and Company, 1892). New York: Harper Torchbooks, Harper & Row.,

Johnson, D. W. (1990) Reaching Out: Interpersonal Effectiveness and Self-Actualization, Englewood Cliffs, New Jersey: Prentice-Hall.

Johnson, D. W. and Johnson R. (1975) Learning Together and Alone: Cooperative, Competitive, and Individualistic Learning. Englewood Cliffs, New Jersey: Prenctice-Hall.

Johnson, D. W. and Johnson R.T. (1986) Computer-assisted Cooperative Learning, 26(1), 12-18, Educational Technology.

Johnson, D. W., Johnson, R. T. and Smith, K. A.(1991) Active Learning: Cooperation in the College Classroom, Interaction Book Company, Edina, Minnesota.

Johnson, W. People in Quandaries.(1946) New York: Harper & Row.

Johnston, J., & Young, S. J. (1999) A pilot test of Workplace Essential Skills & LitTeacher professional development courses (Evaluation Report). Institute for Social Research, University of Michigan.

Johnston, R., and Usher, R. (1997) Retheorising Experience: Adult Learning in Contemporary Social Practices, October, 29, no. 2, 137-153, Studies in the Education of Adults.

Jourard, S. M. (1958) Personal Adjustment: An Approach through the Study of Healthy Personality. New York: The Macmillan Co.

Jung, C. (1921) Psychological Types; or, The Psychology of Individuation, Translated by H. Godwin Baynes, London, Harcourt, Brace and Co. New York, 1923 (Originally published as Psychologische Typen, Rascher, Zurich, Switzerland: Rascher).

Jung, C. (1945) Betrachtungen: Eine Auslese aus den Schriften. Switzerland: Rascher. (First published in English in 1953 by Pantheon Books, New York as Psychological Reflections).

Kagan, J. *Galenâs Prophecy.* New York: Basic Books, 1994.

Kagan, J., and Moss, H. A. (1962) Birth to Maturity. New York: John Wiley & Sons.

Kanter, R. M. The Change Masters: Innovation in the American corporation. Englewood Cliffs, NJ: Simon & Schuster, 1985.

Katz, R. N. (1999) Dancing with the devil: information technology and the new competition in higher education. San Francisco: Jossey-Bass.

Katzenbach, J. R., and Smith, D. K.(1993) The Wisdom of Teams. Boston: Harvard Business School Press, 1993.

Kaufman, R. (1995) If Distance Learning is the Solution, What is the Problem? American Journal of Distance Education.

Keegan, D. (1986) The Foundation of Distance Education. London: Croom Helm.

Keirsey, D.and Bates, M. (1978, 1998) Please Understand Me II, Del Mar, California: Prometheus Nemesis.

Kerka, Sandra. 1993. Women, human development, and learning. ERIC Digest. Columbus, OH: ERIC Clearinghouse on Adult, Career, and Vocational Education. ED 358379.

Kidd, J. R. (1973) How adults learn. New York: Association Press.

Kirkpatrick, D. (1998) Evaluating Training Programs: The Four Levels. San Francisco: Berrett-Koehler Publications.

Kirkpatrick, D. L, Kramer, G., & Salinger, R. (1994) Essentials for Evaluation. In C. Hodell, Instructional Systems Development, 191-207). Alexandria Virginia: American Society for Training and Development.

Kirkpatrick, D. L. (1975) Evaluating Training Programs. Madison. Wisconsin: American Society for Training and Development.

Kirkpatrick, D.L. (1959) Techniques for Evaluating Training Programs, Vol. 13, No. 11, 3-9, Journal of American Society for Training & Development.

Kirkpatrick, D.L. (1959) Techniques for Evaluating Training Programs: Part 2--Learning, Vol. 13, No. 12, pp. 21-26, Journal of American Society for Training & Development

Kirkpatrick, D.L. (1960) Techniques for Evaluating Training Programs: Part 3--Behavior, Vol. 14, No. 11, 13-18, Journal of American Society for Training &

Development.

Kirkpatrick, D.L. (1960) Techniques for Evaluating Training Programs: Part 4-
-Results, Vol. 14, No. 2, pp. 28-32, Journal of American Society for Training
& Development.

Kirkpatrick, D.L. (1967) Evaluation of Training. In Craig, R.L., Bittle, L.R.
(eds.) Training and Development Handbook (87-112). New York: McGraw-
Hill.

Kirkpatrick, D.L. (1977) Evaluating Training Programs, Evidence vs. Proof,
Vol. 31, No. 11, 9-12, Training and Development Journal.

Kirkpatrick, D.L. (1985) Effective Training and Development, Part 2: In-
House Approaches and Techniques, Vol. 62, No. 1, 52-56, Personnel.

Kirkpatrick, D. (1989) Evaluating Training Programs. San Francisco: Berrett-
Koehler Publishers, Inc.

Klatt, B. (1999). The ultimate training workshop handbook: a comprehensive
guide to leading successful workshops & training programs. New York,
McGraw-Hill.

Knowles, M. S. (1975) Self-Directed Learning: A Guide for Learners and
Teachers, New York, Association Press.

Knowles, M. S. (1977, 2nd ed.) The Adult Education Movement in the United
States, Huntington, New York, Krieger Publishing Co.

Knowles, M. S. (1998, 5th ed.) The Adult Learner: A Neglected Species.
Houston, Texas, Gulf Publishing Co.

Knowles, M. S. et el.(1984) Andragogy in Action: Applying Modern Principles
of Adult Learning. San Francisco: Jossey-Bass.

Knowles, M.S. (1980, 2nd ed.) The Modern Practice of Adult Education: From
Pedagogy to Andragogy, New York: Cambridge Books.

Knowles, M.S. 1970. The Modern Practice of Adult Education: Andragogy vs.
Pedagogy. New York: Association Press.

Knox, A. B. (1977) Adult Development and Learning, San Francisco: Jossey-
Bass.

Knox, A. B. (1986) Helping adults learn. San Francisco: Jossey-Bass.

Kolb, D. A. (1984) Experiential Learning: Experience as the Source of
Learning and Development. Englewood Cliffs, New Jersey, Prentice-Hall.

Kopp, K. Evaluate the Performance of Adults. Module N-6 of Category N.
(ERIC Document Reproduction Service No. ED 289 969).

Kozma, R. B. (1991). Learning with media, 61(2), 179-212, Review of Educational Research.

Kozma, R. B. (1994). Will media influence learning? Reframing the debate. Educational Technology.

Kramer, C. (2002). Success in on-line learning. Albany, NY: Delmar Thomson Learning.

Kravetz, D. J. (1990) The Human Resources Revolution, New York: Jossey-Bass.

Krupp, J-A. (1982). The adult learner: a unique entity. Manchester, Connecticut: Adult Development and Learning.

Lamdin, L. S. (1997). Elderlearning: new frontier in an aging society. Phoenix, AZ: Oryx Press.

Landwehr, W. R. (1991) Looking for a Good Investment? Consider Your Employees, October, 168, Plant Engineering.

Lawrence, Gordon. (1982, 2nd ed.) People Types and Tiger Stripes: A Practical Guide to

Lazarus, R. (1961) Adjustment and Personality, New York: McGraw-Hill.

Learning Styles. Gainesville, Florida: Center for Applications of Psychological Type.

Leavitt, H. J.(1964, 2nd ed.) Managerial Psychology. Chicago: The University of Chicago Press.

Levine, M. (1990) Keeping A Head in School, Cambridge: Educators Publishing Service, Inc..

Levinson, D. J. (1978) The Seasons of a Man's Life. New York: Alfred A. Knopf.

Lewin, K. (1951) Field Theory in Social Science. New York: McGraw-Hill.

Likert, R. (1967) The Human Organization: Its Management and Value. New York: McGraw-Hill.

Lindeman, E. C. (1926) The Meaning of Adult Education. New York: New Republic.

Lippitt, G. L.(1969) Organization Renewal. New York: Appleton-Century-Crofts.

Litzinger, M. E., and Osif, B. (1993) Accommodating diverse learning styles: Designing instruction for electronic information sources. In What is Good Instruction Now? Library Instruction for the 90s. ed. Shirato, L.. Ann Arbor, Michigan: Pierian Press.

Longworth, N. (2003) Lifelong learning in action: transforming education in the 21st century. Sterling, Virginia: Kogan Page.

Lumsden, D. B. (1975) Experimental studies in adult learning and memory. Washington, D.C.: Hemisphere Pub. Corp.

Luthan, F. and Kritner, R. (1985) Organizational Behavior Modification and Beyond. Glenview, Illinois: Scott, Foresman & Co.

M. Wittrock, M. Ed. (1986) Handbook of Research on Teaching. New York: Macmillan.

Maddi, S. R.(1968) Personality Theories: A Comparative Analysis. Illinois, Homewood: The Dorsey Press.

Maehl, W. H. (2000) Lifelong learning at its best: innovative practices in adult credit programs. San Francisco: Jossey-Bass.

Mager, R. F. (1988) Making Instruction Work. Lake Books, Belmont, California.

Marion, T. W. and Melvin, E. F. (1995) The Virtual Classroom, Authentic Assessment, and Learning Process Control in Online Teacher Development to Support Internet Telecommunications in Education. PREPS, Inc., Mississippi State University.

Marrelli, A. F. (1993) Ten Evaluation Instruments for Technical Training, July, 7-14, Technical & Skills Training.

Maslow, A. H. (1970, 2nd ed.) Motivation and Personality. New York: Harper & Row.

Massey, M. (1979) The People Puzzle. Reston, Virginia: Reston Publishing Co.

McCarthy B. (1987) The 4MAT System: Teaching to Learning Styles with Right/Left Mode Techniques. Barrington, Illinois: EXCEL, Inc.

McClelland, D. C. (1992) Achievement Motive, Irvington Publishing,.

McClelland, D. C. (1975) Power: The Inner Experience, Irvington Publishers.

McClelland, D. C.(1985) Human Motivation. Glenview, IL: Scott, Foresman.

McClelland, D. C. (1979) Inhibited power motivation and high blood pressure in men. Journal of Abnormal Psychology, *88,* 182-190.

McClelland, D. C. (1977) The impact of power motivation training on alcoholics. Journal of Studies on Alcohol, 38(1), 142-144.

McClelland, D. C. (1982) The need for power, stress, immune function and illness among male prisoners. Journal of Abnormal Psychology,91(1), 61-70.

McClelland, D. C. (1982) The need for power, sympathetic activation and illness. Motivation and Emotion,6(1), 31-41.

McClelland, D. C.(1965) Toward a theory of motive acquisition. American Psychologist, *20,* 321-333.

McClelland, D. C., and Boyatzis, R. E. The leadership motive pattern and long term success in management. Journal of Applied Psychology, 1982, *67*(6), 737-743.

McClelland, D. C., and Burnham, D. H. (1976) Power is the great motivator. Harvard Business *Review,* March-April, 100-110, 159-166.

McClelland, D. C., and Jemmott, J. B., III.(1980) Power motivation, stress and physical illness. Journal of Human Stress, *6*(4), 6-15.

McClelland, D. C., and Teague, G.(1975) Predicting risk preferences among power-related tasks. Journal of Personality, 1975, *43,* 266-285.

McClelland, D. C., and Watson, R. I., Jr.(1973) Power motivation and risk-taking behavior. Journal of Personality, 1973, *41,* 121-139.

McClelland, D. C., Burnham, David H. (1976) Power is the Great Motivator, March-April, Harvard Business Review.

McClelland, D. C., Davidson, R., Saron, C., and Floor, E. (1980) The need for power, brain norephinephrine turnover and learning. Biological Psychology, 10, 93-102.

McClelland, D. C., Miron, David (1979) The Impact of Achievement Motivation Training on Small Businesses, Vol. 21, No. 4, Summer, California Management Review.

McClelland, D. C., Rhinesmith, S., and Kristensen, R. (1975) The effects of power training on community action agencies. *Journal of Applied Behavioral Science, 11,* 92-115.

McGregor, D. (1966) Leadership and Motivation. Cambridge, Massachusetts: The M.I.T. Press.

McKeachie, W.J., Ed. (1980) Learning, Cognition, and College Teaching. New Directions for Teaching and Learning, No. 2. San Francisco: Jossey-Bass.

McNeer, Elizabeth J. (1991) Learning theories and library instruction. *Journal of Academic Librarianship* 17, no. 5: 294-97.

Merisotis, J. P. & Phipps, R. A. (1999) What's the difference? Outcomes of distance vs. traditional classroom based learning, 31(3), 13-17, Change.

Merriam, S. B., and Caffarella, R. S. (1998, 2nd ed.) Learning in Adulthood: A Comprehensive Guid*e*. San Francisco: Jossey-Bass.

Messmer, M. (1990) How to Put Employee Empowerment into Practice, 25, Summer, Woman CPA.

Mezirow, J. (1995) Transformation theory of adult learning. In M. R. Welton (Ed.), In defense of the lifeworld: Critical perspectives on adult learning (39-70). Albany, NY: State University of New York Press.

Mezirow, Jack and associates (eds.) (1990) Fostering Critical Reflection in Adulthood. San Francisco: Jossey-Bass.

Mingle, R. J. & Gold, L. (1996) Should Distance Learning be Rationed? Educom Review.

Moore, M. G. (1973) Toward a Theory of Independent Learning and Teaching. 44, 666-679, Journal of Higher Education.

Moore, M. G. (1990) Recent Contribution to the Theory of Distance Education, 10-15, Open Learning.

Moran, J. J. (2001, Rev ed.) Assessing adult learning: a guide for practitioners. Malabar, FL: Krieger Publishing.

Morgan, R. R. (1996) Enhancing learning in training and adult education. Westport, Connecticut: Praeger.

Mullane, L. (2001) Bridges of opportunity: a history of the Center for Adult Learning and Educational Credentials. Washington, DC: American Council on Education.

Munshi, K. S. (1980) Report on Station-College Executive project in Adult Learning. Washington, DC.: Corporation for Public Broadcasting.

Myers, I.B. and M.H. McCaulley, (1986, 2nd ed.) Manual: A Guide to the Development and Use of the Myers-Briggs Type Indicator. Palo Alto: Consulting Psychologists Press.

Nadler, L. and Nadler, Z.(1989, 3rd ed.) Developing Human Resources. San Francisco: Jossey-Bass.

Naylor, M. (1985) Adult Development: Implications for Adult Education. ERIC Digest No. 41. Columbus: ERIC Clearinghouse on Adult, Career, and Vocational Education, The National Center for Research in Vocational Education, The Ohio State University, (ERIC Document Reproduction Service No. ED 259 211).

Nienstedt, P. R. (1979) Evaluating Perceived Changes Resulting from Participation in a Management Program, Unpublished Doctoral Dissertation. Tempe, Arizona: Arizona State University, College of Business.

(Effectiveness, [one year follow-up] of the Workshop for Effective Management, for Motorola, Robert E. Ripley, Ph.D.)

Ostrand, K. D. (1984) New growth markets in adult learning. Manhattan, Kansas: Learning Resources Network.

Palloff, R. M. (1999) Building learning communities in cyberspace: effective strategies for the online classroom. San Francisco: Jossey-Bass.

Palloff, R. M. (2001) Lessons from the cyberspace classroom: the realities on online teaching. San Francisco: Jossey-Bass.

Papalia, D. E., Sterns, H. L., Feldman, R. D., and Camp, C. J. (2002, 2nd ed.) Adult Development and Aging. New York: McGraw-Hill.

Pascale, R. T. (1990) Managing on the Edge: How successful companies use conflict to stay ahead. London: Viking Penguin

Paterson, R. W. K. (1979) Values, education, and the adult. Boston: Routledge

Perls, F. (1969) Gestalt Therapy Verbatim. Lafayette, California: Real Press People.

Perry, W. (1968) Forms of intellectual and ethical development in the college years. New York: Holt, Rinehart and Winston.

Peters, T. J. and Waterman, R. H. Jr. (1982) In Search of Excellence: Lessons from America's Best Run Companies. New York: Harper & Row.

Peters, T.J. and Austin, N. (1985) A Passion for Excellence. New York: Random House.

Pfeffer, J. (1994) Competitive Advantage through People: Unleashing the power of the workforce. Boston: Harvard Business School Press.

Pfeffer, J. Managing with Power. Boston: Harvard Business School Press, 1994.

Pittman, V. (1986). Station WSUI and the Early Days of Instructional Radio, 67(2), 38-52, The Palimpsest.

Pollack, S. (1989) Four Keys for Empowerment, December, 88-91, Journal for Quality & Participation.

Posner. G. (2000, 5th ed.) Field Experience: A Guide to Reflective Teaching. New York: Longman Publishers.

Powers, B.(1992) Instructor Excellence. San Francisco: Jossey-Bass Inc.

Pratt, D. D. (1998). Five perspectives on teaching in adult and higher education. Malabar, FL: Krieger Publishing Co.

Pratt, D. D. (1988) Andragogy as a Relational Construct, Spring, 38, no. 3, 160-172, Adult Education Quarterly.

Quinnan, T. W. (1997). Adult students "at risk": culture bias in higher education. Westport, CT: Begin & Garvey.

Robert M. Smith .(1991) How people become effective learners, April, 11, Adult Learning.

Roberts, J. M. and Keough, E. M. (Eds.). (1995) Why the Information Highway: Lessons from Open and Distance Learning. Toronto: Trifolium Books.

Rogers, C. R. (1969) Freedom to Learn. Columbus, Ohio: Merrill,

Rogers, C. R.(1961) On Becoming a Person. Boston: Houghton-Mifflin,

Rogers, J. (2001) Adult learning. Philadelphia: Open University Press.

Rosenthal, R. and Jacobson, L. (1968) Pygmalion in the Classroom,. New York: Holt, Rinehart and Winston.

Rowley, D.J. (1998) Strategic choices for the academy: how the demand for lifelong learning will re-create higher education. San Francisco: Jossey-Bass.

Rumble, G. & Harry, K. (1982) The Distance Teaching Universities. London: Croom Helm.

Saltiel, I. M. (2001) Cohort programming and learning: improving educational experiences for adult learners. Malabar, FL: Krieger.

Saltiel, I. M.; Sgroi, A.; and Brockett, R. G., eds. (1998) The Power and Potential of Collaborative Learning Partnerships. New Directions for Adult and Continuing Education, no.79. San Francisco: Jossey-Bass.

Santrock, J. W. (2004, 9th ed.) Life-Span Development. New York: McGraw-Hill.

Savin-Baden, M. (2000) Problem-based learning in higher education: untold stories. Philadelphia: Society for Research into Higher Education: Open University Press.

Schlesinger, L. A. and Heskett, J. L. (1991) Enfranchisement of Service Workers, Summer, 83-100, California Management Review.

Schmeck, R., Ed., (1988) Learning Strategies and Learning Styles. New York: Premm.

Schrum, Lynne (1994). On-line Courses: What Have We Learned? University of Georgia, College of Education.

Senge, P. (1990) The Fifth Discipline. New York: Doubleday.

Shale, D. G. (1988) Toward a reconceptualization of Distance Education, 25, American Journal of Distance Education.

Sharan B. Merriam, Rosemary S. Caffarella (1998) Learning in Adulthood: A Comprehensive Guide, San Francisco, Jossey-Bass.

Shaw, G. B. (1965) Pygmalion. New York: Thor Publications. (Copyright holders, The Public Trustee and The Society of Authors, 84 Drayton Gardens, London SW 10).

Shoen, L. S. (1980) You and Me. Las Vegas: AMERCO.

Silverman, S. L. (2000) Learning and development: making connections to enhance teaching. San Francisco: Jossey-Bass.

Simmons, V. I. (1993) Survey of Attitudes Toward the Indiana Education Telecommunication System. Terre Haute, Indiana: Indiana State University.

Simon, L.. (2002) New beginnings: a reference guide for adult learners. Upper Saddle River, New Jersey: Prentice-Hall.

Singarella, T. A. & Sork, T.J. (1993) Ethical Issues for Adult Education. Adult Education Quarterly.

Skinner, B. F. (1953) Science and Human Behavior. New York: The MacMillan Company.

Smith, R. (1990) Learning to Learn Across the Lifespan. San Francisco: Jossey-Bass.

Smith, R. M. (1991) How people become effective learners, April, 11, Adult Learning..

Sorenson, H. (1938) Adult Abilities. Minneapolis, Minnesota: University of Minnesota Press.

Sperling, J. G. (1997) For-profit higher education: developing a world-class workforce. New Brunswick, New Jersey: Transaction Publications.

Spille, H. A. (1997) External degrees in the information age: legitimate choices. Phoenix, AZ: Oryx Press.

Steinbach, R.L. (1993) The Adult Learner: Strategies for Success. Menlo Park, California: Crisp Publications.

Steinbach, R.L. (1993) The Adult Learner: Strategies for Success. Menlo Park, California: Crisp Publications.

Steiner, C. M. (1974) Scripts People Live. New York: Grove Press.

Stephen, B. (1986) Understanding and Facilitating Adult Learning. San Francisco: Jossey Bass.

Stephen, B. (1990) The Skillful Teacher. San Francisco: Jossey-Bass.

Stice, J. E. (1987) Using Kolb's Learning Cycle to Improve Student Learning, 77, 291-296, Engineering Education.

Stites, R. (1998) Adult learning theory: An argument for technology. In C. E. Hopey (Ed.), Technology, basic skills, and adult education: Getting ready and moving forward (pp. 51-58). Columbus, OH: ERIC Clearinghouse on Adult, Career, & Vocational Education.

Stogdill, R. and Coons, A. E., eds.(1957) Leader Behavior: Its Description and Measurement, Research Monograph No. 88. Columbus, Ohio: Bureau of Business Research, The Ohio State University,

Stoneall, L. (1991) Inquiring Trainers Want to Know, November, 31-39, Training and Development.

Stoneall, L. (1991) Inquiring Trainers Want to Know. November, 31-39. Training and Development.

Stubblefield, H. W. (1994) Adult education in the American experience: from the colonial period to the present. San Francisco: Jossey-Bass.

Sullivan, E. J. (1993) The adult learner's guide to alternative and external degree programs. Phoenix: Oryx Press.

Tannen, D. (1990) You Just Don't Understand. New York: Ballantine Books.

Tapscott, Dan (1998) Growing up Digital: The Rise of the Net generation. New York: McGraw-Hill.

Ticknor, A. E. (1891) A Precursor of University Extension. Book News.

Taylor, E. W. (1998) The Theory and Practice of Transformative Learning: A Critical Review. Information Series no. 374. Columbus: ERIC Clearinghouse on Adult, Career, and Vocational Education, Center on Education and Training for Employment, The Ohio State University.

Taylor, K. (2000) Developing adult learners: strategies for teachers and trainers. San Francisco: Jossey-Bass.

Tennant, M. (1997, 2nd ed.) Psychology and Adult Learning. San Francisco: Jossey-Bass.

Thomas, K. W. and Velthouse, B. A. (1991) Cognitive Elements of Empowerment: An "Interpretive" Model of Intrinsic Task Motivation, October, 666-681, Academy of Management Review.

Thorndike, E. L.(1928) Adult Learning. New York: Macmillan.

Tight, M. (1996). Key concepts in adult education and training. New York: Routledge.

Tisdell, E. J. (1989) Poststructural Feminist Pedagogies: The Possibilities and Limitations of Feminist Emancipatory Adult Learning Theory and Practice, Spring, 48, no. 3, 139-156, Adult Education Quarterly.

Tisdell, E. J. (2003) Exploring spirituality and culture adult and higher education. San Francisco: Jossey-Bass.

Tomasek, H. (1989) The Process of Inverting the Organizational Pyramid, 105-112, Human System Management,

Tuckman, B. W. (1965) Developmental Sequence in Small Groups, 63, 384-399. Psychological Bulletin.

Twigg, A. C. (1994) The changing Definition of Learning. Educom Review.

Usher, R. (1997) Adult education and the postmodern challenge: learning beyond the limits. New York: Routledge.

Vargus, S. B. & Gavette, L. C. (1993) Post-Secondary Educational Services in Central Indiana. Indiana University Public Opinion Laboratory Research Report.

Veillere, M. F. and Harman, S. S. (1991) Reinforcement Theory: A Practical Tool, Vol. 12, No. 2, 27-31, Leadership & Organization Development Journal.

Vella, J. (1994) Learning to Listen, Learning To Teach. San Francisco: Jossey-Bass.

Vella, J. K. (1994) Learning to listen, learning to teach: the power of dialogue in educating adults. San Francisco: Jossey-Bass.

Vella, J. K. (1998) How do they know they know? evaluating adult learning. San Francisco: Jossey-Bass.

Vella, J. K. (2000) Taking learning to task: creative strategies for teaching adults. San Francisco: Jossey-Bass.

Verdun, J. R. (1977) Adult teaching adults: principles and strategies. Austin, Texas: Learning Concepts.

Verdun, J. R. (1980) Curriculum building for adult learning. Carbondale: Southern Illinois University Press.

Verespez, M. A. (1990) When You Put the Team in Charge, December, 30-32, Industry Week.

Verespez, M. A. (1991) No Empowerment Without Education, April, 28-29, Industry Week.

Vetter, H. J.(1969) Language Behavior and Communication. Illinois, Itasca: F. E. Peacock.

Vygotsky, L. S. (1978) Mind in Society: The Development of Higher Psychological Processes. Cambridge, Massachusetts: Harvard University Press.

Wallace, J. (1991) Faculty and Student Perceptions of Distance Education Using Television. Dissertation: Muncie, Indiana: Ball State University.

Walton, M. (1986) The Deming Management Method. New York: Dodd, Mead & Company.

Warr, P. B. Ed. (1971) People at Work. Middlesex, England: Penguin Books.

Watkins, L. B. & Wright, J. S. (1991). The Foundations of American Distance Education: A Century of Collegiate Correspondence Study. Dubuque, Iowa: Kendall/Hunt Publishing Company.

Weinberg, H. L. (1959) Levels of Knowing and Existing. New York: Harper & Row.

Wellins, R. S., Byham, W. C. and Wilson, J. M. (1991) Empowered Teams. San Francisco: Jossey-Bass.

Whitehead, B. M. (2003) Planning for technology: a guide for school administrators, technology coordinators, and curriculum leaders. Thousand Oaks, California: Corwin Press.

Wiesenberg, F. & Hutton, S. (1995) Teaching a Graduate Program Using Computer Mediated Conferencing Software. American Association for Adult and Continuing Education.

Wilimon, W. H. and Naylor, T. H. (1995) The Abandoned Generation: Rethinking Higher Education. Grand Rapids, Michigan: William B. Eerdmans Publishing Co.

Willis, Barry (Ed.) (1994) Distance Education Strategies and Tools. Englewood Cliffs: Educational Technology Publications.

Wilson, M. J. & Mosher, N. D. (1994) Interactive Multimedia Distance Learning (IMDL): The Prototype of the Virtual Classroom. World Conference on Educational Multimedia and Hypermedia, Vancouver, Canada.

Wilson, R.C. (1986) Improving Faculty Teaching: Effective Use of Student Evaluations and Consultants, 57, 196-211, Journal of Higher Education.

Wlodkowski, R. J. (1985, 1999, Rev. ed.) Enhancing adult motivation to learn: a comprehensive guide for teaching all adults. San Francisco: Jossey-Bass.

Wolpe, J. (1969) The Practice of Behavior Therapy. New York: Pergamon Press.

Workplace Training
Youngman, F. (2000) The political economy of adult education and development. New York: Zed Books.
Zander, A.(1977) Groups at Work. San Francisco: Jossey-Bass.
Zigerell, J. (1984) Distance Education: An Information Age Approach to Adult Education. The National Center for Research in Vocational Education. Columbus, Ohio.The Ohio State University.
Zucker, B., Johnson, C., and Flint, T. (1999) Prior Learning Assessment: A Guidebook to American Institutional Practices. Dubuque, Iowa; Kendall-Hunt Publishing.

Bios
ROBERT E RIPLEY, PhD

Experience
Educator
University Graduate Schools Professor.

From Instructor to University Graduate School Merit Professor
Director of institutes and centers – partially retired.
University of Minnesota
Iowa State University
Arizona State University

Currently adjunct professor at Ottawa University and Northern
Arizona University

Director: state and federal grants

Specialty: Careers, Wellness, Personal Success Development

Psychologist
Private Practice licensed Psychologist – 25 years.

Military
Veteran: U.S. Air Force –worldwide communications and security

Education: Combined Business, Education and Psychology – University
of Minnesota

BA – Personnel Psychology, Speech and Education

MA – College Student Personnel Administration

PhD – Developmental Psychology, Counseling Psychology

MARIE J RIPLEY, MA

Experience
Educator
Classroom Teacher to College Professor
Elementary, high school and college

Business
Small business owner
Interior decorating and contemporary furniture

MARIE J RIPLEY, MA, continued

Publisher
Publishing activities from writing, editing, cover design, manufacturing of the finished product, and distributing.

Real Estate
Licensed Real Estate Agent - ABR
New Home designer and director of construction, residential refurbishing. Also, apartment complex owner and manager.

Education:
BA – Architecture – University of Minnesota
Post Graduate – Architecture – Arizona State University
BS - Art Education – University of Minnesota
MA – Guidance and Counseling – Arizona State University
Also attended Valparaiso University and UCLA.

JOINTLY
Co-Authors: for all of their professional books and journal articles with over 40 years of publishing. Award winning and members of the elite British Literati Club.

Primary focus: Wellness, Personal Success and Career Management

Other areas: Parenting, children's ages & stages, understanding and educating adult learners.

Independent Contractors
From start-ups to International Fortune 500 companies. Primarily consulting with CEOs, Presidents and all levels of management. From vision, mission, strategic planning, assessments, to management training and development.

Directors
Of institutes and academies
Educated and trained individuals and groups from over 24 different countries.

Grants
With local, state, regional levels, as well as, the U.S. Departments of Labor, Education, Justice and U.S. Navy.

Consulting Firm:
Coaching/Counseling, Recruiting
Individual and Organizational Assessments
Seminars, Workshops and Retreats

SELF-CARE

Also, the authors have now joined with Desert Health Worldwide, LLC to also consult and assist individuals and organizations worldwide to focus on three areas: Health-Wellness, Success and Careers.

To have a sustainable successful adult life you want to know proven worldwide food supplements and natural products that can best support your unique needs to provide you with high energy, change of habits, and prevention of potential illness or sickness.

Here are 5 dominant areas that people of all ages and stages have wanted the authors to provide them with more information for wellness and sustainable career support.

_____ Natural Supplements, catering to specific health problems

_____ Botanical, Chinese and Ayuvedic Herbs

_____ Foot Care - especially with the increased number of
Diabetics at all ages.

_____ Increasing energy and immune system in one
capsule, rather than several pills.

_____ Pain Management - specific area or the whole body.

If you desire more information in any of these five areas the authors may be contacted at: wellness@deserthealthww.com.

Made in the USA
Lexington, KY
14 February 2011